TOTTENHAM HOTSPUR F.C.   PUBLIC TRIAL

At Brookfield Lane, Cheshunt   SATURDAY 14th AUGUST 1954

WHITES

SMITH

WILLIS 3   HILL 6

HARMER 10   OWEN 11

STOKES 8   J.WOOLFORD 7

TECE 4

KING 5

BOSELEY 9

DUNMORE 9

LAUREL 5   SHAW 2

HOLLOWBREAD 1

SPIVEY 8

WOODS 10

NICHOLSON 3

BAKER 2

L.WARREN 4

MARCHI 6

A.WOOD 7

D.MILTON 11

BLUE and WHITE

Whites v Blue & White,
Single-sheet programme for the Public Trial game held at Cheshunt on 14th August 1954.

(Front Cover):
Tottenham v Aston Villa, 1954-55, Christmas style issue.

(Back Cover):
(top): **Tottenham Juniors v United Glass Bottle (Pantiles),**
Winchester Cup Final, 9th April 1955.

(bottom): **Arsenal v Chelsea,** F.A. Cup 3rd Round, 2nd Replay, 20th January 1947.

i

Tottenham Hotspur

*The Programme &
Handbook Guide
1946-1992*

compiled by
Chris Ward
and
Steve Isaac

**Skript Design
& Publishing**

Published in Great Britain by
Skript Design & Publishing
26 Harebell Drive, Witham, Essex CM8 2XB,
Tel/Fax 0376 502290

ISBN 1-874799-00-8

British Library Cataloguing-in-Publication Data.
A catalogue record for this book is available from the British Library.

The authors wish to thank the following for the co-operation in the production of this book:
Tottenham Hotspur Football Club, for granting us permission to reproduce the programme covers and logos.
John Matthews, Alan Rosenthal and Andy Porter, for their assistance in compiling the listings, and for lending us some of the programmes from their collections.

Designed and Typeset by Skript Design and Publishing, 26 Harebell Drive, Witham, Essex CM8 2XB.
Printed and bound by Banjo Printers & Stationers, 11 Perry Road, Witham, Essex CM8 3YZ.
Cover printed by Bensons Printing Company, 12 Perry Road, Witham, Essex CM8 3YZ.

Introduction

Mention the name "Tottenham Hotspur" to any football supporter virtually anywhere on the planet and he or she will immediately associate it with one of Britains' leading exponents of attractive football. They may not be the most successful club in the history of football, but they have, for many seasons, been the club that has achieved a particular honour first. Henceforth, since entering the Football League back in 1908, they have nearly always been amongst the best supported clubs in the League, with the knock-on effect that their programmes, handbooks and other associated items are amongst the most highly sought after by collectors all over the world. In this volume we hope to be able to inform all those collectors, and supporters, as comprehensive a list as we have been able, of all the programmes, either issued by the club, or just played on the grounds at White Hart Lane, Cheshunt, and Hoddesdon, as possible.

My associate in this publication, Chris Ward, better known to many as Brentside Programmes, has been a regular follower of Tottenham Hotspur since watching his first match at White Hart Lane against Fulham during the 1966-67 season. Like many of us, he immediately became a collector of the clubs' programmes, before, in the early 1980's becoming one of Britains' leading programme dealers.

It was he who first spawned this publication when he produced a list of home programmes, in a duplicated booklet form, in 1981 which covered the seasons from 1946-47 up to and including the 1980-81 season. However it later transpired that this listing missed quite a number of issues, mainly because many collectors were unaware that editions had been produced.

My own association with Tottenham Hotspur as a supporter came in March 1958 when my elder brother, also a Chris, took me from our then home in Palmers Green, to see the Reserves play Queens Park Rangers Reserves. Those being the days when Reserve matches drew bigger gates than most League clubs attract these days. Gates of 7,000 to 10,000 being the norm. At the time I was only six years old, so coming regularly was out of the question, but in the October of the same year I saw my first League match. That was on October 25th against Leeds United, and as if nothing had ever changed since, we were beaten 3-2, but I was hooked, and from that day to this, I was not only a supporter but a collector as well.

It was in 1984 that I first met Chris, when I acquired a copy of his latest catalogue from his pitch outside the Wingate Trading Estate in the High Road, and for the next few seasons I would occasionally ask whether he was going to up date his initial listings booklet. A few more seasons went by, and then in 1991 I was made redundant from my job at London's sole remaining evening newspaper. I began my own small publishing company, and I suggested that we update, and upgrade his booklet into a more comprehensive edition, which I could produce in conjunction with him.

So here we present to you, whether a collector or just a supporter, this edition covering the seasons from 1946-47. In time we hope to go back even further into history, and produce a companion edition covering the seasons from 1908 up to 1946. At present we do have some lists from some of the seasons, but we would welcome any further information from collectors if they would be good enough to contact me at the address given on the page opposite.

Steve Isaac

3

The Programmes

From Pink to Full Colour
From 4 to 48 pages

During the course of the next few pages I shall endeavour to do my best to chart the changing face of the Tottenham Hotspur Football and Athletic Company Limited Official Programme and Record of the Club, as it was in 1946, to the modern day full colour magazines. Interspersed, of course, are many other editions for special matches, friendlies, etc., that were not always produced by the club but by the body that organised the match.

Then as we progess from this section into the main listings section we have also included reproductions of a standard club issue of the season, along with reproductions of some of the more obscure programmes that often have collectors bidding extremely high prices to purchase as and when one emerges from the dark recesses of a cupboard and into the daylight of the open market. We have made no attempt in this publication to estimate values. That would be extremely unwise, as time itself increases prices and in a couple of seasons time any price tag would almost certainly be under-valued. The only comment we make is that any programme only has a value in relation to that price a collector will pay for a copy. Even less than mint copies of rare programmes can command a similar price to a perfect copy simply because, to an avid collector maybe seeking just one issue to complete a seasons collection, any copy is better than none.

1946-47

Whilst not being the first season of football following the ending of World War II, the 1946-47 season was the first with the resumption of Football League matches, during the 1945-46 season Spurs had participated in the Football League South. Spurs resumed in Division Two, where they had been since 1935. This was the first season that Thomas Knight & Co, The Clock House Press, of Hoddesdon had printed the club programme, having taken over from Crusha. In those days paper rationing was still in force, with the result that the quality of paper used varied from edition to edition, as did the shade of the paper. Most 1st XI matches were printed on white paper, but this was not the case with the Reserves. The edition for the Arsenal v Chelsea, F.A. Cup replay was a throwback to the previous seasons by printed on pink paper. Most issues for the season were four page editions, with the occasional single sheet being used for minor games. The two matches played in June of that season are, from that date to this, the last matches to have been played on the ground.

1947-48

There was no discernable change in the design for this season from last seasons editions. However, from issue number 25, the League match against Birmingham City, the fixtures on the back page were removed and replaced by a series of cartoon sketches of the players drawn by Mickey Durling.

1948-49

The programmes for this season again followed the established format, but a change in the typeface used for the body text occurred. The "Official Programme" heading on the first page also changed style. For some club single-sheet issues, as depicted later in this book, no text appeared on the cover but with the Cockerel centred. For some of the Representative matches played on the ground the programmes were produced by the organising body. One example was the Edinburgh City Police v London Metropolitan Police match played on Friday, 8th April, 1949. This was a 16 page edition, printed in blue on white paper. Whilst there is not too much special in that other than the fact that this was probably the first Maybank Press printed issue ever to be sold for a match at Tottenham. You will remember that during the most part of the 1980's they printed the club programme.

4

The programme for the 1949-50 saw the Cockerel motif move up the cover to allow two columns of text to be printed, this format was to remain until the 1959-60 season. For the first time the back page was not confined to 1st and Reserve team fixtures and table, as the 'A' team fixtures in the Eastern Counties League made their first appearance. One club edition to break from the normal four page edition was that for the visit of Grimsby Town in April. To celebrate winning the Division Two Championship an eight page edition was produced and printed on a superior grade of paper. It was still priced as any other League edition though. A special edition was also produced for the England v Italy international in November. Again most minor representative matches had programmes produced by the organising body. One small point of interest, or should I say trivia, but on page 3 of the programme above the teams line-ups the capacity that could be accommodated under cover dropped from 60,000 to 50,000. It does beg us to ask the question, who stole a roof?, as no extra seats had been installed at this time.

1950-51

Our return to the First Division was not greeted with any change to the appearance to the programme other than a quiz being incorporated to the front page, and as ever it was not always discernable from the headline exactly whom the days opponents were. As all supporters are aware this was the season when the First Division Championship was won for the first time, not that the producers of the programme went overboard with enthusiasm. No special edition, just a cartoon style drawing adorning the cover for the final few issues of the season. In the case of the issue for the Liverpool match, this did not reduced the editorial content as the fixtures and tables were removed from the back page.

1951-52

The format remained unchanged for this season, though as usual, there were the occasional changes in cover design, with the Christmas issues having a photograph of the club's Christmas Party on the front page. A special edition was produced for the F.A. Cup Semi-Final between Arsenal and Chelsea. An eight page edition was produced for the planned first meeting on March 29th 1952. The weather intervened however, and the match was postponed a week. In between these matches Spurs had been due to meet Huddersfield Town in a League match on the Monday, but that too had to be postponed two days to the Wednesday. Another edition was produced with the date inside changed. Then came the re-arranged Semi-Final the following Saturday. The original edition was used but with a single-sheet insert containing the up-dated League tables, and a new Half-Time Scoreboard. This all meant that two editions both numbered 48 had appeared before No.47 had gone on sale. A new edition was produced for the Semi-Final replay two days later.

1952-53

Issues for this season remained in the usual format with no variations at all from the previous season. The only noticeable change came during February and March, when the programme broke from tradition and featured an advertisement along the foot of the first page for the National Savings Association. The Schools issues towards the end of the season were, as usual, not produced by the club but by the organising Association.

1953-54

Every match played on the ground during this season had a programme produced by the club and numbered in sequence accordingly, but there was still no change in the design or the pattern of four page issues interspersed by the occasional two page single-sheet edition. The edition was the visit of Newcastle United in February was printed on glossy paper, as was the case when a photograph or two was to be included. This edition sadly recorded the deaths of Tottenham stalwarts, George Wagstaffe Simmons, the Vice-Chairman, and Vivian Woodward.

1954-55

The programme production staff really had their work cut out deciding the formula for this seasons editions. A fifteen second long meeting probably took place to decide to remain with their tried and tested format. It was about this time that most other League clubs had adopted some form of magazine style issue, though with most of those containing mostly advertisements, Tottenham's larger four page format probably contained more reading material than most other programmes. This was the season in which the Floodlit Friendly came to prominence, and often the quiz on the front was replaced by a trailer for a forthcoming "Floodlit Football" match. It was during September that the "Did You Know" disappeared from the cover for good. Most of these Friendly matches featured a photograph of the opposition on the cover until the opening paragraphs of text. As usual, editions around Christmas featured a seasonal touch. Most issues were four page editions with some exceptions, the programmes for the "friendly" matches against Arsenal and F.C. Servette are both single-sheet issues. The final couple of League issues for this season saw a dramatic change to the routine with a street map with revised "Car Parking" arrangements featuring prominently.

1955-56

The programme still retained the same format, and design of four page issues and the occasional single-sheet, though for some matches variations were revealed. The programme for the match against F.C. Vasas was printed on glossy paper with pictures of the opponents on the back page. At the end of another struggling against relegation, the first competitive European match was played at White Hart Lane as a London met Basle in the International Industries Fairs Inter-Cities Cup. This competition being a forerunner to the Inter-Cities Fairs Cup, later to be re-christened as the U.E.F.A. Cup. In those days the teams were drawn from the clubs that played in the City rather than having club sides participate. The edition was this match was a four page issue but was printed in black ink on white glossy paper.

1956-57

Most programmes for this season were four page issues, though the programmes for the match versus Racing Club De Paris and Northampton Town Reserves were amongst the few single sheet issues. Of special note is the programme for the match on April 5th 1957, when the London Police met Edinburgh Police in the Tait Challenge Trophy. The programme for this match is in fact an edition of the Metropolitan Police Football Club, who in those days played in the Spartan League. It is an eight page issue only marginally smaller in size to that of a Tottenham issue, but the vast majority of the issue is advertising.

1957-58

Style, format and price remain unchanged for the umpteenth consecutive season but with occasional variations. Issues for the matches against Vfb. Stuttgart, Aldershot Reserves, Birmingham City Reserves, and Canto Do Rio were printed on glossy paper. In the case of the reserve issues this was because the programme featured a team photograph of Canto Do Rio. The same picture dominating the cover of the programme for the actual match against them. The Christmas issues featured a drawing of Tottenham High Cross in 1804. The programme for the English Schools Shield was a four page duplicated programme produced by the Hackney Schools Athletic Association.

1958-59

Apart from Bill Nicholson taking over from Jimmy Anderson as Manager during October, a fact first noted on the cover of the programme for the visit of Bela Vista, the programme again did not vary in it style or format. A number of reserve programmes were single-sheet issues, but breaking away from the norm were the programmes for the visit of the Bucharest Selected XI, that was printed in black on glossy paper, and the F.A. Cup Semi-Final between Luton Town and Norwich City. That programme formed the basis of the programme that was to be introduced for the 1961-62 season, being a 12-page glossy issue. Of special note is the programme for the London Challenge Cup Final against West Ham United. Although listed in the Fixture lists as a Reserve Team match, both clubs agreed to field their full First XI's, and over 18,000 attended the match. We have, therefore, listed this programme as a 1st XI fixture in the main listing for this season.

1959-60

After over a decade of the same cover layout, the 1959-60 season heralded a change to the design with the cockerel being shrunk and being place at the top centre of the programme. The date and serial numbers also moving to the top of the programme. The first two issues of the season were both printed on glossy paper before returning to the normal paper for Issue No.3. Other issues that season to be printed on glossy paper were Nos. 5, 7, 14, 16, 19, 22, 23, 25, 36, and 47. Perhaps surprising is the fact that most of those editions were for Reserve matches. The programme for the Charity Match on April 27th in aid of the Save The Children Fund was a 16-page glossy programme printed with a red and white cover, but it was not produced by the club. The various unnumbered schools programmes were produced by the home Association. Again a number of the Reserve and Minor matches had single-sheet editions.

1960-61

The most momentous season in the history of Tottenham Hotspur Football Club saw the old-fashioned style programme be issued for the final time when the 'A' team met March Town United at the end of the season. Though that issue was a single-sheet edition. The final four-page issue had appeared for the visit of Nottingham Forest as the final League match of the season against West Bromwich Albion saw a 12 page glossy issue printed to celebrate winning the League Championship, though still priced at 2d. Although the following seasons programme were different in appearance, the size and layout of the centre-page spread were used during the 1961-62 season. The layout of the usual programme for this season was no different to that of the 1959-60 season, with glossy issues again interspersing with plain paper issues. The following editions were all printed on glossy paper, Nos. 1, 4, 5, 8, 11, 13, 14, 27, 41, 43, 44, 47, and 49. A number of the Reserve and other match issues were single-sheet editions as was probably the hardest to come by edition of the season. That being for the friendly in October against The Army, with Spurs fielding a side comprised of First and Reserve team players.

1961-62

12 pages and measuring 215mm x 135mm, glossy paper and priced 3d. That was the new programme unveiled as a new era in Tottenham programmes began with Charity Shield match on August 12th 1961. The Reserve issues for the season were the same overall size but only 4 page issues, and priced 2d. However, the cover was still a throw-back to the old days with the large Cockerel motif again prominent down the left-hand side, with text taking up the remainder of the cover. For issues 1-7 and 9, the title at the top of the front page was blue and featured the outline of a ball, but issue 8, and then from 10 onwards, the panel was changed to feature the League Championship Trophy and the F.A. Cup in outline instead. The only other changes displayed during the season were, firstly, over the Christmas period when issue No.25 gave no indication as to the opposition but included a panel stating "Greetings from Tottenham", whilst issue 27 wished us all a Happy New Year. The next break from routine came for the European Cup Semi-Final against Benfica when a wrap-around coloured cover helped boost the issue to one of 20 pages. They price did rise to 6d for this edition. The next two matches, the visits of the Sheffield duo also broke from the normal. No text on the cover of the Wednesday game other than the fixture, and for the visit of United two days later, only a four page edition was issued, though priced as a normal programme. The visit of Eynesbury Rovers in the Eastern Counties League did not bring about a true home programme, but one of the duplicate large single-sheet programme normally used for matches at Cheshunt. The Schools programmes were again not produced by the club but by the organising Association.

1962-63

Only one obvious change to the cover for this season as a second F.A. Cup replaced the League Championship Trophy in the top panel. The same 12 or 4 page format was retained. The harsh winter weather that disrupted the season during January and February lead to many postponements. Amongst those was the F.A. Cup tie against Burnley, though when the match was played eleven days later the original programme was issued. During March and April a couple of F.A. Cup Second replays were staged on the ground, and for both matches 4 page publications were issued. The only breaks from the standard programme came with the Cup Winners Cup Semi-Final when another wrap around cover boosted the programme to 16 pages, but doubled the price, and for a number of the minor matches when small duplicated single-sheets were issued. One example being the London F.A. Winchester Cup Final against West Ham Juniors. However, perhaps the most sought after Tottenham programme in recent history is the A4 sized pink single-sheet issue for the Friendly matches staged against Arsenal on January 26th. Both 1st and Reserve teams were in action, but an attendance of over 19,000 assured that many attending the game did not acquire a copy. Hardly any come onto the open market these days.

1963-64

The ball reappeared in the front panel now that the club held only the Cup Winners Cup, and the cockerel was much reduced in size at the bottom of a panel containing the clubs' honours. Otherwise the style, size, price and pagination did not alter. The Public Trial match returned that season and that was a normal 12 page issue. The first break with routine came with the re-arranged Cup Winners Cup tie programme against Manchester United. For the second date the programme was only a four page issue, priced as per a reserve match at 2d. Once again minor matches such as the Q.P.R F.A. Youth Cup tie were single-sheets just a shade smaller than the usual programme.

1964-65

This season began with a 4 page Public Trial match programme, from which we could see that the top panel was now bereft of any motif. Instead the club badge was utilised alongside a panel denoting the serial number and date. The first League issue against Sheffield United emerged with a photograph of the ground adorning the cover and for most first team matches this cover designed remained all season. There were a couple of exceptions, one being the John White Memorial Match which was a 16 page edition, completely in black and white and priced at a tanner, the other was for the replayed F.A. Cup tie against Torquay United, which although played five days later than originally intended, was only a four page issue. Another change to the 1st team programme for this season was that the teams line-ups were now only on one page, not spread across the centre pages. The issue for the visit of Ipswich Town in the Cup had a cover that did not include the picture of the ground. Instead a panel marking the tribute to Sir Winston Churchill who had died a few days beforehand. Another unique programme that season was the Football Combination fixture against Mansfield Town, for a few days prior the Chelsea Reserves match had been postponed, so instead of moving from No.37 to No.38, 37a was issued instead. Again most minor matches appeared as duplicated single-sheets but the Corinthian Shield Final programme produced by the London Schools F.A was a four page glossy issue, marginally smaller than the club programme.

1965-66

Programmes for this season for a time followed the pattern of the previous season but from issue No.10 the picture of the ground was to be replaced by an action photograph. That same picture remained for three League editions, but returned for issues 20, 23, 26, 28. A special seasonal design was used for issue 25 though. The programme for the visit of the Hungarian Select XI utilised a coloured wrap around cover though boosting this edition to 16 pages, the page numbering did not include the cover. From issue No.29 the cover picture changed from match to match, apart from issues 36 & 38, whereupon the ground re-appeared. By and large the Reserve issues followed their usual 4 page pattern all season, but at Easter that pattern was broken when a combined issue was printed for the visits of Ipswich and Southampton. The three matches in the Combination after that were all single-sheet affairs until normality returned for the final match against Plymouth Reserves. The programme for the visit of Crystal Palace Juniors in the South East Counties League Cup, Junior Section, was a double-sided duplicated sheet priced at 1d, whilst the programme for the London Boys v Birmingham Boys match in March was slightly smaller than an A5 double-sided single-sheet printed on card by the Tottenham and Edmonton Weekly Herald, and given away free.

1966-67

Absolutely no change to the programme for this particular season. The cover picture on 1st team editions was changed from issue to issue. Another coloured wrap around was used for the visit of the Polish Select XI, again boosting the issue to 16 pages, though the back page was blank, hardly worth doubling the cover price for. From the start of 1967, the cover action photograph was replaced by a picture of that days visitors. There was only one club issued single-sheet that season, that being for the visit of the Metropolitan Police Cadets in the F.A. Youth Cup, even the visit of Brentwood Town in the Metropolitan League merited a four page 'Reserve style' edition. The only other programme issued for a match at White Hart Lane that season was for the Final of the Compton Cup, for that a duplicated large single-sheet was issued by the Haringey Schools Sports Association. Finally, whilst covering this season, a touch of humour, for included in the Met. Police Youth side in the No.7 shirt was a player they would surely never let near any cells or prisons. For his name is A.File!! Spurs had little troubling in breaking out of defence though, they won 14-0.

8

The programme had a complete overhaul during the summer of 1967, and re-emerged in August as the smallest ever, 184mm x 133mm, produced by the club, and for many their own favourite programmes. However the cover price for both types of issue doubled, the Reserve 4 page issues to 2d, and the 16 page first team editions to 6d. The cover design did not alter all season with a picture of Phil Beal tackling Leicester's Mike Stringfellow adorning all the first team editions. Not even a couple of European Cup Winners Cup ties could yield a change in the format. Issues numbered, 20, 40, 42, 47, and 49 were all single-sheet editions. Perhaps the most sought after programme for this season is the one for the postponed match against Burnley in January. Apparently very few copies emerged onto the open market, and even catching a glimpse of one can be considered a privilege. During the season Tottenham also played host to the England v Scotland Schoolboys International as Wembley was not available to stage the match. For this match English Schools F.A produced a 12 page edition in the same style as it would have been had it been played at Wembley. It was printed by Thomas Knight & Co. though, and in the Scotland side that day, one Graeme Souness.

1968-69

The reduced size format was retained for this season, the cockerel returned to the cover to replace the badge, but so did the picture of the ground. Though later in the season two different action shots replaced it. This season began with a friendly against Glasgow Rangers, which to this day is still the only match to have been played at White Hart Lane in the month of July. That issue set the pattern for the season, though from issue No.52, in first team editions, the players full names were used rather than just their surname. All reserve matches were 4 page issues, with the only single-sheet editions being Nos. 20, 25, and 34 (the played game), which were all Youth team matches. Another of those very rare programmes is that for the original visit of Queens Park Rangers at the end of November 1968, again very few found their way onto the market, whereas the other postponed issues are not all that hard to come by.

1969-70

The same design of programme that ended the 1968-69 season re-emerged for the 1969-70 season, with a cover picture that changed from time to time. There was no increase in the cover price of first team issues, but reserve editions edged up to 3d. each. Single sheet editions were produced for issues 9, 17, 28, 34, and 38. The programme for the F.A. Youth Cup Semi-Final against Bristol City was an 8 page edition, whilst an attractive 16 page issue was published for the Final 1st Leg against Coventry City. A 4 page edition came out for the 2nd replay. Tottenham also staged another F.A. Cup Semi-Final as Watford met Chelsea in the mud. For this game a programme of similar dimensions to those of the early 60's was produced. It contained 16 pages, cost a bob, and featured blue and gold prominently on the cover and centre spread.

1970-71

This season saw a return to the larger 215mm x 134mm format, though whilst still a 16 page edition for first team matches, and 4 pages for reserve issues, this season did see a major breakthrough in the history of the Tottenham Hotspur Official Programme, for colour photographs were used from time to time, and the goalscorers and attendances were given for first team matches. The same cover design was used all season for first team issues, whilst the reserves retained the format used almost since time began. The team line-ups on page 9 began against the background of a blue pitch but changed to a white pitch with blue lines from the League Cup Semi-Final programme against Bristol City, though issues numbered 54 & 57 saw a brief reversal to the original. Colour pictures appeared in three issues, Nos, 31, (v Man. Utd), 48, (v Chelsea), and 60 (v Arsenal). Single-sheet editions were issued for programmes 23, 31 (the postponed game), 32, 45, and 55. Another change that occurred during this season was that the programmes by being priced at One Shilling (5p), and Threepence, but after February 15th that became 5p (One Shilling) and 1p, with all references to the old LSD monetary system disappearing after issue No.47.

This season saw what I consider to be just about the most uninspiring cover design ever used for a Tottenham programme. The reserve issues remained as they had been for previous seasons. The only break to the tedium of two blue bands, and one white band, which would have been most appropriate had we been called Queens Park Rangers, came with the design for the U.E.F.A. Cup Final against Wolverhampton Wanderers. Colour was used just once during the season when a team line-up was featured in issue 6 (v Liverpool). Only one single-sheet edition was published that being No.26. One changed forced upon the programme producers was that for all the European matches, the old-fashioned style 2-3-5 team line-up had to be changed to a list from 1 to 17.

1972-73

No change to the cover design, style, size or price of either First Team or Reserve issues. The only items worth mentioning is that issue No.24 was the only single-sheet, and No.5 was the only one to possess a colour photograph. Only the programme for the Goodbye Greaves match broke the mould, cover-wise, but internally it was similar to most other programmes. Two editions did buck the trend altogether but for not the anticipated reason. They were the programmes for the matches against Olympiakos Pireaus and Red Star Belgrade, wherein numbers were not listed against the players names.

1973-74

Supporters and Collectors hoping for a change of cover design for this season were again to be disappointed as the status quo was maintained. No colour appeared until the edition for the U.E.F.A Cup Final against Feyenoord. The only note worthy comments are the unusual 4-3-3 team line-ups used in the Grasshoppers edition, and the moving to the back page of the line-ups in the Lokomotive Leipzig edition. Single sheet editions were published for Nos. 22 & 34. The Philip Beal Testimonial programme was slightly different internally from the norm, but was the same size in every other aspect, except twice the price. It was not until the final two issues of the season that anything substantial happened. A 16 page edition was produced for the F.A. Youth Cup Final with a yellow and blue cover, and yellow and blue used on the team line-ups, and a 20-page large format edition was produced for the Feyenoord Final with a coloured cover and colour pictures on two pages inside.

1974-75

At least the programme changed slightly for this one of the most traumatic seasons in the clubs' history. Price rises decreed 7p and 2p respectively for First Team and Reserve editions, but at least we got a change in cover design, and a change to a team line-up printed vertically. In all other aspects the tried and trusted format was used. Quirks occurred during the season that maybe worthy of mention. Bill Nicholson resigned at the end of August but he was still listed as Manager in all the programmes until Terry Neill replaced him in the programme for the visit of Ipswich Town Reserves. His departure contributed to some changes in the layout for the visit of West Ham United. Colour appeared just once, on the rear of the Gilzean Testimonial Programme, which was a large format 16 page issue. Single sheet editions was fairly common-place due to a plethora of Youth team games. The following were single sheet issues: Nos. 13, 21, 23, 26, 33 (29th January), 37, 39, 40, 43. Number 39 being for the visit of Birmingham City Reserves. A duplicated single-sheet was produced for the South East Counties League Div.2 Cup Semi-Final and Final.

1975-76

At last a change to a cover design of some originality. The team line-ups were moved to the back page and for a couple of issues featured the sketch of a player as a background. On the down-side, the cost rose to 10p, for a programme that was still only 16 pages in content. This season also saw the first step in the demise of the Reserve team programme. Now it had been reduced to a single-sheet, one-sided productions with no reading material whatsoever, and it still cost 2p. One special edition that season was produced for the visit of Manchester City. That match was used to commemorate Pat Jennings breaking the clubs' appearance record, and a colour photograph on the cover, and two coloured pages inside made it the seasons most attractive programme. A large format 16-page issue was produced for the Cyril Knowles Testimonial Match. Duplicated single-sheet editions were produced for all the other matches on the ground. One item of interest but the London v Bristol, Schools Match in October featured one Gary Mabbutt wearing No.6 for the Bristol side, probably his first appearance at White Hart Lane. Clive Allen was playing for the London Boys.

1976-77

No great changes this season other than Tottenham Hotspur on the cover changed from white to blue. The Reserve issues appeared the same as the season before, and even the Pat Jennings Testimonial programme was similar in many ways to the Cyril Knowles Testimonial programme. The only programmes to break the mould were Nos. 24 & 38 for which 4 page editions were produced, priced at 5p. However the season did produce some oddities. Single sided duplicated sheets were produced nearly all the Youth and other matches, with a couple of exceptions. One being them 2nd Leg of the South East Counties League Division One Cup Final, which was changed to be played at White Hart Lane, but the original Queens Park Rangers edition was sold at the ground.

1977-78

Our slide into Division Two at least heralded another new era in the history of the Tottenham Hotspur Official Programme, as colour became standard for the cover of the programme. Priced at 15p, and printed using the large 235mm x 180mm format, it saw Tottenham finally get in line with most other clubs. However, the programme was still only 16 pages from front to back. The Reserve programme also increased to the same size dimensionally but it was still only a single-sided sheet. It at least still only cost 2p. Nine different pictures were used on the cover during the course of the season, with a tenth being used for the John Pratt Testimonial Match, but not in colour. That followed the trend set by the Cyril Knowles programme for size, content and layout. Single sided duplicated sheets were issued for the Youth team & boys matches at White Hart Lane, and for the two Reserve matches played at Cheshunt. For the Police Athletic Association Cup Final between the forces of the Metropolitan and West Midlands areas a 40 page programme was produced, which was printed by James E. James of Liverpool. Priced at 10p, it contains no less than 25 pages of advertising.

1978-79

This was the 33rd and last season that Thomas Knight & Co. Ltd. printed the club programmes, and the last in which the Reserve programmes were printed, as the club took over from the following season with duplicated sheets. It was therefore the last season in which all the seasons programmes were numbered in sequence. First Team editions for this season rose to 20p in price, but whilst still being only 16 pages in content, the quantity of colour pictures rose. Even the cover picture changed from issue to issue once the same picture had been used on issues 2 & 3, and from issue 10 there was a slight change to the team line-ups on the back page. Reserve programmes remained as single-sided glossy sheets, priced at 2p. The edition for the Steve Perryman Testimonial Match was priced at 30p, contained 24 pages, and was printed by the Maybank Press. The other three unnumbered programmes were all duplicated single-sheets.

1979-80

Gasps of horror greeted the first issue of the new season, as Maybanks took over the printing of First Team issues. An extra 4 pages took the total to 20, but the price rose to 25p. Certainly it was an inauspicious start for Maybanks as a complete hash was made of the statistics page with Charlton Athletic's Youth Team fixtures been printed instead of Tottenham's, but horror of horrors to Spurs supporters was the appearance in the programme of advertisements. Issue 21 for the visit of Liverpool was boosted to 24 pages by the inclusion by the inclusion of a National Girobank European Championship Wallchart. For the Terry Naylor Testimonial, a 16 page issue was produced, whilst for the Wimbledon South East Counties League Division Two Cup Final, a 4 page A5 sized programme was sold, priced at 2p. For Reserve matches, Spurs began the season with photocopy of the previous seasons editions, but with changes made where necessary, after that duplicated numbered sheets were produced, priced at 2p, though on occasions the size tended to vary away from A4.

1980-81

The standard League issue for this season rose to 24 pages, with the price moving up to 30p, making this seasons issues far more attractive than the previous season. Another National Girobank insert booster issue number 10 to

11

28 pages, and as we progressed towards the F.A. Cup Final some flair was displayed in the covers of issues 21 & 23. Other issues that season included a 4 page issue for the F.A. Cup replay between Enfield and Barnsley, a 16 page insert bolstered the size to 20 pages overall, price 20p. For the F.A Youth Cup Final against West Ham United, an 8 page A5 sized issue was produced, with 4 page issues appearing for the Semi-Final against Manchester United, and the South East Counties Cup Final against Cambridge United. All three editions were marketed at 10p. The Barry Daines Testimonial programme was 20 pages retailing at 35p. All other programmes were A4 sized single duplicated sheets given away free at the gate. For Reserve issues, neither side on the programme was referred to as Reserves any longer.

1981-82

The inclusion of 8 page inserts in the programme now became a regular feature, but I shall discard them from any figures given as they tended to annoy many supporters and collectors by their presence. As had become normal by now a change of cover design greeted the new season, but the overall size and price remained static. A change in the design of the cover was produced for our European Cup Winners Cup matches. Breaking away from the standard issue were two editions, firstly the special edition for the opening of the New West Stand. This programme, for the visit of Wolves, was increased in price to 50p but it included a special 16 page supplement. Then for the visit of Eintract Frankfurt, two prices appeared on the cover. 30p for the normal issue, but 80p for a copy containing an England World Cup poster. The style of Reserve, Youth team and other matches remained unchanged.

1982-83

The start of the 1982-83 season saw the programme appear with the club title in the style that it appears these days on all the clubs printed matter. Unfortunately the opening of our Centenary Season was greeted with the programmes first three issues having 1981-82 printed on the cover instead of 1982-83. The eight page inserts remained all season to bolster the standard 24 page issue which was now priced at 40p. Of great interest to collectors during this season was the Programme Flashback page. For the two European matches, the colours are the cover were reversed. Other changes to the standard issue through the season included only a 4 page insert in issues 17,18, and 20, and the inclusion 8 page Supporters Survey in issue 21. The Reserve programmes changed appearance mid-season as they reverted from their previous style to include the new style "Tottenham Hotspur" title. Also of interest to collectors is the A5 sized single-sheets that were given away free upon admission to the U.E.F.A Youth Tournament Final between France and Italy. It had originally been intended to play the 3rd Place Play-Off match between Czechoslovakia and England on the ground as well but due to the wet conditions this had been moved to Watford. As far as we are aware this single-sheet is available in five different colours depending on which part of the ground was entered. Each copy has a reference to that area in the bottom left hand side, and each copy is also individually numbered in the bottom right hand corner.

1983-84

In many ways the 1983-84 season was the season in which the greatest variety of Spurs programmes appeared. The issue for the opening League match against Coventry saw only the title "Spurs", white with a blue shadow on a blue background, at the top, but from the next issue the title was made more prominent back changing the shadow to black. The dreaded inserts disappeared from the centre of the programme to leave a standard 28 page issue, costing 50p. Issue number 3, contained a single-sheet ticket application form for the forthcoming introduction of "live" televised football against Nottingham Forest, and from issue number 4 the panel containing the opponents, date and serial numbers etc, was moved in between the club motif and the Spurs title. Perhaps the most strange looking programme, outwardly, at least, was that for the visit of Nottingham Forest for wrapped around the outside was a four page supplement promoting the forthcoming Share Offer. Inside only a 24 page issue was produced. For the visit of Liverpool, issue 10, a 32 page programme emerged, and then from issue 14 onwards, "SPONSORED BY HOLSTEN" appeared in an enlarged Spurs title. Then for the U.E.F.A. Cup Final a 40 page edition appeared, to become the first Spurs programme to ever cost £1. Two Testimonial matches were staged during the season, at the start for Bill Nicholson for which a 24 page issue costing 50p was produced, and then at the end for Keith Burkinshaw for whom a similar sized and priced edition was produced. As the Nicholson Testimonial Match and the Nottingham Forest match were both played on a Sunday, single sided team sheet were also produced and given to supporters as they passed through the turnstiles. The Reserve programmes for this season also changed appearance mid-season. Changing from the duplicated club letter-head style to a the purposefully designed Official

12

Programme style they still use to this day.

1984-85

The standard issue for this season was again 28 pages with the price unchanged at 50p, though a 32 page edition was produced for the visit of Real Madrid. Four page editions, priced at 10p, were produced for the visits of Birmingham City in the F.A Youth Cup, and Arsenal in the Final of the South East Counties League Cup. All the reserve team programmes played at either White Hart Lane or Cheshunt were the now standard free single-sheets. A 12 page edition, at 30p, was produced for the Peter Southey Memorial Match against Fulham at the start of the season.

1985-86

Yet another change on the cover design greeted this season, with a touch of variety being shown by displaying our opponents name in their club colours. The price had now risen to 60p, and for that a 32 page issue was purchased, however for issues 13, 14, and 15, 36 page editions were produced, and issues 28 to 30 were bolstered to 36 pages by the inclusion of a 4 page application form to join the Spurs Members Club. There were also a number of special issues during this season, which began with the Glenn Hoddle Testimonial. For this a smaller sized 24 page programme was produced and printed by Coral Press of St.Albans, it cost £1, but the club also produced a single-sided team sheet. In March the Spurs Staff met a Parliamentary XI at White Hart Lane, and for this Charity Match an eight page, normal size, programme was given away upon admission to the ground at either 50p or 25p. Then in April the club staged the F.A. Cup Semi-Final between Liverpool and Southampton and for £1 a standard sized 36 page issue was purchased. Also costing £1 was the large format 16 page programme for the Ossie Ardiles Testimonial in which Diego Maradona made his one appearance for Spurs. Finally, a 4 page issue, costing 10p, was produced for yet another South East Counties League Cup Final against Arsenal.

1986-87

The cover design for this season was the same as for the 1985-86 season except that instead of a pale blue background, it was now white. The team layouts on the back page had shrunk to allow the half-time scoreboard and future matches to be included, and the cover price moved up to 80p. Most issues were 32 pages, but six issues managed to reach 36 pages, those being issues 15, 23, 26, 27, 28, and 30. However issue 15 also included a copy of the first Woolwich Arsenal v Tottenham programme, as this match was the 100th local derby, and this programme is fairly scarce on the open market. A 32 page programme was also issued for the Paul Miller Testimonial Match, it was also the regulation size, and had a cover similar in design to that for the Ossie Ardiles Testimonial Match. All the Reserve and Youth team programmes were the now standard single-sheet. There was one other match played on the ground at the end of the season when Ridgeway Rovers met Forest United in the Middlesex County Youth F.A Under-12 County Cup Final. Sponsored by Spears Games, a 12 page programme was produced, with a printed cover but duplicated inner pages. It cost 50p.

1987-88

The first programme of the 1987-88 season was for Chris Hughton's Testimonial Match against Arsenal. For this a large format 32 page issue was produced costing £1. It then took five regular issues before a finite pattern for the season emerged. The first four issues of the season saw the cover designs colours vary until No.5 became predominantly Sky Blue with Yellow and Blue trim. The priced remained at 80p and the content remained at 32 pages. A 36 page issue was produced for the friendly against Monaco, and for the League match against Derby. Tony Galvin's Testimonial programme was a standard size 36 page issue again with a cover price of £1. Whilst the Danny Thomas Benefit Match saw a 32 page issue on sale at £1. For the F.A. Cup Semi-Final the club produced a 36 page edition at £1.20, however these two programmes were not printed by Maybanks but by the Valentine Press. Four page programmes, priced 10p were produced for the Youth team matches against Doncaster Rovers and Southampton. Single sheet team-sheets were also available for the Sunday matches against Arsenal and Charlton. The programme for the final League match of the season against Luton Town also included an eight page Season Ticket Application Form. The Club also produced the programme for the Frank Bruno v Joe Bugner clash on the ground in October. Large format, 60 pages and costing £4, it holds the record for being the most expensive programme on sale at White Hart Lane.

1988-89

A change of cover design, a cover price of £1, and a change to having the Valentine Press greeted the new season. The first issue for the aborted visit of Coventry was a 36 page production with the team line-ups on the back cover being back by a full colour picture of the West Stand, with the teams printed in white. However, that was to change from the second issue No.1 of the season when we met Arsenal. Now the picture had been made feint with the printing in black, but for this issue a 40 page programme emerged. However, the norm was the to drop to 32 pages. For the visit of Blackburn Rovers, the "Sponsored by HOLSTEN" was omitted from the cover. A single sided team sheet was also produced for the visit of Nottingham Forest. Also during this season the habit of including the Spurs Shop catalogue in the programme also came to the fore, but for the purposes of this book, we shall ignore them. This cover design was copied by Nottingham Forest a couple of seasons later.

1989-90

The first issue of the 1989-90 season for the visit of Luton saw the cover design of the previous season repeated, but from the second issue the picture was increased to the full depth of the page. Still priced at £1, and still containing 32 pages, the programme displayed little variation from the previous season. A 36 page edition was produced for the visit of Arsenal. For the Youth Team Cup matches against Manchester United and Arsenal, 4 page productions were issued at 10p, whilst for the F.A. Youth Cup Final against Middlesbrough, an eight page programme, at 20p, was on sale. A Benefit Match was also staged for Danny Blanchflower against a Northern Ireland XI, and for £1 a 48 page programme was available. It is also worth noting that from February all numbered Reserve team issues, were incorrectly printed as being Volume 88 instead of 82.

1990-91

Total Graphics Ltd. of Edmonton assumed control of the production of the programme from this season, and by and large, a good job has been done. However, every change has its price, and for this the programme jumped to £1.30 per issue., but at least we are getting 48 pages. The season had begun with the Ray Clemence Benefit match for which a 32 page programme costing £1 was marketed. Other issues this season, saw a 32 page programme, at £1, for the England v Poland Under-21 International. The Peter Shilton International Farewell programme was not produced by the club, but printed by M-Press. It was also a 32 page issue, priced at £1.30. Our home match against Liverpool in November was covered live by The Match, and for this the club programme was also available in advance with an eight-page The Match wrap around. However, unlike some clubs, the programme issued on the day was no different to that produced in advance. Regular collectors will know that the away programmes at Everton and Derby varied from those issued with "The Match" wrappers.

1991-92

The opening issue of the 1991-92 season was the exception to the normal pattern for the season, as a solid panel was printed on the left-hand side of the cover, before it returned to the shaded area as per the 1990-91 season. The back page also featured the team line-ups in a style that was to last just one edition. Still 48 pages, but the cover priced edged up to £1.50. Whilst still often being weighed down the inclusion of 28 page catalogues, this seasons programmes came out very well in the judging of the various Programme of the Year Awards. Other issues this season came for the Cyril Knowles Memorial Match for which a smaller sized 32 page programme, costing £1 was produced, and such was the demand that a re-print was ordered. A re-print had also been carried out after the visit of Manchester United, when another complete sell-out was achieved. For the visits of Manchester United in the F.A. Youth Cup Semi-Final, Arsenal in the Southern Junior Floodlit Cup Final, and Chelsea in the South East Counties League Cup Final, four page editions, priced at 10p, were produced.

Also of interest to collectors may be the fact that two versions exist of the programme for the visit of Oldham Athletic. For on page 13 is a picture of Gordon Durie supposedly in action against Southampton. In many copies half of the picture is blacked out, but some obviously slipped through the net with the picture intact. This only reveals that the picture was actually taken against Sheffield United!!

Reserve programmes for this season changed from having a blue heading to being black.

A 44 page programme was issued for the Chris Eubank v Michael Watson, but this programme was produced by Matchroom.

S.Isaac

The Season by Season
Listing
1946-1992

All first team matches are listed in **bold type**.
Unnumbered programmes are
marked with an asterisk *

1946-47

Volume 39

*	17th August	Whites v Blue & White Hoops	**Public Trial**
*	24th August	Whites v Blue & White Hoops	**Public Trial**
1	**31st August**	**Birmingham City**	**League**
2	2nd September	Ipswich Town Reserves	Football Combination
2	7th September	Reading Reserves	Football Combination

(programme incorrectly numbered, sequence not rectified)

3	**9th September**	**Southampton**	**League**
4	**14th September**	**Newcastle United**	**League**
5	16th September	Crystal Palace Reserves	Football Combination
6	21st September	Birmingham City Reserves	Football Combination
7	**28th September**	**Manchester City**	**League**
8	**5th October**	**Burnley**	**League**
9	**7th October**	**Newport County**	**League**
10	12th October	Plymouth Argyle Reserves	Football Combination
11	14th October	Bromley	London Challenge Cup 1st Round
12	19th October	Norwich City Reserves	Football Combination
13	**26th October**	**Sheffield Wednesday**	**League**
14	28th October	Queens Park Rangers	London Challenge Cup 2nd Round
15	2nd November	Arsenal Reserves	Football Combination
16	4th November	Cardiff City Reserves	Football Combination
17	**9th November**	**Bury**	**League**
18	16th November	Luton Town Reserves	Football Combination
19	18th November	Southend United Reserves	Football Combination
20	**23rd November**	**Plymouth Argyle**	**League**
21	30th November	Millwall Reserves	Football Combination
22	**7th December**	**Chesterfield**	**League**
23	14th December	Northampton Town Reserves	Football Combination
24	**21st December**	**Bradford**	**League**
25	25th December	Queens Park Rangers Reserves	Friendly
26	**26th December**	**Coventry City**	**League**
27	28th December	Charlton Athletic Reserves	Football Combination
28	**4th January**	**West Bromwich Albion**	**League**
29	**11th January**	**Stoke City**	**F.A Cup 3rd Round**
30	18th January	Reading Reserves	Football Combination Cup
31	20th January	Arsenal v Chelsea	F.A Cup 3rd Round 2nd Replay
32	**25th January**	**Arsenal**	**Friendly**
33	**27th January**	**Swansea Town**	**League**
*	1st February (am)	Edmonton Boys v Plymouth Boys	English Schools Shield
34	1st February (pm)	Portsmouth Reserves	Football Combination Cup
35	8th February	Southampton Reserves (postponed)	Football Combination Cup
36	1st March	Arsenal Reserves	Football Combination Cup
37	3rd March	Southend United Reserves	Football Combination Cup
38	**8th March**	**Fulham**	**League**
39	15th March	Brentford Reserves	Football Combination Cup
40	**22nd March**	**Luton Town**	**League**
41	29th March	Fulham 'A'	Friendly
42	**4th April**	**Nottingham Forest**	**League**
43	**5th April**	**Leicester City**	**League**
*	7th April (am)	Edmonton Boys v North Kent Boys	English Schools Shield
44	7th April (pm)	Southampton Reserves	Football Combination Cup
*	12th April (am)	Edmonton Boys v Coventry Boys	English Schools Shield
45	12th April (pm)	West Ham United Reserves	Friendly
46	**19th April**	**Millwall**	**League**
47	26th April	Swindon Town Reserves	Football Combination
48	3rd May	Leyton Orient Reserves	Football Combination
49	10th May	Monteagle	London Minor Cup Final
*	15th May	Edmonton Boys v Heston & Isleworth Boys	Star Shield Final
50	**17th May**	**West Ham United**	**League**
51	26th May	Queens Park Rangers Reserves	Football Combination Cup
52	26th May	Enfield v Hendon	Middlesex Senior Cup Final
*	31st May	Walthamstow Avenue v Dando	Tottenham Charity Cup Junior Final
*	31st May	Devonshire Hill v KB Sports	Tottenham Charity Cup Senior Final
53	**7th June**	**Barnsley**	**League**
54	14th June	Arsenal Reserves v Swansea T. Resrvs.	Football Combination Cup Final

1946-47

TOTTENHAM HOTSPUR

FOOTBALL AND ATHLETIC COMPANY, LIMITED

OFFICIAL PROGRAMME

AND RECORD OF THE CLUB

Chairman : F. J. BEARMAN
Directors :
H. F. CADMAN, GEORGE COX, W. J. HERYET,
G. WAGSTAFFE SIMMONS, F.J.I., FREDK. WALE
E. DEWHURST HORNSBY
Secretary: A. W. TURNER

**ISSUED EVERY
MATCH DAY**

**PRICE
ONE PENNY**

VOL. XXXIX. No. 54   JUNE 14th, 1947

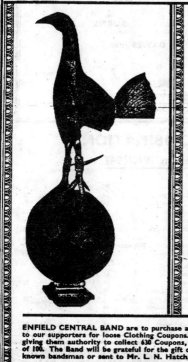

FOOTBALL COMBINATION
CUP FINAL

Fancy a Cup Final Tie in England on June 14th! According to Football Association rules the competition games in this country, save for County and Charity Cups and authorised special matches, should have finished on Saturday, May 3rd. The exceptionally severe winter, plus the intervention of the Government to cancel big football in mid-week, made an extension of the season necessary to enable competitions to be concluded.

That explains why this afternoon we have here the Final Tie of the Football Combination Cup. This was run in four Sections on a home and away basis, and the winners of the four groups were Arsenal, Chelsea, Coventry, and Swansea Town. In the Semi-final Ties played last Saturday, Arsenal defeated Coventry City 1—0, and Swansea Town defeated Chelsea 3—1. The Reserve teams of Arsenal and Swansea Town thus oppose each other here this afternoon, and they will play extra time if necessary.

The Spurs concluded their programme last Saturday with a home game against Barnsley, and the result was a draw. It was a keen, hard match from start to finish. In the first half the Spurs were certainly on top, but after change of ends Barnsley rallied and made a fine fight of it.

A glance at the table will reveal that Tottenham finished sixth, that West Ham United made a fine recovery in the second half of the season and finished in the middle of the table, that Millwall easily escaped the relegation that threatened them for the major part of the season, and that Fulham, although not maintaining their early promise, were always well clear of the danger zone.

Our team, in charge of Mr. W. J. Heryet, a director, left London on Monday according to schedule to play four games in the South of France. They had assurances before starting that arrangements would be made to enable them to fulfil their programme.

ENFIELD CENTRAL BAND are to purchase a new set of 30 Uniforms at a cost of £375, and appeal to our supporters for loose Clothing Coupons. They hold a Board of Trade Licence (IM1F/18908/47) giving them authority to collect 630 Coupons, of which the bandsmen have guaranteed a minimum of 100. The Band will be grateful for the gift of one or more coupons, which may be handed to any known bandsman or sent to Mr. L. N. Hatch, 52 First Avenue, Enfield.

Printed by Thomas Knight & Co., Ltd., The Clock House Press, Hoddesdon, Herts

The latest in the season any match has been played at White Hart Lane, when on Saturday June 14th, **Arsenal Reserves** met **Swansea Town Reserves** in the Football Combination Cup Final.

(see overleaf for the reverse side of the programme)

1946-47

Final, Football Combination Cup   June 14th, 1947   Kick-off 3.15

ARSENAL RESERVES

Red and White Shirts, White Knickers

RIGHT WING				GOAL				LEFT WING
				PLATT				
				1				
				BACKS				
	JONES, S.					WADE		
	2					3		
				HALF-BACKS				
WALLER (Capt.)			SMITH, L.			HORSFIELD		
4			5			6		
				FORWARDS				
HOLLAND	CURTIS			SHARRATT		MORGAN		RUDKIN
7	8			9		·10		11

Referee: **Mr. W. DELLOW** (Surrey)
Linesmen: Mr. F. May, Reading (Blue and White Flag)
Mr. E. Fowler, Hornchurch (Red and White Flag)

11	10			9		8		7
MORRIS	CUMLEY			JAMES, D.		THOMAS		HOPKINS
				FORWARDS				
	6			5		4		
	WILLIAMS			NEWELL		BURNS		
				HALF-BACKS				
		3				2		
		CUMLIFFE				DAVIES (Capt.)		
				BACKS				
				1				
				TARRY				
				GOAL				
LEFT WING								RIGHT WING

SWANSEA TOWN RESERVES

White Shirts, White Knickers

ANY ALTERATION WILL BE NOTED ON THE BOARD

THE FOOTBALL COMBINATION

Final Group Placings—Season 1946-1947

	P.	W.	D.	L.	F.	A.	Pts.		P.	W.	D.	L.	F.	A.	Pts.
Arsenal	14	8	4	2	22	8	20	Swansea Town	14	9	2	3	46	26	20
Tottenham Hotspur	14	4	8	2	22	14	16	Bristol Rovers	14	8	1	5	27	22	17
Queen's Park Rangers	14	5	6	3	19	18	16	Bristol City	14	6	4	4	29	28	16
Portsmouth	14	6	3	5	25	15	15	Aldershot	14	6	3	5	25	26	15
Brentford	14	6	3	5	18	17	15	Plymouth Argyle	14	5	4	5	24	26	14
Southend United	14	5	2	7	18	29	12	Cardiff City	14	5	2	7	31	32	12
Southampton	14	3	5	6	17	23	11	Bournemouth & Boscombe	14	4	2	8	27	39	10
Reading	14	1	5	8	10	27	7	Swindon Town	14	2	4	8	20	30	8
Coventry City	14	8	3	3	34	16	19	Chelsea	14	12	0	2	28	16	24
Leicester City	14	9	0	5	27	19	18	Fulham	14	11	1	2	39	15	23
Norwich City	14	8	1	5	32	20	17	West Ham United	14	5	4	5	26	19	14
Luton Town	14	4	5	5	15	15	13	Brighton & Hove Albion	14	6	2	6	22	26	14
Watford	14	4	5	5	23	26	13	Charlton Athletic	14	5	1	8	24	32	11
Northampton Town	14	4	4	6	24	26	12	Millwall	14	4	2	8	27	34	10
Ipswich Town	14	3	5	6	17	40	11	Leyton Orient	14	4	1	9	24	36	9
Birmingham City	14	3	3	8	16	26	9	Crystal Palace	14	2	3	9	11	23	7

The team line-ups for the Football Combination Cup Final between Arsenal Reserves and
Swansea City Reserves. This is the reverse side of the single-sheet programme issued.
(Cover on Page 17)

18

1946-47

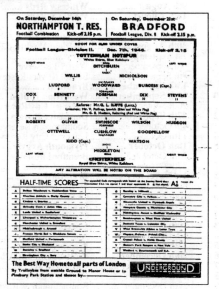

Spurs v Chesterfield, the cover and page three of the four page programme,
for the League match in December

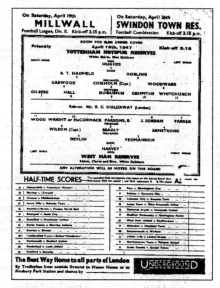

Spurs Reserves v West Ham United Reserves, the cover and page three of
the four page programme for the friendly played in April

1947-48

1   9th August .... Whites v Reds .... **Public Trial**
2   16th August .... Whites v Reds .... **Public Trial**
3   23rd August .... Arsenal Reserves .... Friendly
4   25th August .... Brighton & Hove Albion Reserves .... Football Combination
5   **30th August .... Sheffield Wednesday .... League**
6   **1st September .... Bury .... League**
7   6th September .... Watford Reserves .... Football Combination
8   8th September .... Bristol Rovers Reserves .... Football Combination
9   **13th September .... Bradford .... League**
10   **15th September .... West Ham United .... League**
11   20th September .... Coventry City Reserves .... Football Combination
12   **27th September .... Doncaster Rovers .... League**
13   4th October .... Southampton Reserves .... Football Combination
14   11th October .... Leicester City Reserves .... Football Combination
15   **18th October .... Plymouth Argyle .... League**
16   25th October .... Brentford Reserves .... Football Combination
17   27th October .... Leytonstone .... London Challenge Cup 2nd Round
18   **1st November .... Brentford .... League**
19   8th November .... Swansea Town Reserves .... Football Combination
20   10th November .... Chelsea .... London Challenge Cup Semi-Final
21   **15th November .... Leeds United .... League**
22   22nd November .... Charlton Athletic Reserves .... Football Combination
23   **29th November .... Coventry City .... League**
24   6th December .... Aldershot Reserves .... Football Combination
25   **13th December .... Birmingham City .... League**
26   **20th December .... West Bromwich Albion .... League**
27   **25th December .... Chesterfield .... League**
28   26th December .... Chelsea Reserves .... Football Combination
29   27th December .... Bournemouth & B.Athletic Reserves .... Football Combination
*   3rd January (am).......... Tottenham Boys v Edmonton Boys .... Schools Match
30   3rd January (pm) .... Chelmsford City .... Friendly
31   10th January .... Southend United Reserves .... Football Combination Cup
32   **17th January .... Cardiff City .... League**
33   **24th January .... West Bromwich Albion .... F.A Cup 4th Round**
*   31st January .... Edmonton Boys v Walsall Boys .... Schools Match
34   31st January .... Southampton Reserves .... Football Combination Cup
35   **7th February .... Leicester City .... F.A Cup 5th Round**
*   14th February (am) ...... Tottenham Boys v Enfield Boys .... Schools Match
36   14th February (pm)....... Charlton Athletic Reserves .... Football Combination Cup
37   **21st February .... Southampton .... League**
38   28th February .... Portsmouth Reserves .... Football Combination Cup
39   6th March .... Brentford Reserves .... Football Combination Cup
40   13th March .... Arsenal 'A' .... Friendly
41   **15th March .... Barnsley .... League**
42   20th March .... Portsmouth Reserves .... Football Combination
43   22nd March .... West Ham United Reserves .... Football Combination Cup
44   26th March .... Reading Reserves .... Football Combination Cup
45   **27th March .... Leicester City .... League**
46   **29th March .... Millwall .... League**
47   31st March .... Sea Cadets (England) v Haarlemermeer (Holland) ..... Representative Match
48   3rd April .... Edmonton Boys v Norwich Boys .... English Schools Shield
49   **5th April .... Luton Town .... League**
50   7th April .... British Army v French Army .... Army International
51   8th April .... Bristol City Reserves .... Football Combination
52   **10th April .... Fulham .... League**
53   **12th April .... Nottingham Forest .... League**
*   17th April .... Eire v N.Ireland, Italy v Belguim, England v Holland
                   International Youth Tournament
  (no club programme, as match covered by tournament brochure)
54   19th April .... Fulham .... London Challenge Cup Final
55   **24th April .... Newcastle United .... League**
56   26th April .... Arsenal Reserves .... Football Combination
57   28th April .... L.C.S. Southend v L.C.S. Western .London Co-operative Society Cup Final
*   29th April .... Edmonton Boys v Romford Boys .... Corinthian Shield Final
59   1st May .... Brownco Sports v Eton Manor .... Tottenham Charity Cup Final

20

1947-48

Programme: TWOPENCE.

CORINTHIAN SHIELD
FINAL

EDMONTON BOYS
v.
ROMFORD BOYS

On the TOTTENHAM HOTSPUR F.C. Ground
(by kind permission of Directors)

On THURSDAY EVENING, APRIL 29th, 1948.

Kick-off 6.30

NOTES

To many supporters it may be a surprising admission that, despite the many successful teams representing Edmonton in the past, none has previously qualified for the final of the Corinthian Shield and the London Schools' Championship Competition. The present Edmonton team has gone one step further than any of its predecessors in becoming finalists of this competition.

The Edmonton boys will be opposed by a most capable team from Romford, to whom we give a hearty welcome on their first appearance in this part of London. Outstanding in their team is Andrew Malcolm, captain and centre-half, a long-striding, powerful player, good in defence and attack. He is a schoolboy international, having played for England versus Wales and Scotland, on one of which occasions he was given the captaincy. He is also the captain of the Essex County team. Hearty congratulations to Andrew Malcolm on all these achievements. Whilst Malcolm inspires the Romford boys there are many other prominent players in the team, such as Schooling at right half, and Putter at outside left. By defeating South London (the holders) away, Romford boys proved themselves much above average in the London area.

Records to date:

	Romford				Edmonton.	
Round 1.	v. Leytonstone	(a) 4—2	Round 1.	Bye		
Round 2.	v. St. Pancras	(h) 2—0	Round 2.	v. Bermondsey	(h) 6—0
Round 3.	v. Lewisham	(h) 2—0	Round 3.	v. Dagenham	(h) 2—1
Round 4.	v. South London	(a) 4—1	Round 4.	v. Finchley	(h) 5—0
Semi-Final	v. Willesden	(h) 3—2	Semi-Final	v. Heston	(a) 2—0
		15 5				15 1

Rule 13 of the Competition Rules says:—' In semi-finals and finals the Hon. Gen. Secretary shall have the power, before play commences, to order extra time (30 minutes) to be played, if necessary.' His decision will not be known till just before the kick-off.

Once again we are indebted to the Directors of the Tottenham Hotspur F.C. for the use of their ground on this occasion, and we thank them for their generosity and helpfulness throughout the season.

A pink single-sheet issue for the Corinthian Shield Final between Edmonton Boys and Romford Boys (reverse side on Page 22)

21

1947-48

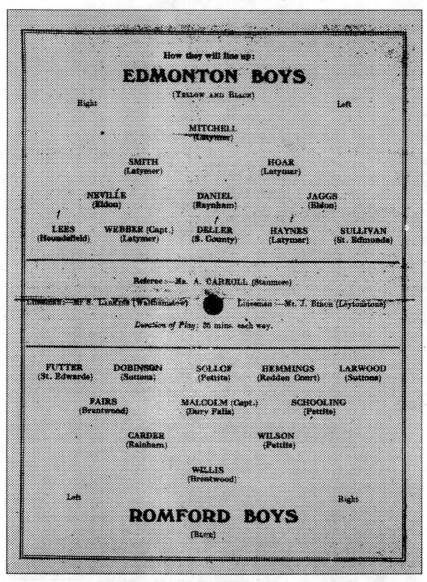

A pink single-sheet issue for the Corinthian Shield Final between Edmonton Boys and Romford Boys
(Cover on Page 21)

22

1947-48

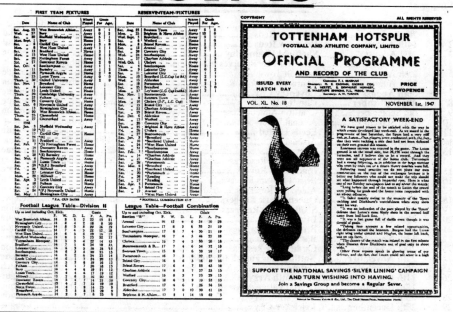

The back and front pages of the programme for the visit of **Brentford** in November 1947. Contrasting with, below left, the back page of the programme for the visit of Southampton, featuring a "Spurs Cartoon" of Freddie Cox.

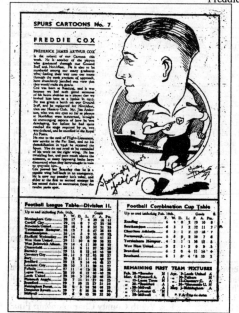

1948-49

Volume 41

*	2nd August	Sweden v Austria	Olympic Games
1	**7th August ....**	**Whites v Reds ....**	**Public Trial**
2	**14th August ....**	**Whites v Reds ....**	**Public Trial**
3	**21st August ....**	**Sheffield Wednesday ....**	**League**
4	23rd August	Leicester City Reserves	Football Combination
5	25th August	Ipswich Town 'A'	Eastern Counties League
6	28th August	Bournemouth & B. Reserves	Football Combination
7	**30th August ....**	**Coventry City ....**	**League**
8	**4th September ....**	**Chesterfield ....**	**League**
9	6th September	Charlton Athletic Reserves	Football Combination
10	11th September	Arsenal Reserves	Football Combination
11	**13th September ....**	**Leeds United ....**	**League**
12	16th September	Arsenal 'A'	Eastern Counties League
13	**18th September ....**	**Bury ....**	**League**
14	25th September	Portsmouth Reserves	Football Combination
15	**2nd October ....**	**Blackburn Rovers ....**	**League**
16	4th October	Bristol Rovers Reserves	Football Combination
17	9th October	Aldershot Reserves	Football Combination
18	**16th October ....**	**Queens Park Rangers ....**	**League**
19	23rd October	Southampton Reserves	Football Combination
20	**30th October ....**	**Bradford ....**	**League**
21	6th November	Bristol City Reserves	Football Combination
22	**13th November..........**	**Barnsley ....**	**League**
23	20th November	Cardiff City Reserves	Football Combination
24	**27th November..........**	**Nottingham Forest (abandoned) ....**	**League**
25	4th December	Oxford University v Cambridge University	Varsity Match
26	**11th December ....**	**Plymouth Argyle ....**	**League**
27	18th December	Crystal Palace Reserves	Football Combination
28	25th December	Millwall Reserves	Football Combination
29	**27th December ....**	**Leicester City ....**	**League**
30	**1st January ....**	**Lincoln City ....**	**League**
31	8th January	Brentford Reserves	Football Combination Cup
32	15th January	West Ham United 'A'	Eastern Counties League
33	**22nd January ....**	**West Bromwich Albion ....**	**League**
34	**29th January ....**	**Middlesbrough ....**	**Friendly**
35	5th February	Chelsea Reserves	Football Combination Cup
36	**12th February ....**	**Nottingham Forest ....**	**League**
37	**19th February ....**	**West Ham United ....**	**League**
38	26th February (am)	London Boys v Birmingham & District Boys ..	Inter-City Schools Challenge
39	26th February (pm)......	Brighton & Hove Albion Reserves	Football Combination
40	**5th March ....**	**Cardiff City ....**	**League**
41	12th March	Leyton Orient Reserves	Football Combination Cup
42	**19th March ....**	**Luton Town ....**	**League**
43	24th March	Reading Reserves	Football Combination Cup
44	26th March	Fulham Reserves	Football Combination Cup
45	**2nd April ....**	**Southampton ....**	**League**
46	6th April	British Army v Belgian Army	Army International
*	8th April	Edinburgh City Police v London Met.Police	Inter-Capital Football Challenge Cup
47	9th April	Queens Park Rangers Reserves	Football Combination Cup
48	11th April	Chelsea v West Ham United	London Challenge Cup Final
49	**15th April ....**	**Brentford ....**	**League**
50	**16th April ....**	**Grimsby Town ....**	**League**
51	18th April	Coventry City Reserves	Football Combination
*	20th April	Metropolitan Police v Edinburgh Police	Representative Match
52	20th April	Marley Youth Centre	London Minor Cup Final
53	21st April	Norwich City 'A'	Eastern Counties League
54	23rd April	Southampton Reserves	Football Combination Cup Semi-Final
55	**25th April ....**	**Hibernian ....**	**Friendly**
56	26th April	Fulham Reserves	Football Combination
57	28th April	Chelsea 'A'	Eastern Counties League
58	**30th April ....**	**Fulham ....**	**League**
59	2nd May....................	Southend United Reserves	Football Combination
60	3rd May....................	Glenville Sports v Sons Athletic	Tottenham Charity Cup Final
61	7th May....................	Arsenal Reserves v Chelsea Reserves ..	Combination Championship Decider
62	9th May....................	Chelsea v West Ham United	London Challenge Cup Final Replay
63	28th May	Middlesex v Liverpool	F.A Youth County Championship Final

24

1948-49

TOTTENHAM HOTSPUR

FOOTBALL AND ATHLETIC COMPANY, LIMITED

OFFICIAL PROGRAMME

AND RECORD OF THE CLUB

ISSUED EVERY MATCH DAY

Chairman : FRED J. BEARMAN
Directors : GEORGE COX, W. J. HERYET,
E. DEWHURST HORNSBY, G. WAGSTAFFE SIMMONS, F.J.I.,
HARRY TAYLOR, FREDK. WALE
Secretary: R. S. JARVIS

PRICE ONE PENNY

VOL. XLI. No. 52   APRIL 20th, 1949

THE ENFIELD CENTRAL BAND WILL PLAY AT EACH HOME GAME

Printed by Thomas Knight & Co., Ltd., The Clock House Press, Hoddesdon, Herts.

The front cover of the **Tottenham Juniors v Marley Youth Centre** programme
(reverse side on Page 26)

25

1948-49

<table>
<tr><td>On Saturday, April 23rd
SOUTHAMPTON RES.
Semi-Final, F.C. Cup   Kick-off 3.00 p.m.</td><td>On Monday, April 25th
HIBERNIAN
Friendly   Kick-off 6.15 p.m.</td></tr>
</table>

ROOM FOR 60,000 UNDER COVER

Final, London Minor Cup   **April 20th, 1949**   **Kick-off 6.15 p.m.**

TOTTENHAM JUNIORS
White Shirts, Blue Knickers

RIGHT WING   GOAL   LEFT WING

R. WARD
1

BACKS

T. WHEELER   **R. FORD**
2   3

HALF-BACKS

J. PONTY   **A. MARCHI**   **K. COLLINS**
4   5   6

FORWARDS

J. WOOLFORD   **N. HARRIS**   **J. SLEE**   **K. WOODCOCK**   **S. SEYMOUR**
7   8   9   10   11

Referee: Mr. A. COOK
Linesmen: Mr. J. Taylor (Blue and White Flag)
Mr. L. Scott (Red and White Flag)

---

11   10   9   8   7
T. O'BRIEN   **J. MOIR**   **A. SCHNEIDER**   **W. RUSSELL**   **B. PALMER**

FORWARDS

6   5   4
M. BENNIE   **J. SMAILES**   **D. HAWKINS**

HALF-BACKS

3   2
J. RAYMOND   **B. DULIEU**

BACKS

1
A. POCOCK

LEFT WING   GOAL   RIGHT WING

MARLEY YOUTH CENTRE
Green Shirts, White Knickers

ANY ALTERATION WILL BE NOTED ON THE BOARD

HOW THE CLUBS HAVE REACHED THE FINAL

TOTTENHAM JUNIORS					MARLEY YOUTH CENTRE		
Bye				1st Round	Bye		
beat Tudor Rose	...	...	... 3—2	2nd Round	beat Eton Manor	... ...	... 3—1
beat Caxton Juniors	...	...	... 5—0	3rd Round	beat Wood Green Youth Club	...	... 3—2
beat Old Bealonians	...	...	... 4—2	4th Round	beat Douglas United	... ...	... 6—1
beat Dockland Settlement	...	...	... 9—1	5th Round	beat Dulwich Hamlet Juniors	...	... 3—2
beat Goresbrook	...	...	... 2—0	Semi-Final	beat R.O.F.S.A.	... ...	... 1—0

The back cover of the **Tottenham Juniors v Marley Youth Centre** single-sheet programme
(front cover on Page 25)

26

1948-49

Tottenham v Bury, League

Chelsea v West Ham United,
London Challenge Cup Final Replay, the front cover
design of this single-sheet was the same as for the
Marley Youth Centre match.

Sweden v Austria, Olympic Games
These programmes were eight pages editions with
the cover design being applied to all Games events.

The first Maybank Press Ltd. programme
on sale at Tottenham?

1949-50

1	**6th August**	...... **Whites v Reds**	.......**Public Trial**
2	**13th August**	...... **Whites v Reds**	.......**Public Trial**
2	20th August	...... West Ham United 'A'	...... Eastern Counties League

(incorrectly numbered, sequence rectified)

4	**22nd August**	...... **Plymouth Argyle**	.......**League**
5	**27th August**	...... **Blackburn Rovers**	.......**League**
6	29th August	...... Brentford Reserves	...... Football Combination
7	3rd September	...... Watford Reserves	...... Football Combination
8	**5th September**	...... **Sheffield Wednesday**	.......**League**
9	**10th September**	...... **Leeds United**	.......**League**
10	**17th September**	...... **Bury**	.......**League**
11	19th September	...... Brighton & Hove Albion Reserves	...... Football Combination
12	24th September	...... Portsmouth Reserves	...... Football Combination
13	26th September	...... Charlton Athletic Reserves	...... Football Combination
14	29th September	...... Ipswich Town 'A'	...... Eastern Counties League
15	**1st October**	...... **Bradford**	.......**League**
16	3rd October	...... Plymouth Argyle Reserves	...... Football Combination
17	8th October	...... Swindon Town Reserves	...... Football Combination
18	**15th October**	...... **Coventry City**	.......**League**
19	17th October	...... Charlton Athletic	...... London Challenge Cup 1st Round Replay
20	20th October	...... Norwich City 'A'	...... Eastern Counties League
21	22nd October	...... Southampton Reserves	...... Football Combination
22	**29th October**	...... **Barnsley**	.......**League**
23	2nd November	...... Eynesbury Rovers	...... Friendly
*	5th November (am)	...... London Boys v Glasgow Boys	...... Inter-City Schools Match
24	5th November (pm)	...... Bristol City Reserves	...... Football Combination
25	**12th November**	...... **Sheffield United**	.......**League**
26	19th November (am)	...... Spurs Juniors v South Shields Ex-Schoolboys	...... Representative Games
26	19th November (pm)	...... Chelsea Reserves	...... Football Combination
27	**26th November**	...... **Queens Park Rangers**	.......**League**
*	30th November	...... England v Italy	...... International
28	3rd December	...... Oxford University v Cambridge University	...... Varsity Match
29	**10th December**	...... **Swansea Town**	.......**League**
30	**17th December**	...... **Brentford**	.......**League**
31	24th December	...... Ipswich Town Reserves	...... Football Combination
32	**26th December**	...... **Chesterfield**	.......**League**
33	27th December	...... Chelsea 'A'	...... Eastern Counties League
34	**31st December**	...... **Cardiff City**	.......**League**
35	7th January	...... F.A Youth XI	...... Friendly
36	14th January	...... Brentford Reserves	...... Football Combination Cup
*	21st January (am)	...... Hornsey Boys v Southampton Boys	...... English Schools Shield 5th Round
37	21st January (pm)	...... Arsenal 'A'	...... Eastern Counties League
38	**28th January**	...... **Sunderland**	.......**F.A Cup 4th Round**
39	**4th February**	...... **Leicester City**	.......**League**
40	11th February	...... Southend United Reserves	...... Football Combination Cup
41	18th February	...... Crystal Palace Reserves	...... Football Combination Cup
42	**25th February**	...... **Southampton**	.......**League**
43	4th March	...... Chelsea Reserves	...... Football Combination Cup
44	**11th March**	...... **Luton Town**	.......**League**
45	18th March	...... Chelsea v Arsenal	...... F.A Cup Semi-Final
46	20th March	...... Brighton & Hove Albion Reserves	...... Football Combination Cup
47	22nd March	...... Chelsea v Arsenal	...... F.A Cup Semi-Final Replay
48	**25th March**	...... **West Ham United**	.......**League**
49	1st April (am)	...... Welsh Juniors	...... Friendly
50	1st April (pm)	...... Queens Park Rangers Reserves	...... Football Combination
51	**7th April**	...... **Hull City**	.......**League**
52	**8th April**	...... **Preston North End**	.......**League**
53	10th April (am)	...... Edmonton Boys v Walthamstow Boys	...... Schools Match
54	10th April (pm)	...... Bournemouth & B. Athletic Reserves	...... Football Combination
55	13th April	...... Arsenal Reserves	...... Football Combination Cup
56	15th April (am)	...... Liverpool Juniors	...... Friendly
57	15th April (pm)	...... West Ham United Reserves	...... Football Combination
58	17th April	...... Aldershot Reserves	...... Football Combination
59	18th April	...... Middlesex Boys v Essex Boys	...... Schools Match
60	**22nd April**	...... **Grimsby Town**	.......**League**
61	26th April	...... Edmonton Boys v Tottenham Boys	...... Hotspur Cup Final
*	28th April	......	...... Tobacco Trades Cup Final
62	29th April	...... Norwich City Reserves	...... Football Combination
63	**1st May**	...... **Hibernian**	.......**Friendly**
64	3rd May	...... Oldham v Reading	...... National Co-op. Sports Assoc. Cup
*	5th May	......	...... Tottenham Charity Cup Final
65	6th May (am)	...... Edmonton Boys v Dagenham Boys	...... Corinthian Shield Final
66	6th May (pm)	...... Harwich & Parkeston	...... East Anglian Cup Final

1949-50

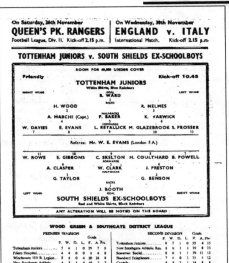

Tottenham Juniors v South Shields Ex-Schoolboys, the team line-ups from the 4-page programme issued for this friendly match.

Tottenham v Grimsby Town, an eight page edition to celebrate the Division Two Championship.

1950-51

1	**12th August**	**Whites v Reds**	**Public Trial**
2	**19th August**	**Blackpool**	**League**
3	21st August	Swindon Town Reserves	Football Combination
4	26th August	Aldershot Reserves	Football Combination
5	**28th August**	**Bolton Wanderers**	**League**
6	2nd September	Charlton Athletic Reserves	Football Combination
7	6th September	Eynesbury Rovers	East Anglian Cup 1st Round
8	**9th September**	**Manchester United**	**League**
9	16th September	Chelsea Reserves	Football Combination
10	**18th September**	**Lovells Athletic**	**Friendly**
11	**23rd September**	**Sunderland**	**League**
12	25th September	Brentford Reserves	Football Combination
12	30th September	Watford Reserves	Football Combination
	(incorrectly numbered, sequence not rectified)		
13	**7th October**	**Burnley**	**League**
14	9th October	Hounslow Town	London Challenge Cup 1st Round
15	14th October	Bristol City Reserves	Football Combination
15	**21st October**	**Stoke City**	**League**
	(incorrectly numbered, sequence not rectified)		
16	23rd October	Crystal Palace	London Challenge Cup 2nd Round
17	28th October	Ipswich Town Reserves	Football Combination
18	**4th November**	**Portsmouth**	**League**
19	11th November	Brighton & Hove Albion Reserves	Football Combination
20	13th November	Brentford	London Challenge Cup Semi-Final
21	**18th November**	**Newcastle United**	**League**
22	25th November	West Ham United Reserves	Football Combination
23	**2nd December**	**Middlesbrough**	**League**
24	9th December	Oxford University v Cambridge University	Varsity Match
25	16th December	Southampton Reserves	Football Combination
26	18th December	Bristol Rovers v Gillingham	F.A Cup 2nd Round 2nd Replay
27	**23rd December**	**Arsenal**	**League**
28	25th December	Norwich City Reserves	Football Combination
29	**26th December**	**Derby County**	**League**
30	**30th December**	**Charlton Athletic**	**League**
31	6th January	Bournemouth & B. Athletic Reserves	Football Combination
32	8th January	Plymouth Argyle Reserves	Football Combination
33	13th January	Portsmouth Reserves	Football Combination
34	**20th January**	**Wolverhampton Wanderers**	**League**
35	3rd February	Crystal Palace Reserves	Football Combination Cup
36	10th February	Brentford Reserves	Football Combination Cup
37	**17th February**	**Aston Villa**	**League**
38	24th February	Southend United Reserves	Football Combination Cup
39	**3rd March**	**Chelsea**	**League**
*	10th March (am)	Southern Youth Clubs v Northern Youth Clubs	Representative Match
40	10th March (pm)	Chelsea Reserves	Football Combination Cup
41	**17th March**	**West Bromwich Albion**	**League**
42	23rd March	Brighton & Hove Albion Reserves	Football Combination Cup
43	**26th March**	**Fulham**	**League**
44	**31st March**	**Everton**	**League**
45	7th April	Queens Park Rangers Reserves	Football Combination Cup
46	**14th April**	**Huddersfield Town**	**League**
47	21st April	West Ham United 'A'	Eastern Counties League
48	23rd April	Arsenal Reserves	Football Combination Cup
49	24th April	Brentford Juniors	Winchester Cup Final
50	26th April	Chelsea 'A'	Eastern Counties League
51	**28th April**	**Sheffield Wednesday**	**League**
52	**5th May**	**Liverpool**	**League**
53	**7th May**	**F.C Austria**	**Festival of Britain Match**
54	8th May	London XI v Provincial XI	Schoolboys Challenge Match
55	**12th May**	**Dortmund Borussia**	**Festival of Britain Match**

1950-51

Tottenham v Middlesbrough,
League match in December.

Tottenham v Liverpool,
a change of cover design to celebrate the League
Championship, the same cover design was used for
the Festival of Britain Match against F.C. Austria,
the team line-ups for which are shown below.

(left): Tottenham v Lovell's Athletic,
Friendly Match.

31

1951-52

Volume 44

1951-52

TOTTENHAM HOTSPUR

FOOTBALL AND ATHLETIC COMPANY, LIMITED
President: The Right Hon. LORD MORRISON, P.C., D.L., J.P.

Official Programme

AND RECORD OF THE CLUB

Secretary: R. S. JARVIS

Team Manager: ARTHUR S. ROWE

Medical Officer: Dr. A. E. TUGHAN

Chairman: FRED J. BEARMAN

Directors: F. JOHN BEARMAN, Wm. J. HERYET, E. DEWHURST HORNSBY, G. WAGSTAFFE SIMMONS, F.J.I., HARRY TAYLOR, FREDK. WALE

PRICE
ONE PENNY

VOL. XLIV. No. 23.   THURSDAY, NOVEMBER 8th, 1951

On Saturday, 10th November	On Saturday, 17th November
PORTSMOUTH RESERVES	**CHELSEA**
Football Combn. Sec. 'B' Kick-off 2.30 p.m.	Football League, Div. I. Kick-off 2.30 p.m.

TOTTENHAM HOTSPUR v. CAMBRIDGE UNIVERSITY

ROOM FOR 50,000 UNDER COVER

Friendly   **November 8th, 1951**   **Kick-off 2.30**

TOTTENHAM HOTSPUR
White Shirts, Blue Knickers

RIGHT WING   GOAL   LEFT WING

REYNOLDS
1

BACKS

HENTY		J. WILLIAMS
2		3

HALF-BACKS

ROBSHAW	KING	RAWLINGS
4	5	6

FORWARDS

CASTLE	A. STOKES	McCLELLAN	MURPHY (Capt.)	N. SULLIVAN
7	8	9	10	11

Referee: Mr. J. W. DYSON (Herts.)

11	10	9	8	7
L. J. BOARDMAN	J. LAYBOURNE	G. WITTEKIND	P. B. H. MAY	R. SUTCLIFFE
(St. Catherine's)	(Emmanuel)	(Downing)	(Pembroke) Capt.	(St. John's)

	6	5	4	
	R. C. VOWELS	G. ALEXANDER	A. SENIOR	
	(Emmanuel)	(Caius)	(Downing)	

3		2
G. TORDOFF		G. WHITEFIELD
(St. John's)		(Emmanuel)

1
J. DAVID
(St. John's)

LEFT WING   RIGHT WING

CAMBRIDGE UNIVERSITY
Light Blue and White Halves, White Knickers

ANY ALTERATION WILL BE NOTED ON THE BOARD

Printed by Thomas Knight & Co. Ltd., The Clock House Press, Hoddesdon Herts.

33

1951-52

On Saturday, 13th October
ARSENAL RESERVES
Football Combn. Sec. 'B' Kick-off 3.15 p.m.

On Saturday, 20th October
ASTON VILLA
Football League, Div. I. Kick-off 3.00 p.m.

ROOM FOR 50,000 UNDER COVER

Friendly　　　October 10th, 1951　　　Kick-off 3.15

TOTTENHAM HOTSPUR
White Shirts, Blue Knickers

RIGHT WING　　　　　　　GOAL　　　　　　　LEFT WING

DITCHBURN
1

BACKS

RAMSEY　　　　　　　　　**WILLIS**
2　　　　　　　　　　　　　　3

HALF-BACKS

NICHOLSON　　　**CLARKE**　　　**BURGESS** (Capt.)
4　　　　　　　5　　　　　　　6

FORWARDS

WALTERS　**BENNETT**　**McCLELLAN**　**BAILY**　**MEDLEY**
7　　　8　　　9　　　10　　　11

Referee: **Mr. A. H. BLYTHE** (Edmonton)
Linesmen: Mr. W. Potts, London (Red Flag)
Mr. F. L. Warburton, London (Yellow Flag)

11　　　10　　　9　　　　8　　　7
KNUDSEN　**LUNDBERG**　**JENSEN**　**HANSEN, J. W.**　**HOLM**

FORWARDS

6　　　　　5　　　　　4
NIELSEN, S.　　**ANDERSEN**　　**HANSEN, E.**

HALF-BACKS

3　　　　　　2
BASTRUP-BIRK　　　**PETERSEN**

BACKS
1
NEILSEN, E.

LEFT WING　　　　GOAL　　　　RIGHT WING

COPENHAGEN COMBINATION
Light Blue Shirts

ANY ALTERATION WILL BE NOTED ON THE BOARD

HALF-TIME SCORES
The appended Code corresponds with letters on the Scoring Board thus
first-named Club has scored 1 and their opponents 0.　★ Not played

A		O		
B		P		
C		Q		
D		R		
E		S		
F		T		
G		U		
H		V		
J		W		
K		X		
L		Y		
M		Z		
N				

Supporters are reminded that this season there are no prematch bookings for the Stands. 2,000 seats are available at the turnstiles on match days.

YOUR BEST WAY HOME IS BY
LONDON TRANSPORT
Trolleybuses from outside the ground serve Manor House and Finsbury Park Stations

(above) The team line-ups of the **Tottenham v Copenhagen Combination** programme
(overleaf) The cover of the single-sheet **Tottenham v Cambridge University** programme

34

1951-52

Tottenham v Hibernian, Friendly

Tottenham v Newcastle United,
F.A. Charity Shield

Single-sided insert in the F.A. Cup
Semi-Final programme for the
re-arranged match on April 5th 1952.

Arsenal v Chelsea,
F.A. Cup Semi-Final

1952-53

Volume 45

1	**16th August**	**Whites v Blues**	**Public Trial**
2	**23rd August**	**West Bromwich Albion**	**League**
3	30th August	Arsenal Reserves	Football Combination
4	**1st September**	**Manchester City**	**League**
5	**6th September**	**Cardiff City**	**League**
6	8th September	Birmingham City Reserves	Football Combination
7	13th September	Southampton Reserves	Football Combination
8	**15th September**	**Liverpool**	**League**
9	**20th September**	**Arsenal**	**League**
10	22nd September	West Ham United Reserves	Football Combination
11	**27th September**	**Burnley**	**League**
12	29th September	Cardiff City Reserves	Football Combination
13	4th October	Fulham Youth	Middlesex Invitation Cup
14	11th October	Charlton Athletic Reserves	Football Combination
15	13th October	Plymouth Argyle Reserves	Football Combination
16	**18th October**	**Blackpool**	**League**
17	25th October	Chelsea Reserves	Football Combination
18	**1st November**	**Manchester United**	**League**
19	8th November	Fulham Reserves	Football Combination
20	10th November	Norwich City Reserves	Football Combination
21	**15th November**	**Bolton Wanderers**	**League**
22	22nd November	Norwich City 'A'	Eastern Counties League
23	**29th November**	**Sunderland**	**League**
24	6th December	Northampton Town Reserves	Football Combination
25	**13th December**	**Charlton Athletic**	**League**
26	20th December	Portsmouth Reserves	Football Combination
27	**25th December**	**Middlesbrough**	**League**
28	27th December	Coventry City Reserves (postponed)	Football Combination
29	**3rd January**	**Newcastle United**	**League**
30	**12th January**	**Tranmere Rovers**	**F.A Cup 3rd Round Replay**
31	17th January	Reading Reserves	Football Combination
32	21st January	Coventry City Reserves	Football Combination
33	**24th January**	**Sheffield Wednesday**	**League**
34	31st January	Tottenham Boys v Bristol Boys	English Schools Shield
35	**4th February**	**Preston North End**	**F.A Cup 4th Round Replay**
36	7th February	Queens Park Rangers Reserves	Football Combination Cup
37	14th February	Brentford Reserves	Football Combination Cup
38	**21st February**	**Preston North End**	**League**
39	28th February	Waltham Cross Boys Club	Winchester Cup 3rd Round
40	**4th March**	**Birmingham City**	**F.A Cup 6th Round Replay**
41	7th March	Brighton & Hove Albion Reserves	Football Combination Cup
42	**12th March**	**Derby County**	**League**
43	**14th March**	**Chelsea**	**League**
44	21st March	Chelsea Reserves	Football Combination Cup
45	**28th March**	**Portsmouth**	**League**
46	30th March	Millwall Reserves	Football Combination
47	**3rd April**	**Stoke City**	**League**
48	4th April	Crystal Palace Reserves	Football Combination Cup
49	6th April	Brighton & Hove Albion Youth	Middlesex Invitation Cup
50	8th April	Southend United Reserves	Football Combination Cup
51	**11th April**	**Aston Villa**	**League**
52	16th April	West Ham United 'A'	Eastern Counties League
*	18th April (am)	London Schools v Midland Counties Federation	Representative Match
53	18th April (pm)	Arsenal Reserves	Football Combination Cup
*	23rd April	Dagenham Boys v S.London Boys	Sun Shield Final
54	**25th April**	**Wolverhampton Wanderers**	**League**
*	30th April	Tottenham Boys v Edmonton Boys	Star Shield Final

1952-53

TOTTENHAM HOTSPUR

FOOTBALL AND ATHLETIC COMPANY, LIMITED

President: The Right Hon. LORD MORRISON, P.C., D.L., J.P.

Official Programme

AND RECORD OF THE CLUB

Secretary: R. S. JARVIS

Team Manager: ARTHUR S. ROWE

Medical Officer: Dr. A. E. TUGHAN

Chairman: FRED J. BEARMAN

Directors: F. JOHN BEARMAN, Wm. J. HERYET, E. DEWHURST HORNSBY, G. WAGSTAFFE SIMMONS, F.J.I., HARRY TAYLOR, FREDK. WALE

PRICE ONE PENNY

VOL. XLV. No. 13.   SATURDAY, OCTOBER 4th, 1952

On Saturday, October 11th	On Monday, October 13th
CHARLTON ATH. Reserves	**PLYMOUTH ARGYLE RES.**
Football Combn. Div. I. Kick-off **3.15** p.m.	Football Combn. Div. I. Kick-off **3.15** p.m.

TOTTENHAM HOTSPUR YOUTH v FULHAM YOUTH

Middx. Invitation Cup   October 4th, 1952   **Kick-off 3.15**

TOTTENHAM HOTSPUR YOUTH

White Shirts, Blue Knickers

RIGHT WING   LEFT WING

GOAL
L. MELLOWS
1

BACKS
M. HOPKINS (Capt.)   **R. COWLING**
2   3

HALF-BACKS
M. CONROY   **J. LAURELS**   **F. TEECE**
4   5   6

FORWARDS
A. WOOD   **A. WOODS**   **C. McGILLICUDDY**   T. CLISS   **K. BIRKS**
7   8   9   10   11

Referee: Mr. R. O. HOUNSELL (Wood Green)

Linesmen: (Red Flag)
              (Yellow Flag)

AUSTIN   **BARTON**   **LOASBY**   **HAINES**   **O'KEEFE**
11   10   9   8   7

FORWARDS
BROUGHTON   **LAMPE**   **EDWARDS**
6   5   4

HALF-BACKS
MALLABURN   **COLLINGS**
3   2

BACKS
TWICKENHAM
GOAL
1

LEFT WING   RIGHT WING

FULHAM YOUTH

Blue Shirts, Black Knickers

ANY ALTERATION WILL BE NOTED ON THE BOARD

Printed by Thomas Knight & Co Ltd The Clock House Press, Hoddesdon Herts

Tottenham Youth v Fulham Youth, the single-sheet programme for the Middlesex Invitation Cup. The reverse side is on the next page.

1952-53

THE SPURS' GOSSIP OF THE WEEK

TODAY'S MATCH

The fixture this afternoon is a Junior game between Tottenham Youth team and Fulham Youth team in the Middlesex Invitation Cup competition. This competition is run on a League basis; there are seven clubs competing, and each club plays its opponents once only and has three home games and three away games. When the final League table is made up the top club then plays the second club for the Challenge Cup, which is known as the "G.R. Hawes Cup."

Last season the winners were Portsmouth, and Fulham were runners-up. The competition is restricted to players who are under 18 years of age on September 1st in the current season.

In their first game, played at Cheshunt, our juniors lost 0—3 against the Crystal Palace Youth team.

The following is the table of results to date:—

	P.	W.	D.	L.	Goals F.	A.	Ps.
Brentford	2	1	1	0	11	8	3
Chelsea	1	1	0	0	5	0	2
Fulham	1	1	0	0	2	0	2
Crystal Palace	2	1	0	1	6	6	2
Portsmouth	1	0	1	0	5	5	1
Tottenham Hotspur	1	0	0	1	0	3	0
Brighton	2	0	0	2	0	7	0

We look forward to an attractive game and welcome the Fulham lads to our enclosure in this encounter between our respective under 18's.

OUR WIN LAST SATURDAY

Although we won our match with Burnley last Saturday we cannot feel happy with the form shown. It was not a great game, and although the visitors forced three corners to our two we had slightly the best of matters in the first half but our passing was not up to the usual standard. In the early stages our left wing showed up well, but afterwards the right wing came into the picture. The visitors quite rightly have the reputation of having one of the best defences in the League, and in this game they certainly broke up many attempts of our forwards, but whether it is that our players have not yet got the feel of our new turf or the fact that they were supported by a strong wind in the second half, many of the passes made both by forwards and halves to open spaces would have needed a racing car to reach them.

Of the two goalies, Ditchburn had the more difficult shots to deal with during the first half, when we faced the strong wind, and a blank score sheet at half-time was a fair reflection of the game. The second half provided an early thrill as after some 5 minutes' play Withers took a return pass from Medley and sensing an opening he, contrary to the accepted standards of a full-back's play, made his way to the corner flag from which an accurate centre was pushed on to the bar by the goalie only for Duquemin to head through from the rebound. This goal served to inspire both teams to put more into attack, and both goalies had more to do, but not for another 20 minutes was there any further scoring, when the visitors reserve outside-left, Pilkington, who had a good game, fastened on to a weak pass back and ran on to test Ditchburn with a hard shot which he did well to stop, but Holden running up on to the rebound equalised for the visitors.

Both teams made some good efforts to get the lead, but we had the better opportunities and both Duquemin and Bennett missed golden opportunities, and it certainly looked as if it was not our day; however, 2 minutes from the end Medley took the ball to the corner flag, and what looked like a high centre swerved in with the wind and surprisingly beat the visitors' goalie, giving us a rather lucky win by 2 goals to 1.

WE VISIT PRESTON

To-day we meet Preston North End at Deepdale, and our lads will have to improve on their showing of last Saturday

to secure any points. At the moment we are a point ahead in the League table but our hosts have a match in hand, and a superior goal average of 13 for, 11 against. Our last two meetings have resulted as under:—

1952—February 23rd (home): won 1—0 (Harmer).
April 14th (away): drew 1—1 (Ramsey).

THE RESERVES

Our visit to Coventry Reserves in a 1st Division Combination fixture last Saturday resulted in a draw of two goals each. At the interval we were losing by a goal to nil, but a good rally in the second half secured us a point. Our team was: Reynolds; Henty, Willmott; Marchi, Gibbins, Brittan; Castle, Uphill, Gibbons, Dicker, Adams.

The scorers were Castle and Gibbons.

On Monday last they received Cardiff City Reserves in the return Combination game. In the first game, on the opening day of the season, we lost at Cardiff by the solitary goal, and our visitors who had up to our meeting last Monday only lost one game, were then at the top of the Combination table with 13 points for eight games. This time we proved superior and won easily by 6 goals to 1, after Cardiff had scored in the first few minutes.

The team was: Reynolds; P. Baker, Hopkins; Robshaw, Farley, Brittan; Adams, Uphill, Gibbons, McClellan, Quinlan.

Goal scorers were McClellan 3, Adams (penalty), Quinlan, and Gibbons.

To-day we visit Portsmouth Reserves in another Combination fixture.

"A" TEAM

After last Wednesday week's game with the Arsenal "A" at Hendon, which yielded us a point, we visited Chelmsford City Reserves in another Eastern Counties League game on Saturday last and were successful by 3 goals to 1 after leading by 1—0 at the interval. Our team was: Ames; Shaw, Pitcher; Neill, King, Rawlings; Dowsett, A. Stokes, Boseley, Spivey, Quinlan. Our scorers were A. Stokes (2) and Boseley. To-day they visit Yarmouth Town in the return League fixture. The previous game on September 13th resulted in a goalless draw.

"B" TEAM

This team were without a game last Saturday, but the previous Thursday they entertained Hastings United Reserves in the return Metropolitan League fixture, at Cheshunt, winning by 2 goals to 1. The attendance was, however, disappointing and we can assure our supporters who can visit these midweek games that they will find them well worth while, and will in all probability be watching some young player who in the course of a few years may be a first-team star.

On Wednesday last they met Tonbridge Reserves in the return League fixture, which resulted in a win for Tonbridge by 2 goals to nil.

To-day they visit Dunstable Town in a League game.

EXCURSION TO DERBY

Henry Coaches Ltd. will operate coaches to Derby for our away match next Saturday. Coaches will leave 1 Broad Lane, Tottenham, N.15, at 8 a.m. and Whitehall Street (opposite ground) at 8.15 a.m., the fare being only 10/6. For further particulars phone Stamford Hill 1138.

VARIA

We are being favoured with many important visitors of late, and last Saturday was no exception, as in addition to the Mayors of Southgate and Tottenham, Mr. Walter Winterbottom, the English Team Manager, was an interested spectator.

The first team will be away again next Saturday when they are visiting Derby County. Our next home game is a very attractive one as the visitors are Blackpool, who are in such devastating form at present with Stanley Matthews shining as brightly as ever.

Tottenham Youth v Fulham Youth, the single-sheet programme for the Middlesex Invitation Cup. The reverse side is on the next page.

1952-53

Tottenham Reserves v Coventry City Reserves, team line-ups in the programme for the postponed match in December.

Tottenham v Birmingham City, F.A. Cup 6th Round Replay

Cover of the small 4 paged programme for the Star Shield Final between Tottenham Boys and Edmonton Boys.

(right):
Whites v Blues,
Public Trial Match

1953-54

1	**15th August**	.... **Whites v Colours**	.... **Public Trial**
2	**19th August**	.... **Aston Villa**	.... **Legaue**
3	22nd August	.... Chelsea Reserves	.... Football Combination Cup
4	**26th August**	.... **Charlton Athletic**	.... **League**
5	**29th August**	.... **Middlesbrough**	.... **League**
6	2nd September	.... Southend United Reserves	.... Football Combination Cup
7	5th September	.... Brighton & Hove Albion Reserves	.... Football Combination Cup
8	9th September	.... Arsenal Reserves	.... Football Combination Cup
9	**12th September**	.... **Liverpool**	.... **League**
10	**16th September**	.... **Burnley**	.... **League**
11	19th September	.... Crystal Palace Reserves	.... Football Combination Cup
12	23rd September	.... Queens Park Rangers Reserves	.... Football Combination Cup
13	**26th September**	.... **Manchester United**	.... **League**
14	**29th September**	.... **Racing Club de Paris**	.... **Friendly**
15	3rd October	.... Brentford Reserves	.... Football Combination Cup
16	5th October	.... Fulham	.... London Challenge Cup 1st Round
17	**10th October**	.... **Arsenal**	.... **League**
18	14th October	.... Football Association XI v Royal Air Force	.... Representative Match
19	17th October	.... Portsmouth Reserves	.... Football Combination
20	22nd October	.... London Boys v Manchester Boys	.... Inter-City Schools Challenge
21	**24th October**	.... **Manchester City**	.... **League**
22	**28th October**	.... **F.C Austria**	.... **Friendly**
23	31st October	.... Millwall Reserves	.... Football Combination
24	**7th November**	.... **Chelsea**	.... **League**
25	10th November	.... Amateur International XI	.... Friendly
26	14th November	.... Chelsea Reserves	.... Football Combination
27	**21st November**	.... **Huddersfield Town**	.... **League**
28	28th November	.... Ipswich Town Reserves	.... Football Combination
29	**5th December**	.... **Wolverhampton Wanderers**	.... **League**
30	12th December	.... Fulham Reserves	.... Football Combination
31	**19th December**	.... **Sheffield Wednesday**	.... **League**
32	**25th December**	.... **Portsmouth**	.... **League**
33	26th December	.... Norwich City Reserves	.... Football Combination
34	2nd January	.... Charlton Athletic Reserves (postponed)	.... Football Combination
35	9th January	.... Leicester City Reserves	.... Football Combination
36	**13th January**	.... **Leeds United**	.... **F.A Cup 3rd Round Replay**
37	**16th January**	.... **West Bromwich Albion**	.... **League**
38	23rd January	.... West Ham United Reserves	.... Football Combination
39	30th January	.... Chelsea 'A'	.... Metropolitan League
40	**6th February**	.... **Newcastle United**	.... **League**
41	13th February	.... Plymouth Argyle Reserves	.... Football Combination
42	20th February	.... Brighton & Hove Albion 'A'	.... Metropolitan League
43	**24th February**	.... **Hull City**	.... **F.A Cup 5th Round Replay**
44	27th February	.... Tottenham Boys v Edmonton Boys	.... Hotspur Cup Final
45	**3rd March**	.... **Bolton Wanderers**	.... **League**
46	**6th March**	.... **Cardiff City**	.... **League**
47	13th March	.... Crook Town v Walthamstow Avenue	.... F.A Amateur Cup Semi-Final
48	**20th March**	.... **Sunderland**	.... **League**
49	27th March	.... Arsenal Reserves	.... Football Combination
50	31st March	.... Charlton Athletic Reserves	.... Football Combination
51	**3rd April**	.... **Blackpool**	.... **League**
52	**5th April**	.... **Hibernian**	.... **Friendly**
53	10th April	.... Reading Reserves	.... Football Combination
54	12th April	.... Cardiff City Reserves	.... Football Combination
55	16th April	.... Luton Town Reserves	.... Football Combination
56	**17th April**	.... **Sheffield United**	.... **League**
57	**19th April**	.... **Preston North End**	.... **League**
58	24th April	.... Bournemouth & B. Athletic Reserves	.... Football Combination

1953-54

TOTTENHAM HOTSPUR

FOOTBALL AND ATHLETIC COMPANY LIMITED

Official Programme

AND RECORD OF THE CLUB

Secretary: R. S. JARVIS
Team Manager: ARTHUR S. ROWE
Medical Officer: Dr. A. E. TUGHAN

Chairman: FRED. J. BEARMAN
Vice-Chairman: E. DEWHURST HORNSBY
Directors: F. JOHN BEARMAN, Wm. J. HERYET
FREDK. WALE

**PRICE
TWOPENCE**

VOL. XLVI. No. 44   SATURDAY, FEBRUARY 27th, 1954

'HOTSPUR' CHALLENGE CUP

Tottenham and Edmonton boys join battle to-day to decide the destination of the "Hotspur" Cup for season 1953-54. At the moment the trophy is held jointly as the 1952 game produced a 1—1 draw here. Tottenham have yet to win this cup, Edmonton having been successful on the three previous occasions.

The teams have already met twice this season, on both occasions in the second round of the Middlesex *Star* Shield. The first meeting resulted in a 1—1 draw at the Barrass Stadium and Tottenham won the replay convincingly by 6 goals to 2.

The teams are skippered by their outstanding personalities —Ray Wright leads Tottenham and John Petts leads Edmonton. Incidentally, both are English Schools' international trialists, and both have represented London and Middlesex.

Terence Harrison, the Tottenham left-winger, has been "capped" by London and Middlesex. John Clarkson, the young Edmonton centre-forward, is not on show to-day as he is playing in the Junior International Trial at Birmingham.

RECORDS THIS SEASON

Tottenham have played eight competition games, winning five, drawing one and losing two, while Edmonton have played nine, won five, drawn one and lost three.

The Tottenham senior team, on show to-day, have reached the semi-final stage of the *Star* Shield and play Harrow on March 6th at the Lordship Enclosure, kick-off 10.30 a.m. Both Edmonton's and Tottenham's under-13 sides are enjoying a very successful season—they are unbeaten to date and Tottenham have reached the final of the Middlesex "Compton" Cup.

DURATION OF PLAY

The duration of play will be 40 minutes each way and extra time of 10 minutes each way if necessary.

SUBSTITUTES

Substitutes will be allowed up to the 39th minute in cases of injury.

PRESENTATION OF TROPHY

The Lady Morrison, Mayor of Tottenham, has kindly consented to present the trophy at the conclusion of the match.

APPRECIATION

The Tottenham and Edmonton Schools' Football Associations are very grateful to the Directors of the Tottenham Hotspur Football Club for their continued generosity in offering the use of their ground. The interest taken by the Club in schoolboy football has always been greatly appreciated.

AND AN APPEAL

The co-operation of all in ensuring that no damage is done to the Club's property will be appreciated, as it is only through the generosity of the Club that the match is being played. Spectators, young and old, are asked to refrain from throwing any kind of litter on the playing area and from climbing over the rails during the interval or after the match.

CUP TIE ARRANGEMENTS

The Cup-tie with West Bromwich Albion, which is a Sixth Round tie, on March 13th, will not be an all-ticket match and admission to the ground will be by payment at the turnstiles, 1/9 and 2/3. Admission to the Stand and Paddock will be by ticket only, and the prices of the seats will be 7/6 and for the Paddock 5/-.

As this is not an all-ticket match our allocation of tickets will be comparatively small and it is feared that in view of the heavy volume of inquiries it will not be possible to meet all requests for tickets. Nevertheless, it is emphasised that there is a capacity of 60,000 at the Hawthorns and that ample standing accommodation will be available by payment at the turnstiles.

In our next issue we shall have available the particulars of the excursions by British Railways and by motor coaches.

AMATEUR CUP SEMI-FINAL HERE

On Saturday, March 13th, we have the pleasure of staging one of the Amateur Cup Semi-finals when Crook Town will meet either Finchley or Walthamstow Avenue. This should be an exceptionally fine match and a large crowd is expected. Further details will be published in a later programme. The kick-off is timed for 3 p.m.

Tottenham Schoolboys v Edmonton Schoolboys, the single-sheet programme for the Hotpsur Challenge Cup Final. The reverse side is on the next page.

1953-54

On Wednesday, March 3rd	On Saturday, March 6th
BOLTON WANDERERS	**CARDIFF CITY**
Football League Div. I Kick-off **3** p.m.	Football League, Div. I Kick-off **3.15** p.m.

ROOM FOR 50,000 UNDER COVER

Hotspur Challenge Cup (Final)   **February 27th, 1954**   **Kick-off 3.15 p.m.**

TOTTENHAM SCHOOLBOYS
White Shirts, Blue Knickers

RIGHT WING

WITTEY
(South Grove)
1

LEFT WING

HILLS
(Rowland Hill)
2

JENKINS
(Downhills)
3

D'EATH
(Tottenham County)
4

HACKETT
(St. Thomas More)
5

HAMMOND
(Downhills)
6

TAYLOR
(Rowland Hill)
7

WRIGHT (Capt.)
(Downhills)
8

HUNT
(Page Green)
9

DUKE
(St. Thomas More)
10

HARRISON
(Rowland Hill)
11

Referee: **Mr. F. C. KING**, W. Middlesex
Linesmen: **MR. A. GROTTICK**, N. Middlesex (Red Flag)
MR. K. WHITEHEAD, N. Middlesex (Yellow Flag)

WHYMAN
(Elden)
11

PURDY
(Latymer)
10

TAYLOR
(Croyland)
9

MACDONALD
(Croyland)
8

WATSON
(Latymer)

SAVAGE
(Silver Street)
6

PETTS (Capt.)
(Raynham)
5

GREEN
(Elden)
4

JEPPS
(Edmonton County)
3

HINSBY
(Raynham)
2

LEFT WING

MORRELL
(Latymer)
1

RIGHT WING

EDMONTON SCHOOLBOYS
Black and Amber Quarters

ANY ALTERATION WILL BE NOTED ON THE BOARD

HALF-TIME SCORES
The appended Code corresponds with letters on the Scoring Board thus **A¹** means the first-named Club has scored I and their opponents 0.   ★ Not played **A₀**

A	Arsenal v. Tottenham Hotspur	O	Bristol Rovers v. Leeds United
B	Aston Villa v. Liverpool	P	Bury v. Rotherham United
C	Blackpool v. Charlton Athletic	Q	Derby County v. Fulham
D	Cardiff City v. Preston North End	R	Doncaster Rovers v. Leicester City
E	Chelsea v. Sheffield Wednesday	S	Everton v. Plymouth Argyle
F	Huddersfield Town v. West Bromwich Albion	T	Hull City v. Luton Town
G	Manchester City v. Bolton Wanderers	U	Lincoln City v. Birmingham City
H	Portsmouth v. Burnley	V	Notts County v. Nottingham Forest
J	Sheffield United v. Middlesbrough	W	Oldham Athletic v. Swansea Town
K	Sunderland v. Manchester United	X	Bournemouth & B.A. v. Crystal Palace
L	Wolverhampton Wdrs. v. Newcastle United	Y	Leyton Orient v. Swindon Town
M	Blackburn Rovers v. Stoke City	Z	Millwall v. Aldershot
N	Brentford v. West Ham United		

On Saturday, March 13th   **Amateur Cup Semi-final**   **Kick-off 3 p.m.**

CROOK TOWN v FINCHLEY or WALTHAMSTOW AV.

Tottenham Schoolboys v Edmonton Boys, the single-sheet programme for
the Hotspur Challenge Cup Final. The front cover is on the previous page.

1953-54

Tottenham Reserves v Plymouth A. Reserves,
Football Combination.

Tottenham v Huddersfield Town,
League.

Tottenham v F.C.Austria,
Friendly.

Football Association XI v Royal Air Force,
Representative Match.

43

1954-55

1	**10th August**	**Blue & White Stripes v Whites**	**Public Trial**
*	14th August	Blue & White Stripes v Whites	Public Trial
2	(no programme issued with this number)		
3	21st August	Arsenal Reserves	Football Combination Cup
4	**25th August**	**Wolverhampton Wanderers**	**League**
5	**28th August**	**Sunderland**	**League**
6	4th September	Brentford Reserves	Football Combination Cup
7	**8th September**	**Manchester United**	**League**
8	11th September	Chelsea Juniors	South East Counties League
9	15th September	Southend United Reserves	Football Combination Cup
10	**18th September**	**Portsmouth**	**League**
11	22nd September	Brighton & Hove Albion Reserves	Football Combination Cup
12	25th September	Queens Park Rangers Reserves	Football Combination Cup
13	**2nd October**	**Charlton Athletic**	**League**
14	4th October	Millwall	London Challenge Cup 1st Round
15	6th October	Chelsea Reserves	Football Combination Cup
16	**9th October**	**West Bromwich Albion**	**League**
17	13th October	Crystal Palace Reserves	Football Combination Cup
18	16th October	Cardiff City Reserves	Football Combination
19	**18th October**	**Sportklub Wacker Vienna**	**Friendly**
20	**23rd October**	**Preston North End**	**League**
21	25th October	London Boys v Manchester Boys	Inter-City Schools Challenge
22	30th October	Millwall Reserves	Football Combination
23	**2nd November**	**Essen Rot-Weiss**	**Friendly**
24	**6th November**	**Cardiff City**	**League**
25	13th November	Leicester City Reserves	Football Combination
26	**15th November**	**Finchley**	**Friendly**
27	**20th November**	**Leicester City**	**League**
28	27th November	Chelsea Reserves	Football Combination
29	**4th December**	**Everton**	**League**
30	11th December	Luton Town Reserves (postponed)	Football Combination
31	**18th December**	**Aston Villa**	**League**
32	25th December	Bristol City Reserves	Football Combination
33	**27th December**	**Bolton Wanderers**	**League**
34	1st January	Arsenal Juniors	South East Counties League
35	8th January	Bournemouth & B. Athletic Reserves	Football Combination
36	**15th January**	**Arsenal**	**League**
37	**22nd January**	**Sheffield Wednesday**	**League**
38	**29th January**	**Port Vale**	**F.A Cup 4th Round**
39	5th February	Portsmouth Reserves	Football Combination
40	**12th February**	**Blackpool**	**League**
41	19th February	London Schoolboys v Birmingham Schoolboys	Schools Challenge Match
42	26th February	Brighton & Hove Albion Reserves	Football Combination
43	**2nd March**	**Arsenal**	**Friendly**
44	**5th March**	**Manchester City**	**League**
45	**9th March**	**Racing Club de Paris**	**Friendly**
46	12th March	Hendon v Hounslow Town	F.A Amateur Cup Semi-Final
47	16th March	Coventry City Reserves	Football Combination
48	**19th March**	**Sheffield United**	**League**
49	23rd March	West Ham United Reserves	Football Combination
50	26th March	Birmingham City Reserves	Football Combination
51	**30th March**	**F.C Servette**	**Friendly**
52	**2nd April**	**Chelsea**	**League**
53	4th April	Luton Town Reserves	Football Combination
54	8th April	Arsenal Reserves	Football Combination
55	9th April	United Glass Bottle (Pantiles)	Winchester Cup Final
56	**11th April**	**Huddersfield Town**	**League**
57	**16th April**	**Burnley**	**League**
*	21st April	Tottenham Schools v Edmonton Schools	Bower Cup Final
*	23rd April (am)	Tottenham Schools v Edmonton Schools	Hotspur Cup
58	23rd April (pm)	Norwich City Reserves	Football Combination
*	25th April	Enfield A v Higham United	Tottenham Charity Cup Final
59	26th April	Charlton Athletic Reserves	Football Combination
*	28th April	Middlesex Boys v Essex Boys	Home Counties Championship Final
60	**30th April**	**Newcastle United**	**League**

1954-55

TOTTENHAM HOTSPUR

FOOTBALL AND ATHLETIC COMPANY, LIMITED

Official Programme

AND RECORD OF THE CLUB

Secretary: R. S. JARVIS
Team Manager:
ARTHUR S. ROWE
Medical Officer:
Dr. A. E. TUGHAN

Chairman: FRED. J. BEARMAN
Vice-Chairman: E. DEWHURST HORNSBY
Directors: F. JOHN BEARMAN, Wm. J. HERYET, FREDK. WALE

PRICE
TWOPENCE

VOL. XLVII. No. 43   WEDNESDAY, MARCH 2nd, 1955

TOTTENHAM HOTSPUR v ARSENAL

On Saturday, March 5th	On Wednesday, March 9th
MANCHESTER CITY	**RACING CLUB DE PARIS**
Football League Div. I Kick-off 3.15 p.m.	Friendly FLOODLIT Kick-off 7.30 p.m.

Friendly (Floodlit)   **March 2nd, 1955**   **Kick-off 7.30 p.m.**

TOTTENHAM HOTSPUR
White Shirts, Blue Shorts

RIGHT WING   GOAL   LEFT WING

REYNOLDS
1
BACKS

RAMSEY (Capt.)   **HOPKINS**
2   3

HALF-BACKS

BLANCHFLOWER   **CLARKE**   **MARCHI**
4   5   6

FORWARDS

GAVIN   **BAILY**   **DUQUEMIN**   **BROOKS**   **RELPH**
7   8   9   10   11

Referee: Mr. A. H. BLYTHE, London
Linesmen: Mr. J. H. BROOKS, London (Red Flag)
Mr. F. M. WILSON, Middlesex (Yellow Flag)

MARDEN   **BLOOMFIELD**   **ROPER**   **TAPSCOTT**   **CLAPTON**
11   10   9   8   7

FORWARDS

FORBES   **FOTHERINGHAM**   **GORING**
6   5   4

HALF-BACKS

EVANS   **BARNES (Capt.)**
3   2

BACKS

KELSEY
1
GOAL

LEFT WING   RIGHT WING

ARSENAL
Red and White Shirts, White Shorts

ANY ALTERATION WILL BE NOTED ON THE BOARD

Printed by Thomas Knight & Co. Ltd., The Clock House Press, Hoddesdon, Herts.

Tottenham v Arsenal, the single-sheet programme for the friendly match
on March 2nd 1955. The reverse side is on the next page.

1954-55

CLUB GOSSIP

To-night we have pleasure in welcoming our friends from Highbury in a friendly floodlit match, and we can be certain of witnessing a keen and interesting game. No matter when we meet, whether it be in League or Cup or a friendly, the games are fought out in that keen spirit of friendly rivalry that always gives a thrill to the spectators.

We have met twice in the League this season and the Arsenal won on both occasions, for at Highbury on September 4th they scored two goals without reply and then on January 15th they came to Tottenham and took away the two points by scoring the only goal of the match.

For most of the season both clubs have been fighting hard to get away from the relegation zone, and at the moment we are slightly better placed than the Arsenal, but we expect both clubs to hold a fairly reasonable position when the final League table is made up in May.

Again, both clubs have introduced many fresh faces to their supporters during the season as the old stalwarts, who brought many honours to both the Arsenal and the Spurs, have found "time marches on" and "waits for no man." However, we feel confident that the young players of both clubs will fight hard to emulate their predecessors and again bring some of the honours of the game to North London.

Like the rest of the country's activities, floodlit matches recently have been "under the weather" but we hope for a fine night so that we can enjoy a good sporting game.

AMATEUR CUP SEMI-FINAL

The Football Association have selected our ground as the venue for one of the Semi-final ties of the Amateur Cup, that between Hendon and Hounslow Town.

The match will be played on Saturday, March 12th, kick-off 3 p.m.

RACING CLUB TO VISIT US AGAIN

Our next floodlit fixture will be on Wednesday, March 9th, when the opposition will be furnished by our old friends and rivals, Racing Club de Paris. This will be our fifth meeting with the famous Paris club, three matches having been played in Paris and one previously at Tottenham. The three games in Paris resulted in two wins for us and one drawn game; it will be recollected that when Racing Club visited us in September, 1953, we were the winners by 5 goals to 3.

From the particulars we have received of their probable team it is evident that there have been changes in the playing personnel of Racing Club, for we note that of the team that played here in 1953 there are only four members due to visit us next Wednesday. These are Pivois (goal), Lelong (right-back), Cisowski (centre-forward), and Curyl (outside-left). Racing Club, who have evidently been much occupied with team-building, expect to field five full Internationals and one "B" International, so that a keenly contested match is in prospect.

After a short spell in Division Two, Racing Club were promoted at the end of last season to the Premier Division of the French League, and according to all accounts are holding their own both in League and Cup. The kick-off will be at 7.30 p.m., and tickets may be obtained from the Club's office at 7/- each for numbered and reserved seats. The admission to the ground will be 2/-.

F.C. AUSTRIA COMING?

Our old friends from Austria hope to visit us for a floodlight game on Wednesday, March 30th, kick-off 7.30. Negotiations are not yet completed and so full particulars will be given in a future programme. Last season they visited Tottenham on October 28th, when we beat them in a very exciting match by 3—2.

NEW DATES

Owing to the weather we were unable to play our League game with West Bromwich Albion last Saturday, and we shall now visit the Hawthorns on Wednesday, April 27th. The visit to Charlton, which has twice been held up by wintry weather, has been fixed for Thursday, May 5th. It will be an evening match and will give our supporters a good opportunity of getting over to The Valley.

IN A GOOD CAUSE

A match has been arranged between an International XI and a combined Sheffield XI for the benefit of Derek Dooley, the Sheffield Wednesday centre-forward who, our supporters will remember, met with an accident playing for his club which resulted in his having to have a leg amputated. Derek was a very promising player and we hope this match will be a great financial success. Alf Ramsey has been chosen to play in this match.

FOOTBALL LEAGUE—DIV. I

Up to and incl. Feb. 26th

	P.	W.	D.	L.	F.	A.	Ps.
Wolverhampton W.	30	15	8	7	71	52	38
Sunderland	30	11	15	4	49	38	37
Chelsea	30	13	9	8	60	46	35
Portsmouth	30	13	8	8	55	39	34
Charlton Athletic	29	15	4	10	63	46	34
Manchester City	30	14	6	10	57	51	34
Everton	29	13	7	9	46	42	33
Manchester United	30	14	5	11	61	59	33
Burnley	31	12	8	11	40	40	32
Preston North End	29	12	5	12	63	43	29
Huddersfield Town	29	10	9	10	50	51	29
Sheffield United	29	13	3	13	48	60	29
Newcastle United	29	12	4	13	64	62	28
Tottenham Hotspur	29	11	6	12	54	54	28
Cardiff City	28	11	6	11	50	55	28
Aston Villa	29	11	6	12	45	58	28
Arsenal	30	10	7	13	49	52	27
West Bromwich Alb.	28	10	7	11	55	63	27
Bolton Wanderers	27	8	9	10	43	45	25
Blackpool	31	8	7	16	41	56	23
Leicester City	29	6	9	14	51	67	21
Sheffield Wed.	31	4	6	21	45	81	14

FOOTBALL COMB.—DIV. I

Up to and incl. Feb. 26th

	P.	W.	D.	L.	F.	A.	Ps.
Chelsea	17	10	3	4	41	25	23
Tottenham Hotspur	18	9	4	5	40	28	22
Norwich City	19	10	2	7	36	29	22
Bristol City	19	7	6	6	26	23	20
West Ham United	18	7	6	5	40	42	20
Birmingham City	17	8	3	6	36	36	19
Portsmouth	20	7	5	8	37	39	19
Millwall	20	8	3	9	33	40	19
Brighton & H.A.	19	8	3	8	31	41	19
Coventry City	19	7	5	7	27	38	19
Luton Town	15	7	3	5	43	25	17
Arsenal	16	6	4	6	36	28	16
Leicester City	19	7	2	10	34	38	16
Charlton Athletic	18	5	4	9	23	31	14
Cardiff City	17	3	7	7	24	27	13
Bournemouth & B.	19	4	4	11	25	42	12

EASTERN COUNTIES LEAGUE

Up to and incl. Feb. 28th

	P.	W.	D.	L.	F.	A.	Ps.
Arsenal	26	17	5	4	57	31	39
Colchester United	28	15	6	7	60	36	36
Cambridge United	26	13	6	7	63	42	32
Clacton Town	28	14	4	10	52	42	32
March Town Un.	22	13	2	7	59	30	28
Crittall Athletic	24	12	4	8	36	35	28
Gorleston	20	11	5	4	42	31	27
Tottenham Hotspur	21	11	4	8	40	32	26
Eynesbury Rovers	20	12	2	6	43	35	26
Lowestoft Town	24	10	4	10	39	38	24
Yarmouth Town	27	9	5	13	39	48	23
Peterborough Un.	22	9	4	9	38	33	22
Chelmsford City	24	6	7	11	50	51	19
West Ham United	23	6	6	11	30	43	18
Stowmarket	26	6	6	14	34	65	18
Norwich City	20	5	1	14	22	50	11
Bury Town	21	3	4	14	24	52	10
Harwich & Park'n.	22	0	7	15	18	52	7

Tottenham v Arsenal, the reverse side of the single-sheet programme for the friendly match on March 2nd 1955. The front page is overleaf.

1954-55

(right): **Tottenham v Burnley,** Car parking arrangements feature on the cover of the programme for the League match.

(left): **Tottenham Res. v Arsenal Reserves,** Combination Cup match in August.

(left): **Tottenham v Finchley,** Friendly match in November.

(below): **Hendon v Hounslow Town,** F.A. Amateur Cup Semi-Final.

1955-56

1	15th August	**Whites v Blues**	**Public Trial**
2	20th August	**Burnley**	**League**
3	24th August	Aldershot Reserves	Football Combination
4	27th August	Plymouth Argyle Reserves	Football Combination
5	31st August	**Manchester United**	**League**
6	3rd September	**Charlton Athletic**	**League**
7	7th September	Crystal Palace Reserves	Football Combination
8	10th September	**Arsenal**	**League**
9	14th September	Southampton Reserves	Football Combination
10	17th September	Charlton Athletic Juniors	South East Counties League
11	21st September	Arsenal Reserves	Football Combination
12	24th September	**Newcastle United**	**League**
13	1st October	Birmingham City Reserves	Football Combination
14	8th October	**Bolton Wanderers**	**League**
15	10th October	Coventry City Reserves	Football Combination
16	12th October	**F.C Vasas**	**Friendly**
17	15th October	Watford Reserves	Football Combination
18	22nd October	**Sunderland**	**League**
19	24th October	London Boys v Manchester Boys	Inter-City Schools Challenge
20	29th October	Leicester City Reserves	Football Combination
21	5th November	**Cardiff City**	**League**
22	12th November	England v Germany	Amateur International
23	19th November	**Wolverhampton Wanderers**	**League**
24	26th November	Leyton Orient Reserves	Football Combination
25	3rd December	**Blackpool**	**League**
26	6th December	**Swansea Town**	**Friendly**
27	10th December	Reading Reserves	Football Combination
28	17th December	Swansea Town Reserves	Football Combination
29	24th December	**Luton Town**	**League**
30	26th December	**West Bromwich Albion**	**League**
31	31st December	Queens Park Rangers Reserves	Football Combination
32	7th January	**Boston United**	**F.A Cup 3rd Round**
33	21st January	**Everton**	**League**
34	28th January	**Middlesbrough**	**F.A Cup 4th Round**
35	4th February	Chelsea Reserves (postponed)	Football Combination
36	11th February	**Birmingham City**	**League**
37	15th February	Chelsea v Burnley	F.A Cup 4th Round 4th Replay
38	18th February	Cardiff City Reserves	Football Combination
39	25th February	**Chelsea**	**League**
40	3rd March	**West Ham United**	**F.A Cup 6th Round**
41	10th March	**Portsmouth**	**League**
42	17th March	Southend United Reserves	Football Combination
43	19th March	Northampton Town Reserves	Football Combination
44	24th March	**Manchester City**	**League**
45	30th March	**Preston North End**	**League**
46	31st March	Brentford Reserves	Football Combination
47	2nd April	Ipswich Town Reserves	Football Combination
48	7th April	**Aston Villa**	**League**
49	10th April	London Boys v Berlin Boys	European Inter-City Challenge Match
50	11th April	Gorleston	Eastern Counties League Cup Final 1st Leg
51	14th April (am)	Brentford Youth	South East Counties League Cup Semi-Final 1st Leg
52	14th April (pm)	Norwich City Reserves	Football Combination
53	21st April	**Huddersfield Town**	**League**
54	25th April	Eton Manor Juniors	London Minor Cup Final
55	26th April	Chelsea Reserves	Football Combination
56	28th April	**Sheffield United**	**League**
57	30th April	Portsmouth Reserves	Football Combination
*	1st May	Brimsdown Rovers v Enfield 'A'	Tottenham Charity Cup Final
*	3rd May	Edmonton Schools v E.London Schools	Bower Cup Final
58	4th May	London v Basle	Inter-Cities Cup
59	5th May	Arsenal Youth	South East Counties League Cup Final

1955-56

TOTTENHAM HOTSPUR
FOOTBALL AND ATHLETIC COMPANY LIMITED

Official Programme
AND RECORD OF THE CLUB

Secretary: R. S. JARVIS

Team Manager:
J. ANDERSON

Chairman: FRED J. BEARMAN
Vice-Chairman: E. DEWHURST HORNSBY
Directors: F. JOHN BEARMAN, Wm. J. HERYET
FREDK. WALE

**PRICE
ONE PENNY**

VOL. XLVIII. No. 54   WEDNESDAY, APRIL 25th, 1956

TOTTENHAM JUNIORS
v
ETON MANOR JUNIORS

(Final London Minor Cup)   April 25th, 1956   Kick-off 6.30 p.m.

TOTTENHAM HOTSPUR JUNIORS
White Shirts, Blue Knickers

RIGHT WING   LEFT WING

GOAL
P. SHEARING
1
BACKS

E. SPEIGHT   D. EMSON
2   3

HALF-BACKS
A. KING   A. HOARE   F. SHARPE
4   5   6

FORWARDS
J. WHITE   G. THOMSON   J. TITT   R. KING   D. MILTON
7   8   9   10   11

Referee: Mr. A. C. SIMMONS, London
Linesmen: Mr. W. BOWYER, London (Red Flag)
Mr. M. BIRNBAUN, London (Yellow Flag)

11   10   9   8   7
R. YOUNG   K. GUTTRIDGE   D. MADDAMS   A. KNOWLES   B. CLARK
FORWARDS

6   5   4
R. RUSHBROOK   K. BRAND   G. BAILEY
HALF-BACKS

3   2
F. BARRETT   A. HUNT

BACKS
1
T. LUCY
GOAL

LEFT WING   RIGHT WING

ETON MANOR JUNIORS
Light Blue and Dark Blue Shirts, White Knickers

ANY ALTERATION WILL BE NOTED ON THE BOARD

Printed by Thomas Knight & Co. Ltd., The Clock House Press, Hoddesdon, Herts

Tottenham Juniors v Eton Manor Juniors, the single-sheet programme for Final of the London Minor Cup. The reverse side of the programme was, as per most issues, the fixtures and tables.

49

1955-56

TOTTENHAM HOTSPUR

FOOTBALL AND ATHLETIC COMPANY LIMITED

Official Programme

AND RECORD OF THE CLUB

Secretary: R. S. JARVIS

Team Manager:
J. ANDERSON

Chairman: FRED J. BEARMAN
Vice-Chairman: E. DEWHURST HORNSBY
Directors: F. JOHN BEARMAN, Wm. J. HERYET,
FREDK. WALE

**PRICE
TWOPENCE**

VOL. XLVIII. No. 58

FRIDAY, MAY 4th, 1956

LONDON v BASLE

This evening it is our pleasure to stage on our Ground the inter-city fixture between London and Basle, which is the return match for that played in Basle early in the season when London won by 5 goals to nil. The International Industries Fairs Inter-Cities Cup —to give the competition its full title came into being early in 1955 under the Presidency of Mr. E. Thommen, a Vice-President of the Executive Committee of F.I.F.A., in collaboration with Dr. Barassi, President of the Italian Football Association, and Sir Stanley Rous, C.B.E., J.P., Secretary of the Football Association.

The object of the competition is to further international sporting relations, and to contribute to the friendship among nations, particularly between cities who annually hold Industries Fairs. There are 12 cities taking part, and they have been placed in four groups of three in the qualifying competition, as follows:

GROUP A
Barcelona, Vienna, Copenhagen.
GROUP B
Cologne, Leipzig, Lausanne.
GROUP C
London, Basle, Frankfurt.
GROUP D
Milan, Zagreb, Birmingham.

The teams in each group play each other on a home and away basis, and the eventual winners of the

four groups go forward to the Semi-finals which will also be played on a home and away basis. The eventual winners will be presented with a trophy which cannot be won permanently, but the winners of the Final Tie will receive a souvenir cup as their permanent reward.

The competition is conducted by a Committee comprising one member from each of the competing cities, and the representative of the London F.A. is Mr. J. H. Mears, Chairman of the Chelsea Football Club, and a member of the Council of the Football League Management Committee. The headquarters of the competition is in Basle and is under the authority of the Union of the European Football Associations.

London, who draw their players from the 11 professional clubs in membership with them, have played two matches to date, having beaten Basle in Switzerland by 5 goals to nil, and Frankfurt at Wembley by 3 goals to 2. It will be remembered that this latter match took place at Wembley Stadium last October, and was the first match to be played under floodlights at the Stadium.

As far as is known, the only other match played in the competition has been between Barcelona and Copenhagen, which was won by the former by 6 goals to 2.

PEN PICTURES OF THE LONDON PLAYERS

Jack Kelsey, goal (Arsenal). Joined Arsenal in August, 1949, from Llanslet (Swansea), and made his debut in

An aerial view of Basle, Switzerland

Printed by Thomas Knight & Co. Ltd., The Clock House Press, Hoddesdon, Herts.

London v Basle, the cover of the 4 page programme for the first ever competitive European match played at White Hart Lane. This match was in the Inter-Cities Cup "Group C" qualifying round.

1955-56

(right):
**Tottenham v
Boston United,**
F.A. Cup 3rd Round

(left):
**Tottenham v
F.C. Vasas,**
Friendly

(left):
Tottenham v Swansea Town,
Friendly, the team line-ups
featuring famous names from
Spurs past and future in the
Swansea side.

(right):
**London Boys v
Berlin Boys,**
European Inter-City
Challenge

(left):
England v Germany,
Amateur International

51

1956-57

Volume 49

1	11th August	Whites v Blues	Public Trial
2	18th August	Southampton Reserves	Football Combination
3	22nd August	Southend United Reserves	Football Combination
4	25th August	Leeds United	League
5	29th August	Manchester City	League
6	1st September	Norwich City Reserves	Football Combination
7	8th September	Wolverhampton Wanderers	League
8	11th September	Racing Club de Paris	Friendly
9	12th September	Ipswich Town Reserves	Football Combination
10	15th September	Charlton Athletic Reserves	Football Combination
11	22nd September	Luton Town	League
12	26th September	Partick Thistle	Floodlit Challenge
13	29th September	Crystal Palace Reserves	Football Combination
14	6th October	Aldershot Reserves	Football Combination
15	13th October	Cardiff City	League
16	15th October	Brentford	London Challenge Cup 2nd Round
17	20th October	Millwall Reserves	Football Combination
18	23rd October	England v Hungary	Youth International
19	27th October	Burnley	League
20	29th October	London Boys v Manchester Boys	Inter-City Schools Challenge
21	31st October	Hibernian	Floodlit Challenge
22	3rd November	Leicester City Reserves	Football Combination
23	10th November	Newcastle United	League
24	12th November	Heart of Midlothian	Floodlit Challenge
25	17th November	Brighton & Hove Albion Reserves	Football Combination
26	24th November	Manchester United	League
27	26th November	Bexleyheath & Welling Juniors	Southern Junior Floodlit Cup 2nd Round
28	1st December	Swindon Town Reserves	Football Combination
29	3rd December	Red Banner	Friendly
30	8th December	West Bromwich Albion	League
31	15th December	Preston North End	League
32	22nd December	Luton Town Reserves	Football Combination
33	25th December	Everton	League
34	26th December	Leyton Orient Reserves	Football Combination
35	29th December	Bolton Wanderers	League
36	5th January	Leicester City	F.A Cup 3rd Round
37	12th January	London Boys v Birmingham Boys	Inter-City Schools Challenge
38	19th January	Aston Villa	League
39	26th January	Chelsea	F.A Cup 4th Round
40	2nd February	Coventry City Reserves	Football Combination
41	9th February	Sunderland	League
42	16th February	Norwich City 'A'	Eastern Counties League
43	20th February	Chelsea	League
44	23rd February	Bristol Rovers Reserves	Football Combination
45	2nd March	Biggleswade Town	Eastern Counties League
46	9th March	Portsmouth Reserves	Football Combination
47	13th March	Arsenal	League
48	16th March	Portsmouth	League
49	19th March	Chelsea Juniors	Southern Junior Floodlit Cup Semi-Final
50	23rd March	Arsenal Reserves	Football Combination
51	30th March	Sheffield Wednesday	League
*	5th April	London Police v Edinburgh Police	Tait Challenge Trophy
52	6th April	Watford Reserves	Football Combination
53	13th April	Birmingham City	League
*	15th April	Tottenham Schools v East London Schools	Star Shield Final
		& Tottenham (Primary) Boys v Islington (Primary) Boys	Gardiner Memorial Trophy
54	19th April	Fulham Reserves	Football Combination
55	20th April	Birmingham City Reserves	Football Combination
56	22nd April	Charlton Athletic	League
*	25th April	Highfield v Chase F.C	Tottenham Charity Cup Final
57	27th April	Blackpool	League
58	29th April	Northampton Town Reserves	Football Combination
*	1st May	Edmonton Schools v Hackney Schools	Bower Cup Final
59	4th May	Barking & Dist.League v S.Eastern Dist. League	Myrtle Shield Final

1956-57

TOTTENHAM HOTSPUR
FOOTBALL AND ATHLETIC COMPANY LIMITED

Official Programme
AND RECORD OF THE CLUB

Secretary: R. S. JARVIS

Team Manager:
J. ANDERSON

Medical Officer:
Dr. T. A. TUGHAN

Chairman: FRED J. BEARMAN
Vice-Chairman: E. DEWHURST HORNSBY
Directors: F. JOHN BEARMAN, Wm. J. HERYET,
FREDK. WALE

**PRICE
TWOPENCE**

VOL. XLIX. No. 8

TUESDAY, SEPTEMBER 11th, 1956

On Wednesday, September 12th	On Saturday, September 15th
IPSWICH TOWN RES.	**CHARLTON ATHLETIC RES.**
Football Combination — Kick-off 6 p.m.	Football Combination — Kick-off 3 p.m.

TOTTENHAM HOTSPUR v RACING CLUB DE PARIS

ROOM FOR 50,000 UNDER COVER

Floodlit Fixture — September 11th, 1956 — **Kick-off 7.15 p.m.**

TOTTENHAM HOTSPUR
White Shirts, White Knickers

RIGHT WING

GOAL
DITCHBURN
1

LEFT WING

BACKS
BAKER 2   **HOPKINS** 3

HALF-BACKS
BLANCHFLOWER 4   **CLARKE** (Capt.) 5   **MARCHI** 6

FORWARDS
MEDWIN 7   **HARMER** 8   **SMITH** 9   **STOKES** 10   **ROBB** 11

Referee: **Mr. A. H. BLYTHE**, London
Linesmen: **Mr. L. COOK**, Surrey (Red Flag)
Mr. D. LEWIS, London (Yellow Flag)

GUILLOT 11   **DALLA CIECA** 10   **PILLARD** 9   **CISOUSKY** 8   **GRILLET** 7

FORWARDS
MAHJOUB 6   **SOSA** 5   **GABET** 4

HALF-BACKS
MARCHE 3   **LELONG** 2

BACKS
TAILLANDIER
1
GOAL

LEFT WING

RIGHT WING

RACING CLUB DE PARIS
Blue and White Hoops, Blue Knickers

ANY ALTERATION WILL BE NOTED ON THE BOARD

Printed by Thomas Knight & Co. Ltd., The Clock House Press, Hoddesdon, Herts.

Tottenham v Racing Club De Paris, the single-sheet programme for Friendly match played at White Hart Lane on Monday, September 11th, 1956.

53

1956-57

FRIDAY, 5th APRIL 1957   Kick-Off 7.30 p.m.   OFFICIAL PROGRAMME 6d.

INTER-CAPITAL CUP TIE   *TAIT CHALLENGE TROPHY*

LONDON POLICE versus **EDINBURGH POLICE**

FLOODLIGHT   *"SPURS" GROUND, WHITE HART LANE, TOTTENHAM.*
(By kind permission of the Tottenham Hotspur Football Club)

London Police v Edinburgh Police, the cover of the 8 page programme, issued by the Metropolitan Police F.C., but played at White Hart Lane, for the Tait Challenge Trophy.

1956-57

Tottenham v Red Banner, Friendly

Tottenham v Everton, League
The last League match to be played at
White Hart Lane on Christmas Day

Tottenham v Heart of Midlothian,
Anglo-Scottish Floodlit Challenge,
one of three matches played at home
in this ill-fated tournament.

England v Hungary,
Youth International.

1957-58

1	**17th August**	**Whites v Blues**	**Public Trial**
2	**24th August**	**Chelsea**	**League**
3	28th August	Arsenal Reserves	Football Combination
4	31st August	Reading Reserves	Football Combination
5	**4th September**	**Portsmouth**	**League**
6	**7th September**	**Burnley**	**League**
7	11th September	Swindon Town Reserves	Football Combination
8	14th September	Colchester United Reserves	Eastern Counties League
9	**18th September**	**Birmingham City**	**League**
10	**21st September**	**Sheffield Wednesday**	**League**
11	28th September	Southampton Reserves	Football Combination
12	30th September	Finchley	East Anglian Cup 2nd Round
13	2nd October	Portsmouth Reserves	Football Combination
14	**5th October**	**Nottingham Forest**	**League**
15	7th October	Dulwich Hamlet	London Challenge Cup 1st Round
16	**12th October**	**Arsenal**	**League**
17	15th October	England v Rumania	Youth International
18	19th October	Millwall Reserves	Football Combination
19	21st October	West Ham United	London Challenge Cup 2nd Round
20	24th October	London Boys v Manchester Boys	Inter-City Schools Challenge
21	**26th October**	**Leeds United**	**League**
22	2nd November	West Ham United Reserves	Football Combination
23	**9th November**	**Everton**	**League**
24	**11th November**	**Vfb. Stuttgart**	**Friendly**
25	16th November	Luton Town Reserves	Football Combination
26	**23rd November**	**Luton Town**	**League**
27	30th November	Fulham Reserves	Football Combination
28	**7th December**	**Leicester City**	**League**
29	14th December	Ipswich Town Reserves	Football Combination
30	21st December	Northampton Town Reserves	Football Combination
31	25th December	Southend United Reserves	Football Combination
32	**26th December**	**Wolverhampton Wanderers**	**League**
33	**28th December**	**Newcastle United**	**League**
34	**4th January**	**Leicester City**	**F.A Cup 3rd Round**
35	11th January	Charlton Athletic Reserves	Football Combination
36	**18th January**	**Preston North End**	**League**
37	**25th January**	**Sheffield United**	**F.A Cup 4th Round**
38	1st February	Norwich City Reserves	Football Combination
39	**8th February**	**Manchester City**	**League**
40	15th February	Leyton Orient Reserves	Football Combination
41	22nd February	Leicester City Reserves	Football Combination
42	**1st March**	**Partick Thistle**	**Friendly**
43	8th March	Queens Park Rangers Reserves	Football Combination
44	**12th March**	**Bolton Wanderers**	**League**
45	**15th March**	**Sunderland**	**League**
46	22nd March	Plymouth Argyle Reserves	Football Combination
47	24th March	F.A Amateur XI	Friendly
48	**29th March**	**Aston Villa**	**League**
*	2nd April	Hackney Schools v Swansea Schools	English Schools Shield Semi-Final Replay
49	**4th April**	**West Bromwich Albion**	**League**
50	5th April	Aldershot Reserves	Football Combination
51	7th April	Birmingham City Reserves	Football Combination
52	**12th April**	**Manchester United**	**League**
53	**14th April**	**Hibernian**	**Friendly**
*	19th April (am)	Tottenham Schools v Colchester Schools	Hotspur Cup
54	19th April (pm)	Biggleswade Town	Eastern Counties League
55	21st April	Bournemouth & B. Athletic Reserves	Football Combination
*	23rd April	Enfield 'A' v Eastley Athletic	Tottenham Charity Cup Final
56	**24th April**	**Canto Do Rio**	**Friendly**
57	**26th April**	**Blackpool**	**League**
58	28th April	Norwich City 'A'	East Anglian Cup Final

1957-58

TOTTENHAM HOTSPUR

FOOTBALL AND ATHLETIC COMPANY LIMITED

Official Programme

AND RECORD OF THE CLUB

Secretary: R. S. JARVIS

Team Manager:
J. ANDERSON

Medical Officer:
Dr. A. E. TUGHAN

Chairman: FRED. J. BEARMAN

Vice-Chairman: FREDK. WALE

Directors:
F. JOHN BEARMAN, D. H. DEACOCK, S. A. WALE

PRICE
TWOPENCE

VOL. L. No. 56   THURSDAY, 24th APRIL, 1958

CANTO DO RIO F.C. (BRAZIL)

1956-57

(RIO DE JANEIRO CITY CHAMPIONS)

Top Row: PAULO (right back), ISMAEL (centre-half), GARCIA (goal), FLORIANO (left back), RAMOS (left-half), VICTOR (right-half). *Lower Row:* MILTON (outside-right), OSMAN (inside-right), GELIO (centre-forward), VOS ANJOS (inside-left), PINHEIRO (outside-left.)

Printed by Thomas Knight & Co. Ltd., The Clock House Press, Hoddesdon, Herts.

Tottenham v Canto Do Rio, Friendly.

57

1957-58

TOTTENHAM HOTSPUR

FOOTBALL AND ATHLETIC COMPANY LIMITED

Official Programme

AND RECORD OF THE CLUB

Secretary: R. S. JARVIS
Team Manager:
J. ANDERSON
Medical Officer:
Dr. A. E. TUGHAN

Chairman: FRED. J. BEARMAN

Directors: F. JOHN BEARMAN, Wm. J. HERYET,
FREDK. WALE

PRICE

TWOPENCE

VOL. L. No. 24

MONDAY, 11th NOVEMBER, 1957

WELCOME TO OUR GERMAN VISITORS

This evening we welcome to our enclosure the famous Vfb. Club of Stuttgart with whom it will be our first meeting at Tottenham, although we have played them twice previously in Stuttgart, in May, 1954 when we were on tour in Austria and Germany, when we lost by three goals to one, and on August 3rd of this year when we drew two goals each.

Fussball-Mannschaft des VfB Stuttgart. Left to right: RETTER, SAWITZKI, LIEBSCHWAGER, SIMON, KANIBER, HINTERSTOCKER, STROHMAIER, PRAXL, WALDNER, BUSCH, BLESSING.

IN THE INTERESTS OF GROUND CONDITIONS, PLAYERS ON EITHER SIDE WILL NOT SIGN AUTOGRAPHS ON THE FIELD

Printed by Thomas Knight & Co. Ltd. The Clock House Press, Hoddesdon, Herts.

Tottenham v Vfb. Stuttgart, Friendly.

58

1957-58

England v Rumania,
Youth International

Hackney Boys
v
Swansea Boys,
English Schools' Shield
Semi-Final Replay.
This programme is a
stencil duplicated 4 page
issue with the teams
printed across the middle
pages, with a brief
editorial on the back page.

Tottenham v Partick Thistle,
Friendly,
Cover is typical of that
for a League match.

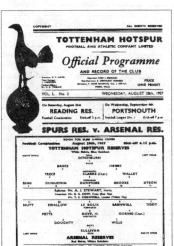

Tottenham Res. v Arsenal Res.,
Football Combination,
single sheet issue.

Tottenham "A" v Norwich City "A",
East Anglian Cup Final,
for which a single-sheet issue was
produced, with the fixtures and Tables on
the reverse side.

1958-59

1	16th August	Whites v Blues	Public Trial
2	23rd August	Blackpool	League
3	27th August	Chelmsford City Reserves	Eastern Counties League Cup
4	30th August	Arsenal Reserves	Football Combination
5	3rd September	Chelsea	League
6	6th September	Newcastle United	League
7	13th September	Eynesbury Rovers	Eastern Counties League Cup
8	17th September	Nottingham Forest	League
9	20th September	Portsmouth Reserves	Football Combination
10	24th September	Bristol City Reserves	Football Combination
11	27th September	Wolverhampton Wanderers	League
12	4th October	West Ham United Reserves	Football Combination
13	6th October	Charlton Athletic	London Challenge Cup 1st Round
14	11th October	Everton	League
15	14th October	Bela Vista	Friendly
16	18th October	Swansea Town Reserves	Football Combination
17	20th October	Finchley	London Challenge Cup 2nd Round
18	25th October	Leeds United	League
19	27th October	Luton Town Youth	Southern Junior Floodlit Cup 1st Round Replay
20	29th October	London Boys v Manchester Boys	Inter-City Schools Challenge
21	1st November	Birmingham City Reserves	Football Combination
22	3rd November	Queens Park Rangers	London Challenge Cup Semi-Final
23	8th November	Bolton Wanderers	League
24	10th November	Hibernian	Friendly
25	15th November	Leyton Orient Reserves	Football Combination
26	22nd November	Birmingham City	League
27	29th November	Fulham Reserves	Football Combination
28	1st December	West Ham United	London Challenge Cup Final
29	6th December	Preston North End	League
30	8th December	Bucharest Selected XI	Friendly
31	13th December	Ipswich Town Reserves	Football Combination
32	20th December	Brighton & Hove Albion Reserves	Football Combination
33	26th December	West Ham United	League
34	27th December	Southampton Youth	Southern Junior Floodlit Cup 2nd Round
35	3rd January	Blackburn Rovers	League
36	10th January	West Ham United	F.A Cup 3rd Round
37	17th January	Bury Town	Eastern Counties League
38	24th January	Newport County	F.A Cup 4th Round
39	31st January	Arsenal	League
40	7th February	Manchester United	League
41	14th February	Norwich City	F.A Cup 5th Round
42	21st February	Portsmouth	League
43	28th February	Bristol Rovers Reserves	Football Combination
44	7th March	Leicester City	League
45	14th March	Luton Town v Norwich City	F.A Cup Semi-Final
46	18th March	Nottingham Forest Reserves	Football Combination
47	21st March	Manchester City	League
48	27th March	Aston Villa	League
49	28th March	Barnet v Walthamstow Avenue	F.A Amateur Cup Semi-Final Replay
50	30th March	Charlton Athletic Reserves	Football Combination
51	4th April	Luton Town	League
52	8th April	Burnley	League
*	10th April	London Police v Edinburgh Police	Challenge Match
53	11th April	Peterborough United Reserves	Eastern Counties League Cup Final 1st Leg
54	13th April	Eynesbury Rovers	Eastern Counties League
55	16th April	Luton Town Reserves	Football Combination
56	18th April	West Bromwich Albion	League
*	21st April	Tottenham Boys v Islington Boys	Hotspur Cup
		& Tottenham Boys v Islington Boys	Gardner Cup
57	23rd April	Cardiff City Reserves	Football Combination
58	25th April	Chelsea Reserves	Football Combination
59	27th April	Leicester City Reserves	Football Combination

1958-59

TOTTENHAM HOTSPUR
FOOTBALL AND ATHLETIC COMPANY LIMITED

Official Programme
AND RECORD OF THE CLUB

Secretary: R. S. JARVIS

Team Manager:
W. E. NICHOLSON

Medical Officer:
Dr. A. E. TUGHAN

Chairman: FRED. J. BEARMAN

Vice-Chairman: FREDK. WALE

Directors:
F. JOHN BEARMAN, D. H. DEACOCK, S. A. WALE

PRICE
TWOPENCE

VOL. LI. No. 15   TUESDAY, 14th OCTOBER, 1958

BELA VISTA F.C. (BRAZIL)

This evening we give a cordial welcome to our visitors from Brazil, the Bela Vista Club, who are here tonight to play the remaining match of their tour in England. Prior to coming to this country they had also had a tour in Europe.

The Bela Vista Club has its headquarters in the town of Sete Lagoas, in the state of Minas Gerais, the most

Bela Vista Football Club of State of Minas Gerais, Brazil. Headquarters and Stadium in Sete Lagoas. *Standing left to right:* DELIO (right back), ADELMAR (goalkeeper), GAIA (left back), SALVATORE (centre-half), LICO (centre-half), EDESIO (left-half), *Seated left to right:* ORLANDO RODRIGUES (trainer), MURILO (outside-left), NAVARRO (outside-right), NENEZAO (inside forward), JERINGHO (centre-forward), ASSIS (outside right).

Printed by Thomas Knight & Co. Ltd., The Clock House Press, Hoddesdon, Herts.

Tottenham v Bela Vista F.C. (Brazil), Friendly.

1958-59

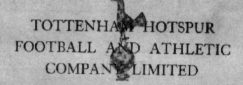

TOTTENHAM HOTSPUR
FOOTBALL AND ATHLETIC
COMPANY LIMITED

AERIAL VIEW OF THE SPURS GROUND

FOOTBALL ASSOCIATION CHALLENGE CUP
SEMI-FINAL TIE
SATURDAY, MARCH 14th, 1959

LUTON TOWN
v.
NORWICH CITY

Kick-off 3.30 p.m.

THE OFFICIAL **6**D. PROGRAMME

Luton Town v Norwich City, F.A. Cup Semi-Final, a 12 page glossy issue.

1958-59

Tottenham Res. v Nottingham Forest Res.,
only a single-sheet issue for this Football
Combination match.

Tottenham v West Ham United,
London Challenge Cup Final, usually a Reserve
team match, but on this occasion the match was
played between the two clubs' League teams.

(above): **Tottenham v Bucharest Selected XI**,
the team line-ups for the Friendly Match.
(right): **Barnet v Walthamstow Avenue**,
F.A. Amateur Cup Semi-Final Replay

1959-60

Volume 52

1	**15th August**	**Whites v Blues**	**Public Trial**
2	22nd August	Southampton Reserves	Football Combination
3	**26th August**	**West Bromwich Albion**	**League**
4	**29th August**	**Birmingham City**	**League**
5	5th September	Arsenal Reserves	Football Combination
6	**9th September**	**West Ham United**	**League**
7	12th September	Charlton Athletic Reserves	Football Combination
8	**19th September**	**Preston North End**	**League**
9	26th September	Leicester City Reserves	Football Combination
10	**3rd October**	**Burnley**	**League**
11	5th October	Brentford	London Challenge Cup 1st Round
12	**10th October**	**Wolverhampton Wanderers**	**League**
13	12th October	Watford Youth	Southern Junior Floodlit Cup 1st Round
14	17th October	Swansea Town Reserves	Football Combination
15	19th October	Queens Park Rangers	London Challenge Cup 2nd Round
16	**24th October**	**Nottingham Forest**	**League**
17	26th October	Luton Town Youth	Southern Junior Floodlit Cup 2nd Round
18	28th October	Middlesex Boys v Staffordshire Boys	Inter-County Schools Challenge
19	31st October	Luton Town Reserves	Football Combination
20	2nd November	Chelsea	London Challenge Cup Semi-Final
21	**7th November**	**Bolton Wanderers**	**League**
22	14th November	Bournemouth & B. Athletic Reserves	Football Combination
23	**16th November**	**Torpedo Club, Moscow**	**Friendly**
24	**21st November**	**Everton**	**League**
25	28th November	Portsmouth Reserves	Football Combination
26	**5th December**	**Blackburn Rovers**	**League**
27	12th December	Brighton & Hove Albion Reserves	Football Combination
28	**19th December**	**Newcastle United**	**League**
29	26th December	West Ham United Reserves	Football Combination
30	**28th December**	**Leeds United**	**League**
31	2nd January	Birmingham City Reserves	Football Combination
32	9th January	Fulham Reserves	Friendly
33	**16th January**	**Arsenal**	**League**
34	**23rd January**	**Manchester United**	**League**
35	30th January	Spalding United	Eastern Counties League
36	**3rd February**	**Crewe Alexandra**	**F.A Cup 4th Round Replay**
37	6th February	Bristol City Reserves	Football Combination
38	**13th February**	**Leicester City**	**League**
39	**20th February**	**Blackburn Rovers**	**F.A Cup 5th Round**
40	27th February	Ipswich Town Reserves (postponed)	Football Combination
41	**5th March**	**Sheffield Wednesday**	**League**
42	12th March	Leyton Orient Reserves	Football Combination
43	**19th March**	**Fulham**	**League**
44	26th March	Nottingham Forest Reserves	Football Combination
45	**2nd April**	**Luton Town**	**League**
*	6th April	Tottenham Schools v West London Schools	Bower Cup Final
*	7th April	Middlesex Youth v London Youth	F.A County Youth Championship
46	9th April	Chelsea Reserves	Football Combination
47	13th April	Great Britain v Netherlands	Olympic Games Qualifying
48	14th April	London Boys v Manchester Boys	Inter-City Schools Challenge
49	15th April	Southend United Reserves	Football Combination
50	**16th April**	**Manchester City**	**League**
51	**18th April**	**Chelsea**	**League**
*	23rd April (am)	Tottenham Schools v Reading Schools	Hotspur Cup
52	23rd April (pm)	Harwich & Parkeston	Eastern Counties League
*	27th April	T.V All Stars v International Sportsmens XI	Charity Match
*	28th April	West Ham United Juniors	Winchester Cup Final
53	**30th April**	**Blackpool**	**League**
54	2nd May	Ipswich Town Reserves	Football Combination

1959-60

MONDAY, NOV. 16th 1959

COPYRIGHT

VOL. LII. NO. 23

ALL RIGHTS RESERVED

Secretary:
R. S. JARVIS

Team Manager:
W. E. NICHOLSON

Medical Officer:
Dr. A. E. TUGHAN

Chairman:
FRED. J. BEARMAN

Vice-Chairman:
FREDK. WALE

Directors:
F. JOHN BEARMAN, D. H. DEACOCK
S. A. WALE

TOTTENHAM HOTSPUR

FOOTBALL AND ATHLETIC COMPANY LIMITED

Official Programme

AND RECORD OF THE CLUB

WELCOME TO THE TORPEDO CLUB (MOSCOW)

Standing (left to right): G. GUSAROV, N. SENUKOV, TEREKNOV, V. SHUSTIKOV, J. FALIN, V. IVANOV.
Seated: V. VELEKANOV, S. METREVELI, L. OSTROVSKY, A. DENESANKO, A. MEDAKENIN.

PRICE TWOPENCE

Printed by Thomas Knight & Co. Ltd.,
The Clock House Press, Hoddesdon, Herts.

Tottenham v Torpedo Club (Moscow), Friendly.

1959-60

WEDNESDAY
27TH APRIL
1960

TV ALL STARS XI
AD JUVO TOTUS HOMO

OFFICIAL SOUVENIR PROGRAMME

T.V. All Stars XI v The International Sportsmen's XI,
Charity Match in aid of The Save The Children Fund.

1959-60

(left):
**Tottenham "A"
v Harwich &
Parkeston,**
Eastern Counties
League.

(right):
**Tottenham v
Crewe Alexandra,**
the 13-2, F.A. Cup 4th
Round Replay.

(left):
Tottenham Schools v West London Schools,
"A.G. Bower" Cup Final.
A 4-page duplicated programme, which featured
the team line-ups on Page 2

(left):
**Great Britain v
Netherlands,**
Olympic Qualifying
Match.

(right):
**Middlesex Boys v
Staffordshire Boys,**
Inter-County
Challenge.

1960-61

1960-61

TOTTENHAM HOTSPUR
FOOTBALL AND ATHLETIC
COMPANY LIMITED

SATURDAY, APRIL 29th, 1961   **PRICE TWOPENCE**

A Message from the Chairman

MY co-Directors join me to-day, at the end of this unforgettable season, in congratulating our players on their success in winning the Championship of the League. They have indeed written another memorable page in the history of the Club, and by the high skill and excellence of their play they have delighted countless followers of the game both at Tottenham and on the grounds of other clubs. Looking back over the season we have many memories of the dramatic quality of their football, which has received so many tributes from supporters. Congratulations also to our Manager, Mr. W. Nicholson, who has been such an inspiring personality in this happy season, his second in the capacity of Manager, and incidentally his 25th season with the Club. This is a proud day for him, and for all associated with the Club, and may Tottenham Hotspur continue to win new fame in the future. That is the wish of us all.

At the conclusion of to-day's game the League trophy and medals will be presented by a member of the League Management Committee.

FRED J. BEARMAN

The Football League
Div. I Championship Cup

Souvenir Programme

Tottenham v West Bromwich Albion, The cover of the 12 page glossy Championship edition.

1960-61

MONDAY, 24th OCT., 1960

COPYRIGHT

VOL. LIII. NO. 16

ALL RIGHTS RESERVED

Secretary:
R. S. JARVIS

Manager:
W. E. NICHOLSON

Medical Officer:
Dr. A. E. TUGHAN

Chairman:
FRED. J. BEARMAN

Vice-Chairman:
FREDK. WALE

Directors:
F. JOHN BEARMAN, D. H. DEACOCK
S. A. WALE

TOTTENHAM HOTSPUR

FOOTBALL AND ATHLETIC COMPANY LIMITED

Official Programme

AND RECORD OF THE CLUB

TOTTENHAM HOTSPUR v. THE ARMY

Floodlit Friendly   October 24th, 1960   **Kick-off 7.30 p.m.**

TOTTENHAM HOTSPUR
White Shirts, Blue Shorts

RIGHT WING

GOAL

LEFT WING

BROWN
1

BACKS

BAKER
2

HENRY
3

HALF-BACKS

DODGE
4

NORMAN
5

MARCHI (Capt.)
6

FORWARDS

JONES or **AITCHISON**
7

COLLINS
8

SAUL
9

ALLEN
10

DYSON
11

Referee: Major W. R. ECCLES, R.A.O.C.

Linesmen: R.S.M. L. PENTNEY, R.A.O.C. (Red Flag)   Sgt. R. A. PEARSON, R.A. (Yellow Flag)

Pte. J. SYDENHAM
(R.A.M.C.)   11

Pte. G. STRONG
(R.A.O.C.)   9

L/Cpl. J. BYRNE
(R.A.O.C.)   7

Pte. C. CROWE
(R.A.S.C.)   10

FORWARDS

Pte. A. YOUNG
(R.A.O.C.)   8

Pte. J. SMITH
(R.A.M.C.)   6

Pte. R. YEATS
(R.A.S.C.)   5

HALF-BACKS

Pte. M. SCOTT
(R.A.M.C.)   4

Pte. D. FERGUSON
(R.A.S.C.)   3

BACKS

L/Cpl. B. HILL
(Royal Signals)   2

Spr. J. OGSTON
(R.A.)   1

GOAL

LEFT WING

RIGHT WING

THE ARMY
Red Shirts, White Shorts

ANY ALTERATION WILL BE NOTED ON THE BOARD

PRICE TWOPENCE

Printed by Thomas Knight & Co. Ltd,
The Clock House Press, Hoddesdon Herts.

Tottenham v The Army, highly sought after single sheet programme for the Friendly Match.

1960-61

Tottenham v Tbilisi Dynamo, Friendly.

Tottenham v Manchester City, League.

Tottenham "A" v Bury Town,
Eastern Counties League Cup Semi-Final.

England v West Germany,
Under-23 International,
the team line-ups.

London Boys v Manchester Boys, (left), the match switched to Cheshunt in October, and (right), the match played at Tottenham in April.

1961-62

Volume 54

1	**12th August**	**F.A. Selected XI**	**F.A Charity Shield**
2	19th August	West Ham United Reserves	Football Combination
3	**23rd August**	**West Ham United**	**League**
4	**26th August**	**Arsenal**	**League**
5	**2nd September**	**Cardiff City**	**League**
6	9th September	Crystal Palace Reserves	Football Combination
7	**16th September**	**Wolverhampton Wanderers**	**League**
8	**20th September**	**Gornik Zabrze**	**European Cup Preliminary Round 2nd Leg**
9	23rd September	Nottingham Forest Reserves	Football Combination
10	**30th September**	**Aston Villa**	**League**
11	2nd October	Crystal Palace	London Challenge Cup 1st Round
12	7th October	Plymouth Argyle Reserves	Football Combination
13	**14th October**	**Manchester City**	**League**
14	16th October	Queens Park Rangers	London Challenge Cup 2nd Round
15	21st October	Leicester City Reserves	Football Combination
*	23rd October	London Boys v Manchester Boys	Inter-City Schools Challenge
16	**28th October**	**Burnley**	**League**
17	30th October	Queens Park Rangers Youth	Southern Junior Floodlit Cup 2nd Round
18	4th November	Notts County Reserves	Football Combination
19	**11th November**	**Fulham**	**League**
20	**15th November**	**S.C. Feijenoord**	**European Cup 8th Final 2nd Leg**
21	18th November	Peterborough United Reserves	Football Combination
22	**25th November**	**Leicester City**	**League**
23	2nd December	Ipswich Town Reserves	Football Combination
24	**9th December**	**Birmingham City**	**League**
25	**16th December**	**Blackpool**	**League**
26	23rd December	Arsenal Reserves	Football Combination
27	**30th December**	**Chelsea**	**League**
28	**10th January**	**Birmingham City**	**F.A Cup 3rd Round Replay**
29	13th January	Cardiff City Reserves	Football Combination
30	**20th January**	**Manchester United**	**League**
31	27th January	Colchester United Reserves	Football Combination
32	3rd February	Northampton Town Reserves	Football Combination
33	**10th February**	**Nottingham Forest**	**League**
34	12th February	Bexleyheath & Welling Youth	Southern Junior Floodlit Cup 2nd Round
35	17th February	Bristol Rovers Reserves	Football Combination
36	**24th February**	**Bolton Wanderers**	**League**
37	**26th February**	**Dukla Prague**	**European Cup Quarter Final 2nd Leg**
38	3rd March	Luton Town Reserves	Football Combination
39	**10th March**	**Aston Villa**	**F.A Cup 6th Round**
40	**14th March**	**Ipswich Town**	**League**
41	17th March	Mansfield Town Reserves	Football Combination
42	**24th March**	**Everton**	**League**
43	31st March	Shrewsbury Town Reserves	Football Combination
44	**5th April**	**Benfica**	**European Cup Semi-Final 2nd Leg**
45	**7th April**	**Sheffield Wednesday**	**League**
46	**9th April**	**Sheffield United**	**League**
*	13th April	Eynesbury Rovers	Eastern Counties League
*	14th April	Tottenham Schools v Willesden Schools	Schools Match
47	**20th April**	**Blackburn Rovers**	**League**
48	**21st April**	**West Bromwich Albion**	**League**
49	28th April	Norwich City Reserves	Football Combination

1961-62

EUROPEAN CUP

Semi-Final, Second Leg

TOTTENHAM
HOTSPUR

VERSUS

BENFICA

(PORTUGAL)

Thursday, 5th April, 1962

Kick-off 7.45 p.m.

OFFICIAL
PROGRAMME

6d.

Tottenham v Benfica, The cover of the 20 page special edition for the European Cup Semi-Final.

73

1961-62

TOTTENHAM HOTSPUR
FOOTBALL AND ATHLETIC COMPANY LIMITED

MEMBERS OF THE FOOTBALL LEAGUE

WINNERS OF THE F.A. CUP 1900-1, 1920-1

Telephone: TOTTENHAM No. 1020

Telegrams: SPURS, LOWER TOTTENHAM

Secretary
R. S. JARVIS.

748 HIGH ROAD   **TOTTENHAM, N.17**

WHITE HART LANE, TOTTENHAM, N.17.

PROGRAMME — PRICE 1d.

FRIDAY 13TH APRIL 1962.   THE EASTERN COUNTIES LEAGUE   KICK-OFF 7.15 P.M.

V. EYNESBURY ROVERS.

R.   'SPURS "A"   L.
(White shirts, Blue shorts)

BROWN (R)

D. WALKER   DENNIS
2.   3.

BEAL   A. BETSON   LYE
4.   5.   6.

THOMSON   ROFFMAN   BROWN (C)   PIPER   FITTOCK
7.   8.   9.   10.   11.

Referee:- Mr. D. Maitland.   Linesmen:- Mr.   (Amber Flag)
(Essex)   Mr.   (Red Flag)

11.   10.   9.   8.   7.
JENNINGS (B)   BAILEY   STAPLETON   JENNINGS (D)   AGER

6.   5.   4.
GILL   WETTON   SKINN

3.   2.
BYATT   GARNER

DENTON

(Blue & White Stripes)

L.   EYNESBURY ROVERS   R.

.......oOo.......

Tottenham "A" v Eynesbury Rovers, Eastern Counties League match played
at White Hart Lane but with a "Cheshunt style" programme.

74

1961-62

Tottenham v Sheffield Wednesday,
League.

Tottenham v F.A. Selected XI,
F.A. Charity Shield,
The normal cover design.

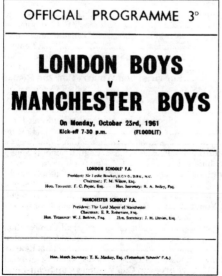

London Boys v Manchester Boys,
4-page large format, not produced by Spurs.

Tottenham v Blackpool, League,
Jimmy Greaves debut.

1962-63

Volume 55

1	**18th August**	**Birmingham City**	**League**
2	25th August	Bristol Rovers Reserves	Football Combination
3	**29th August**	**Aston Villa**	**League**
4	**1st September**	**Manchester City**	**League**
5	8th September	Luton Town Reserves	Football Combination
6	**12th September**	**Wolverhampton Wanderers**	**League**
7	**15th September**	**Blackburn Rovers**	**League**
8	22nd September	Ipswich Town Reserves	Football Combination
9	**29th September**	**Nottingham Forest**	**League**
10	1st October	Arsenal	London Challenge Cup 1st Round
11	**6th October**	**Arsenal**	**League**
12	13th October	Shrewsbury Town Reserves	Football Combination
*	20th October	London Boys v Liverpool Boys	Schools Match
13	**24th October**	**Manchester United**	**League**
14	27th October	Mansfield Town Reserves	Football Combination
15	**31st October**	**Glasgow Rangers**	**European Cup Winners Cup 1st Round**
16	**3rd November**	**Leicester City**	**League**
17	10th November	Leicester City Reserves	Football Combination
18	**17th November**	**Sheffield Wednesday**	**League**
19	24th November	Norwich City Reserves	Football Combination
20	**1st December**	**Everton**	**League**
21	8th December	Arsenal Reserves	Football Combination
22	15th December	West Ham United Reserves	Football Combination
23	**22nd December**	**West Ham United**	**League**
24	**26th December**	**Ipswich Town**	**League**
25	**5th January**	**Burnley**	**F.A Cup 3rd Round**
	(match played on 16th January)		
26	**19th January**	**Blackpool**	**League**
*	**26th January**	**Arsenal**	**Friendly**
		& Arsenal Reserves	Friendly
27	2nd February	Nottingham Forest Reserves (postponed)	Football Combination
28	**9th February**	**Sheffield United (postponed)**	**League**
29	16th February	Northampton Town Reserves	Football Combination
30	23rd February	Cardiff City Reserves	Football Combination
31	**2nd March**	**West Bromwich Albion**	**League**
32	4th March	West Ham United Youth	Southern Junior Floodlit Cup
33	9th March	Plymouth Argyle Reserves	Football Combination
34	**14th March**	**F.C. Slovan Bratislava**	**European Cup Winners Cup 2nd Round**
35	16th March	Peterborough United Reserves	Football Combination
36	19th March	Portsmouth v Coventry City	F.A Cup 4th Rnd 2nd Replay
37	23rd March	Notts County Reserves	Football Combination
38	25th March	Chelsea Youth	Southern Junior Floodlit Cup Semi-Final
39	**27th March**	**Leyton Orient**	**League**
40	**30th March**	**Burnley**	**League**
*	2nd April	Tottenham Schools v Cardiff Schools	English Schools Shield
41	8th April	Nottingham Forest v Southampton	F.A Cup 6th Rnd 2nd Replay
*	10th April	Tottenham Schools v Brighton Schools	English Schools Shield
42	**13th April**	**Fulham**	**League**
43	**15th April**	**Liverpool**	**League**
	17th April	England Youth v USSR Youth	International Youth Tournament
	(no club programme, as match covered by tournament brochure)		
44	18th April	Nottingham Forest Reserves	Football Combination
45	20th April	Crystal Palace Reserves	Football Combination
46	**27th April**	**Bolton Wanderers**	**League**
*	29th April	Tottenham Schools v Stoke Schools	English Schools Shield Semi-Final
47	**1st May**	**O.F.K. Belgrade**	**European Cup Winners Cup Semi-Final**
48	**4th May**	**Sheffield United**	**League**
*	6th May	West Ham United Juniors	London Winchester Cup Final
49	9th May	Colchester United Reserves	Football Combination

1962-63

EUROPEAN CUP WINNERS' CUP

Semi-Final, Second Leg

TOTTENHAM HOTSPUR

VERSUS

O.F.K. Belgrade

Wednesday, May 1st, 1963

Kick-off 7.45 p.m.

OFFICIAL PROGRAMME

6d.

Tottenham v O.F.K. Belgrade, European Cup Winners' Cup Semi-Final 2nd Leg.

1962-63

TOTTENHAM HOTSPUR FOOTBALL & ATHLETIC COMPANY LIMITED

SATURDAY 26TH JANUARY 1963.   FRIENDLY MATCHES.   WHITE HART LANE.

'SPURS RES. v. ARSENAL RES. - KICK-OFF 1.30 P.M. (One Hour)

```
R.                      ' S P U R S   R E S .                    L.
                       (White shirts, Blue shorts)
                            HOLLOWBREAD
                  BARTON                HOPKINS
            SMITH (J)        SMITH (A)         SHARPE
AITCHISON      PIPER           ALLEN           SAUL           DYSON

Referee:- Mr. F. Sheppard.   Linesmen:-              (Yellow Flag)
          (London)                                  (Red Flag)

ANDERSON      BLOOMFIELD       KANE          WARD          KINSELLA
            GROVES           FERRY        SMITHSON
                 CLARKE              BACUZZI
                            BLACK
                  (Red shirts, White shorts)
L.                     A R S E N A L   R E S .                    R.
```

.......oOo.......

'SPURS v. ARSENAL - KICK-OFF 2.45 P.M.

```
R.                      ' S P U R S                              L.
                       (White shirts, Blue shorts)
                              BROWN
                  BAKER                 HENRY
            MARCHI            NORMAN            MACKAY
MEDWIN        CLAYTON         SMITH (R)      GREAVES        JONES

Referee:- Mr. A. J. Sturgeon.   Linesmen:- Mr. S. Christie. (Yellow Flag)
          (London)                         Mr. S. Campton.  (Red Flag)

MACLEOD       EASTHAM         BAKER         STRONG         COURT
            SNEDDON          BROWN        BARNWELL
                 McCULLOUGH           MAGILL
                            McCLELLAND
                  (Red shirts, White shorts)
L.                     A R S E N A L                              R.
```

.......oOo.......

Tottenham v Arsenal, The single-sheet programme for the Friendly matches played
on January 26th, 1963. One of the hardest programmes to come across these days.

1962-63

**Tottenham Juniors v
West Ham Juniors,**
London F.A. Winchester Cup Final,
a duplicated single-sheet programme

Tottenham v Sheffield United,
The postponed League match, most League and
Combination programmes had covers similar to this.

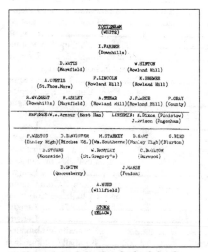

Tottenham Schools v Stoke Schools,
English Schools Shield Semi-Final,
this is page 2 of the four page
programme.

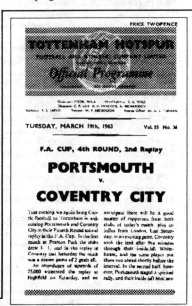

Portsmouth v Coventry City,
F.A. Cup 4th Round, 2nd Replay.

A four page issue, a similar programme was issued for
the Forest v Southampton, 6th Round 2nd Replay.

1963-64

Volume 56

1	**17th August**	**Whites v Blues**	**Public Trial**
2	24th August	Arsenal Reserves	Football Combination
3	**31st August**	**Nottingham Forest**	**League**
4	**4th September**	**Wolverhampton Wanderers**	**League**
4	7th September	Colchester United Reserves	Football Combination
	(programme incorrectly numbered)		
6	**14th September**	**Blackpool**	**League**
7	21st September	West Ham United Reserves	Football Combination
8	**28th September**	**West Ham United**	**League**
9	**2nd October**	**Birmingham City**	**League**
10	5th October	Bristol Rovers Reserves	Football Combination
11	9th October	Millwall	London Challenge Cup 1st Round
12	12th October	Shrewsbury Town Reserves	Football Combination
13	**19th October**	**Leicester City**	**League**
14	21st October	West Ham United	London Challenge Cup 2nd Round
15	26th October	Luton Town Reserves	Football Combination
16	**2nd November**	**Fulham**	**League**
17	4th November	Fulham	London Challenge Cup Semi-Final
18	9th November	Ipswich Town Reserves	Football Combination
19	**16th November**	**Burnley**	**League**
20	23rd November	Plymouth Argyle Reserves	Football Combination
21	**27th November**	**Manchester United (postponed)**	**European Cup Winners Cup 1st Rnd**
22	**30th November**	**Sheffield Wednesday**	**League**
23	**3rd December**	**Manchester United**	**European Cup Winners Cup 1st Rnd**
24	7th December	Mansfield Town Reserves	Football Combination
25	**14th December**	**Stoke City**	**League**
26	21st December	Nottingham Forest Reserves	Football Combination
27	**28th December**	**West Bromwich Albion**	**League**
28	**4th January**	**Chelsea**	**F.A Cup 3rd Round**
29	**11th January**	**Blackburn Rovers**	**League**
30	18th January	Cardiff City Reserves	Football Combination
31	**25th January**	**Aston Villa**	**League**
*	29th January	Queens Park Rangers Youth	F.A Youth Cup 3rd Rnd Replay
32	**1st February**	**Chelsea**	**League**
33	8th February	Norwich City Reserves	Football Combination
34	**15th February**	**Sheffield United**	**League**
35	**22nd February**	**Arsenal**	**League**
36	24th February	British Olympic XI	Friendly
37	29th February	Crystal Palace Reserves	Football Combination
38	**7th March**	**Everton**	**League**
39	14th March	Notts County Reserves	Football Combination
40	16th March	Chelsea	London Challenge Cup Final
41	**21st March**	**Manchester United**	**League**
42	**27th March**	**Liverpool**	**League**
43	28th March	Leicester City Reserves	Football Combination
44	30th March	Peterborough United Reserves	Football Combination
45	**4th April**	**Ipswich Town**	**League**
*	11th April	Crawley Town	Metropolitan League Challenge Cup Semi-Final
46	**18th April**	**Bolton Wanderers**	**League**
*	21st April	Tottenham Schools v Hackney Schools	Blaxland Cup Final
		& Tottenham Schools v Islington Schools	Gardner Cup Final
47	25th April	Northampton Town Reserves	Football Combination
*	27th April	Charlton Athletic "A"	Metropolitan League Challenge Cup Final 1st Leg

1963-64

PRICE THREEPENCE

TOTTENHAM HOTSPUR
FOOTBALL AND ATHLETIC COMPANY LIMITED

Official Programme

COPYRIGHT ALL RIGHTS RESERVED

Chairman: FREDK. WALE   Vice-Chairman: S. A. WALE
Directors: C. F. COX, D. H. DEACOCK, A. RICHARDSON
Secretary: R. S. JARVIS   Manager: W. E. NICHOLSON   Medical Officer: Dr. A. E. TUGHAN

MONDAY, FEBRUARY 24th, 1964   Vol. 56 No. 36

RECORDS

F.A. CUP
Winners 1901, 1921, 1961, 1962
Semi-finalists 1922, 1948, 1953, 1956

F.A. CHARITY SHIELD
Winners 1921, 1952, 1961, 1962

FOOTBALL LEAGUE DIVISION I
CHAMPIONS
1950–51........60 points
1960–61........66 points
RUNNERS-UP
1921–22........51 points
1951–52........53 points
1956–57........56 points
1962–63........55 points

DIVISION II
CHAMPIONS
1919–20........70 points
1949–50........61 points
RUNNERS-UP
1908–09........51 points
1932–33........55 points

EUROPEAN CUP
Semi-finalists 1962
(lost to Benfica 4—3)

EUROPEAN CUP WINNERS' CUP
Winners 1962-63 (beat Atletico Madrid 5—1)

FRIENDLY MATCH

TOTTENHAM HOTSPUR

v.

BRITISH OLYMPIC XI

Kick-off 7.30 p.m.

Tottenham v British Olympic XI, 4-page programme for this Reserve Team friendly.

81

1963-64

TOTTENHAM HOTSPUR FOOTBALL & ATHLETIC COMPANY LTD.

WHITE HART LANE GROUND

F.A. YOUTH CUP   PROGRAMME   Price - 1d.
3RD ROUND REPLAY.

Wed. 29th January, 1964.   Kick-off 7.15 p.m.

v. QUEEN'S PARK RANGERS.   (Extra-time if necessary)

Gardner & Blaxland Cup Finals,
4-page programme for the Tottenham Schools
Association Cup Finals between Tottenham and
Islington for the Gardner Cup, and Rowland Hill &
Edith Cavell for the Blaxland Cup.

Tottenham v Queens Park Rangers,
A single duplicated sheet for the
F.A. Youth Cup 3rd Round Replay.

PUBLIC TRIAL MATCH

Public Trial Match,
The team line-ups
from the 12 page
programme for the
seasons' curtain
raiser. The Whites
v Blues junior
match was played
at Cheshunt.

1963-64

TOTTENHAM HOTSPUR

FOOTBALL AND ATHLETIC COMPANY LIMITED

Official Programme

COPYRIGHT   ALL RIGHTS RESERVED

Chairman: FREDK. WALE   Vice-Chairman: S. A. WALE
Directors: C. F. COX, D. H. DEACOCK, A. RICHARDSON
Secretary: R. S. JARVIS   Manager: W. E. NICHOLSON   Medical Officer: Dr. A. E. TUGHAN

TUESDAY, DECEMBER 3rd, 1963   Vol. 56 No. 23

RECORDS

F.A. CUP
Winners 1901, 1921, 1961, 1962
Semi-finalists 1922, 1948, 1953, 1956

F.A. CHARITY SHIELD
Winners 1921, 1952, 1961, 1962

FOOTBALL LEAGUE DIVISION I
CHAMPIONS
1950–51 . . . . 60 points
1960–61 . . . . 66 points
RUNNERS-UP
1921–22 . . . . 51 points
1951–52 . . . . 53 points
1956–57 . . . . 56 points
1962–63 . . . . 55 points

DIVISION II
CHAMPIONS
1919–20 . . . . 70 points
1949–50 . . . . 61 points
RUNNERS-UP
1908–09 . . . . 51 points
1932–33 . . . . 55 points

EUROPEAN CUP
Semi-finalists 1962
(lost to Benfica 4—3)

EUROPEAN CUP WINNERS' CUP
Winners 1962–63 (beat Atletico Madrid 5—1)

Our Visitors tonight

MANCHESTER UNITED

THIS evening we again welcome our visitors, Manchester United, in the first leg of the European Cup Winners Cup, First Round, having had no more than a glimpse of them as they filed on and off the field last Wednesday when we had the melancholy experience of the match being postponed owing to fog. This was a great disappointment for all present, including the contingent who had travelled from Manchester, and again the Club pays tribute to the sporting way in which the hazard of the climate was accepted. Only a few tickets have been returned for the re-arranged game tonight, and it is good to know that the great majority of those who were here last Wednesday will again be here this evening. If the fates should once more be unkind, and tonight's match abandoned through weather, it would be played tomorrow. Similar provisional arrangements have been made at Old Trafford for the second leg on Tuesday, December 10th; if the match has to be postponed through fog, it would be played on the following day, December 11th. Tickets are on sale at our offices for the return match at Old

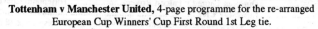

Tottenham v Manchester United, 4-page programme for the re-arranged European Cup Winners' Cup First Round 1st Leg tie.

1964-65

1964-65

TOTTENHAM HOTSPUR

FOOTBALL AND ATHLETIC COMPANY LIMITED

PRICE THREEPENCE

Vol. 57 No. 29

Official Programme

SATURDAY, JAN. 30th, 1965

OUR VISITORS TODAY

IPSWICH TOWN

SIR WINSTON CHURCHILL

This afternoon on sports grounds and football grounds throughout the country, tribute will be paid to the memory of Sir Winston Churchill. Prior to the start of today's match there will be a one minute's silence, and we ask all supporters to join us in this tribute to a great man whose recent death has saddened us all.

Tottenham v Ipswich Town, F.A. Cup 4th Round. Covers were usually as for the 1965-66 season.

1964-65

OUR VISITORS TONIGHT

Q. PARK RANGERS YOUTH XI

THIS evening we welcome Queen's Park Rangers in the first leg of the Final Tie of the Southern Junior Floodlight Cup. The second leg will be played at the White City Stadium on Wednesday, April 28th, the final result depending on goal aggregate. The competition is restricted to players who are under the age of 18 years on September 1st of the current season.

The following shows the progress of the two teams to the Final:

Queen's Park Rangers:

1st Round beat Watford 3—2.

2nd Round beat West Ham 5—1.

Semi-Final beat Charlton A. 3—1.

Tottenham Hotspur:

1st Round beat Reading 4—0.

2nd Round beat Luton Tn. 4—2.

Semi-Final beat Fulham 2—0.

Some of the visiting players have had quite an amount of experience in senior football. Tony Hazell has been a regular member of the Queen's Park Rangers League side, and has been selected to go with the England Youth Team to Germany for the forthcoming International Youth Tournament.

Roger Morgan, and his twin-brother Ian, have also figured in Rangers' League side, and Roger, also, will be with the England party to visit Germany. Mike Leach is at the present moment in the First Team, and has been under the eye of the England Youth Selectors. Frank Sibley has also made five appearances to date in the League side at wing-half. Davies, at centre-forward, is their leading marksman, and has recently scored his 50th goal in Junior football this season.

In our own team this evening no fewer than five of the players have

Tottenham Youth v Queen's Park Rangers Youth, The 4-page programme for the Southern Junior Floodlight Cup Final, 1st Leg, a match which was postponed and not replayed as the Final was reduced to one leg, and played at the, now demolished, White City Stadium.

1964-65

Edmonton, Enfield & Southgate
v East London,
the glossy 4-page programme for the
Corinthian Shield Final.

Tottenham v Scotland XI,
the glossy 16-page programme for the
John White Memorial Match, which
was delayed by one day by fog.

Tottenham v England Amateur XI,
the team line-ups from 4-page programme
for this Friendly played by the Reserves.

Whites v Blues,
the team line-ups from 4-page programme for
the Public Trial match, the last such match to
be staged at White Hart Lane.

87

1965-66

1965-66

TOTTENHAM HOTSPUR GROUND, HIGH ROAD
Tottenham, N.17

TOTTENHAM HOTSPUR

versus

HUNGARIAN SELECT XI

THURSDAY
18th NOVEMBER, 1965
Kick-off 7.30 p.m.

Official
Souvenir Programme **6d**

Tottenham v Hungarian Select XI, Friendly, a 16-page special issue.

1965-66

TOTTENHAM HOTSPUR

FOOTBALL AND ATHLETIC COMPANY LIMITED

Chairman: FREDK. WALE   Vice-Chairman: S. A. WALE
Directors: C. F. COX, D. H. DEACOCK, A. RICHARDSON
Secretary: R. S. JARVIS   Manager: W. E. NICHOLSON   Medical Officer: Dr. BRIAN CURTIN

    PRICE THREEPENCE

Vol. 58   No. 26

Official Programme

SATURDAY, JAN. 1st, 1966

OUR VISITORS TODAY

EVERTON

AERIAL VIEW OF GROUND

Tottenham v Everton, League.
The standard 12-page programme issued during seasons '64-'65, '65-'66, and '66-'67.

1965-66

LONDON SCHOOLS FOOTBALL ASSOCIATION.

President: S. E. TYE, ESQ.
Chairman: F. M. WILSON, ESQ.   *Secretary:* R. A. BAILEY, ESQ.
Match Secretary: T. K. MACKAY, ESQ. (Haringey S.F.A.)

LONDON BOYS v BIRMINGHAM BOYS

SATURDAY, 12th MARCH, 1966.   Kick-off 3.0 p.m.

The London Schools F.A. extends a very warm welcome to the Birmingham and District Association this afternoon. Our Associations first met in 1915 at Highbury when London won by 7 goals to 0. Today's game will be the thirty-ninth in the series, of which London have won 21, lost 13 and drawn 4. Last season's game, at St. Andrew's was won by the home side by 2 goals to 1, thus ending a run of 7 victories by the London Boys.

APPRECIATION.—Grateful thanks are accorded to the Tottenham Hotspur F.C. for the use of the ground and all its amenities for today's match. Scarcely a season goes by without a representative game being played at Tottenham and the interest and support given to Schools' football by the Club is indeed deeply appreciated. Please help us to show our gratitude by keeping off the playing area at all times.

It is with much pleasure that we record our thanks to the directors of the Tottenham & Edmonton Weekly Herald who have so kindly donated the programmes for the game.

The arrangements for today's game were undertaken by the Haringey and Tottenham Associations, and we tender our sincere gratitude for the valuable work done for this match and for many others in past seasons.

R. A. BAILEY,
Hon. Sec.

London Boys v Birmingham Boys,
Schools Match.

Tottenham "A" v Sheppey United,
Metropolitan League Challenge
Cup Semi-Final. A typical
single-sheet issue.

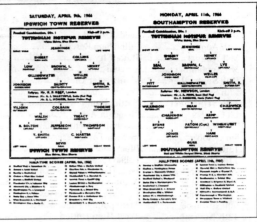

Tottenham Res. v Ipswich Res. & Southampton Res.,
The centre spread of the unusual double issue for the Football
Combination matches over the Easter holiday.

Tottenham Juniors v Crystal Palace Juniors,
A double-sided duplicated single-sheet for the South East
Counties League Cup Final 2nd Leg, Junior Section.

91

1966-67

Volume 59

1966-67

TOTTENHAM HOTSPUR
FOOTBALL AND ATHLETIC COMPANY LIMITED

Chairman: FRED. WALE   Vice-Chairman: S. A. WALE
Directors: C. F. COX, D. H. DEACOCK, A. RICHARDSON
Secretary: R. S. JARVIS   Manager: W. E. NICHOLSON   Medical Officer: Dr. BRIAN CURTIN

COPYRIGHT
ALL RIGHTS RESERVED   PRICE TWOPENCE

Official Programme   Vol. 59 No. 16   Wednesday, Nov. 9th, 1966

F.A. Youth Cup, 1st Round   **Kick-off 7.30 p.m.**

TOTTENHAM HOTSPUR YOUTH XI
White Shirts, Blue Shorts

RIGHT WING   GOAL   LEFT WING
                            HOWARD
                              1

                            BACKS
            COLLINS   **BISH**
               2   3

                        HALF-BACKS
        CUTBUSH   **EVANS**   **WANT**
            4   5   6

        BUNKELL   FORWARDS   **PARKINSON**
            8   10
SHOEMARK   **TURNER**   **CLANCY**
    7   9   11

Referee: **Mr. J. L. J. PRESS**, Herts
Linesmen: **Mr. D. J. HOLDEN**, Herts (Red Flag)
Mr. B. J. BROMLEY, Herts (Yellow Flag)

        11   9   7
R. TURNBULL   **C. BUCK**   **A. FILE**
        10   8
    D. WATSON   FORWARDS   **R. TREHEARNE**

        6   5   4
    T. TRIPP **W. CRUDGINGTON** **B. WILLEY**
                    HALF-BACKS

        3   2
J. O'DONNELL (Capt.)   **J. MARSHALL**
        BACKS

                        1
                    G. PORTER
LEFT WING   GOAL   RIGHT WING

METROPOLITAN POLICE CADETS
Blue Shirts, White Shorts

Tottenham Youth XI v Metropolitan Police Cadets,
F.A. Youth Cup 1st Round, single-sheet issue.

93

1966-67

TOTTENHAM HOTSPUR
FOOTBALL AND ATHLETIC COMPANY LIMITED

Chairman: FREDK. WALE   Vice-Chairman: S. A. WALE
Directors: C. F. COX, D. H. DEACOCK, A. RICHARDSON
Secretary: R. S. JARVIS   Manager: W. E. NICHOLSON   Medical Officer: Dr. BRIAN CURTIN

COPYRIGHT
ALL RIGHTS RESERVED

PRICE TWOPENCE

Vol. 59 No. 37

Official Programme

MONDAY, FEB. 27th, 1967

WELCOME TO
ENGLAND AMATEUR XI

THIS evening we extend a warm welcome to the England Amateur XI, and to the officials accompanying the team. Their visit adds a touch of variety to our fixture list, and we welcome the opportunity of testing our strength against the stars of the amateur world.

Tonight's match is part of the England Amateur Team's preparation for international fixtures with the Republic of Ireland on March 11th, and with Scotland on March 31st.

HELD BRENTFORD

Matches against professional teams provide the right kind of preparation for England's amateurs, and tonight's match is one of three during their present intensive spell of collective training. A fortnight ago this evening, England's amateurs held Brentford's first team to a 2—2 draw at Griffin Park.

The team at Brentford was: J. Shippey (Oxford City); D. Hogwood (Hendon), B. Moffatt (Leytonstone); A. D'Arcy (Enfield), D. Gradi (Sutton United), R. Haider (Kingstonian); C. Townsend (Wealdstone), K. Gray (Leytonstone), L. Pritchard (Sutton), D. Andrews (Leytonstone), and R. Sleap (Hendon). The goals were scored by Larry Pritchard and Dave Andrews.

A third match will be played against West Ham United on March 20th.

Mr. J. W. Bowers, Vice-President of the Football Association, is the Member-in-Charge of the England Amateur XI this evening, and the team manager is Mr. Charles Hughes of the F.A. coaching staff.

The trainer is Mr. Jack Jennings, who has attended England's amateurs for many years. Formerly trainer to Northampton Town, he was a noted full-back with Cardiff City, Middlesbrough and Preston North End before the war.

Here are pen pictures of the visiting team tonight:

JOHN SWANNELL (Hendon)
Goalkeeper. Has played in every amateur international since coming into the side in September, 1964. Also played in the Amateur Cup Finals of 1965 and 1966. Played for Manchester University and Corinthian Casuals before joining Hendon.

DAVID HOGWOOD (Hendon)
Right-back. A newcomer to the England squad who has yet to gain his first amateur international cap. He has played consistently well for Hendon, and was in their Cup Final teams of 1965 and 1966.

Tottenham Reserves v England Amateur XI, Friendly.
A typical 4-page Reserve issue for this postponed match.

94

1966-67

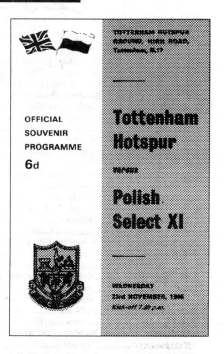

Haringey v West London, Compton Cup Final.
Single duplicated sheet for this
Under-13 district schools match.

Tottenham Reserves v Arsenal Reserves,
The team line-ups from the programme for the
postponed Combination match on January 7th 1967.

Tottenham "A" v Brentwood Town,
The team line-ups from the 4-page programme
for the Metropolitan League match
played at White Hart Lane.

1967-68

1	19th August	Leicester City Reserves	Football Combination
2	**23rd August**	**Everton**	**League**
3	**26th August**	**West Ham United**	**League**
4	2nd September	Peterborough United Reserves	Football Combination
5	**6th September**	**Wolverhampton Wanderers**	**League**
6	**9th September**	**Sheffield Wednesday**	**League**
7	16th September	Northampton Town Reserves	Football Combination
8	23rd September	Birmingham City Reserves	Football Combination
9	**27th September**	**N.K.Hajduk Split**	**European Cup Winners Cup 1st Round 2nd Leg**
10	**30th September**	**Sunderland**	**League**
11	**7th October**	**Sheffield United**	**League**
12	14th October	Coventry City Reserves	Football Combination Cup Group
13	**25th October**	**Nottingham Forest**	**League**
14	28th October	Luton Town Youth	F.A Youth Cup 1st Round
15	**4th November**	**Liverpool**	**League**
16	11th November	Walsall Reserves	Football Combination Cup Group
17	**18th November**	**Chelsea**	**League**
18	25th November	Gillingam Reserves	Football Combination Cup Group
19	**2nd December**	**Newcastle United**	**League**
20	4th December	Oxford United Youth	F.A Youth Cup 2nd Round
21	9th December	Birmingham City Reserves (abandoned)	Football Combination Cup Group
22	**13th December**	**Olympique Lyonnais**	**European Cup Winners Cup 2nd Round 2nd Leg**
23	**16th December**	**Leicester City**	**League**
24	23rd December	West Ham United Reserves	Football Combination
25	**26th December**	**Fulham**	**League**
26	28th December	Birmingham City Reserves	Football Combination Cup Group
27	**6th January**	**Burnley (postponed)**	**League**
27	**20th January**	**Arsenal**	**League**
28	27th January	Ipswich Town Reserves	Football Combination
29	**31st January**	**Manchester United**	**F.A Cup 3rd Round Replay**
30	**3rd February**	**Manchester United**	**League**
31	10th February	Coventry City Reserves	Football Combination
32	**17th February**	**Preston North End**	**F.A Cup 4th Round**
33	21st February	Gillingham Reserves	Football Combination
34	24th February	Swindon Town Reserves	Football Combination
*	26th February	Haringey Boys v Bristol Boys	English Schools Shield
35	**1st March**	**West Bromwich Albion**	**League**
36	**9th March**	**Liverpool**	**F.A Cup 5th Round**
*	16th March	England v Scotland	Schools International
37	**23rd March**	**Stoke City**	**League**
38	27th March	Bristol City Reserves	Football Combination Cup Semi-Final
39	**30th March**	**Burnley**	**League**
40	1st April	Walsall Reserves	Football Combination
41	**6th April**	**Southampton**	**League**
42	8th April	Hatfield Town	Metropolitan League Challenge Cup Semi-Final
43	10th April	Plymouth Argyle Reserves	Football Combination
44	**12th April**	**Leeds United**	**League**
45	13th April	Arsenal Reserves	Football Combination
46	**20th April**	**Coventry City**	**League**
47	22nd April	Orient Youth	London Youth Cup Semi-Final
48	27th April	Chelsea Reserves	Football Combination
49	29th April	Bury Town	Metropolitan League Challenge Cup Final 1st Leg
50	1st May	Arsenal Reserves	Football Combination Cup Final 2nd Leg
51	**4th May**	**Manchester City**	**League**
52	11th May	Southampton Reserves	Football Combination

96

1967-68

Official Programme

Price SIXPENCE

TOTTENHAM HOTSPUR
v.
BURNLEY

FOOTBALL LEAGUE—DIVISION ONE

Saturday, 6th January, 1968

KICK-OFF 3 p.m.

SEASON
1967—68

Vol. 60
No. 27

Tottenham v Burnley
The programme for the postponed League match on 6th January, 1968.

97

1967-68

English Schools' Football Association

SCHOOLS' INTERNATIONAL

(Under the auspices of the London Schools' Football Association)

ENGLAND

v

SCOTLAND

Official Programme   *One Shilling*

England v Scotland, Schools International

1967-68

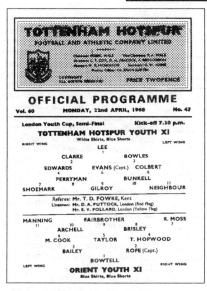

Tottenham Youth XI v Orient Youth XI,
London Youth Cup, Semi-Final.

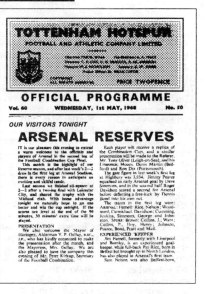

Tottenham Reserves v Arsenal Reserves,
Combination Cup Final, 2nd Leg.

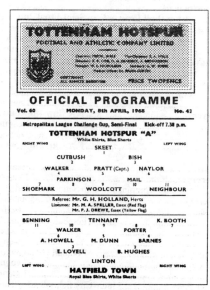

Tottenham "A" v Hatfield Town,
Metropolitan League Challenge Cup,
Semi-Final

Tottenham "A" v Bury Town,
Metropolitan League Challenge Cup,
Final, 1st Leg

1968-69

1	**31st July** .... **Glasgow Rangers** .... **Friendly**
2	**10th August** .... **Arsenal** .... **League**
3	17th August .... Norwich City Reserves .... Football Combination Cup Group
4	**21st August** .... **West Bromwich Albion** .... **League**
5	**24th August** .... **Sheffield Wednesday** .... **League**
6	31st August .... Crystal Palace Reserves .... Football Combination Cup Group
7	**7th September** .... **Burnley** .... **League**
8	11th September .... Gillingham Reserves .... Football Combination Cup Group
9	14th September .... Fulham Reserves .... Football Combination Cup Group
10	**21st September** .... **Nottingham Forest** .... **League**
11	**25th September** .... **Exeter City** .... **Football League Cup 3rd Round**
12	28th September .... Ipswich Town Reserves .... Football Combination Cup Group
13	30th September .... Dagenham .... London Challenge Cup 1st Round
14	**5th October** .... **Leicester City** .... **League**
15	**9th October** .... **Manchester United** .... **League**
16	12th October .... Gillingham Reserves .... Football Combination
17	14th October .... Millwall .... London Challenge Cup 2nd Round
18	**16th October** .... **Peterborough United** .... **Football League Cup 4th Round**
19	**19th October** .... **Liverpool** .... **League**
20	23rd October .... Charlton Athletic Youth .... London Youth Cup 1st Round
21	26th October .... Luton Town Reserves .... Football Combination
22	28th October .... Enfield .... London Challenge Cup Semi-Final
23	**30th October** .... **Southampton** .... **Football League Cup 5th Round**
24	**2nd November** .... **Stoke City** .... **League**
25	6th November .... Harpenden Town Youth .... F.A Youth Cup 1st Round
26	9th November .... Oxford United Reserves .... Football Combination
27	**16th November** .... **Sunderland** .... **League**
28	18th November .... West Ham United .... London Challenge Cup Final
29	23rd November .... Cardiff City Reserves .... Football Combination
30	**30th November** .... **Queens Park Rangers (postponed)** .... **League**
30	**4th December** .... **Arsenal** .... **Football League Cup Semi-Final 2nd Leg**
31	7th December .... Northampton Town Reserves .... Football Combination
32	**14th December** .... **Manchester City** .... **League**
33	21st December .... Reading Reserves .... Football Combination
34	**28th December** .... **Ipswich Town (postponed)** .... **League**
34	1st January .... Bristol City Youth .... Southern Junior Floodlight Cup 2nd Rnd Replay
35	4th January .... Plymouth Argyle Reserves .... Football Combination
36	11th January .... Bristol Rovers Reserves .... Football Combination
37	**18th January** .... **Leeds United** .... **League**
38	**25th January** .... **Wolverhampton Wanderers** .... **F.A Cup 4th Round**
39	**29th January** .... **Queens Park Rangers** .... **League**
40	1st February .... Swansea Town Reserves .... Football Combination
41	**8th February** .... **Aston Villa** .... **F.A Cup 5th Round**
	(match played 12th February)
42	**19th February** .... **Southampton (postponed)** .... **League**
43	**22nd February** .... **Wolverhampton Wanderers** .... **League**
44	26th February .... Southampton Reserves .... Football Combination Cup Semi-Final 2nd Leg
45	1st March .... Peterborough United Reserves .... Football Combination
46	**8th March** .... **Everton** .... **League**
47	15th March .... Bournemouth Reserves .... Football Combination
48	**18th March** .... **Ipswich Town** .... **League**
49	**22nd March** .... **Chelsea** .... **League**
50	29th March .... Arsenal Reserves .... Football Combination
51	**2nd April** .... **Newcastle United** .... **League**
52	**4th April** .... **Coventry City** .... **League**
53	9th April .... London Boys v Manchester Boys .... Inter-City Schools Challenge
54	12th April .... Swindon Town Reserves .... Football Combination
55	**19th April** .... **West Ham United** .... **League**
56	**22nd April** .... **Southampton** .... **League**

100

1968-69

TOTTENHAM HOTSPUR
FOOTBALL AND ATHLETIC COMPANY LIMITED

Chairman: FREDK. WALE   Vice-Chairman: S. A. WALE
Directors: C. F. COX, A. RICHARDSON
Manager: W. E. NICHOLSON   Secretary: G. W. JONES
Medical Officer: Dr. BRIAN CURTIN

League Champions: 1950-51, 1960-61
F.A. Cup Winners: 1901, 1921, 1961, 1962, 1967
Winners of European Cup Winners Cup: 1963

COPYRIGHT ALL RIGHTS RESERVED   PRICE TWOPENCE

OFFICIAL PROGRAMME

Vol. 61   WEDNESDAY, 6th NOVEMBER, 1968   No. 25

F.A. Youth Cup, 1st Round   Kick-off 7.30 p.m.

TOTTENHAM HOTSPUR YOUTH XI
White Shirts, Blue Shorts

RIGHT WING   LEFT WING

DAINES
1

A. MANLEY   HOLDER, P. (Capt.)
2   3

DILLON   A. BENNETT   EDWARDS
4   5   6

PERRYMAN   CHARKER
7   8   9   10   11
J. OLIVER   CLARKE   NEIGHBOUR

Referee: **Mr. S. F. LOVER**, London
Linesmen: **Mr. B. KUTEREBA**, London (Red Flag)
Mr. W. G. BRADFORD, London (Yellow Flag)

C. CRAWLEY   P. McHALE   M. SMOUT
11   9   8   7
P. EVEREST   M. EVEREST
6   5   4
A. BAILEY   D. MORLEY (Capt.)   P. CRAWLEY
3   2
S. CROSBY   D. ISAACS
1
P. HARVEY

LEFT WING   RIGHT WING

HARPENDEN TOWN YOUTH XI
Yellow Shirts, Yellow Shorts

Tottenham Youth XI v Harpenden Town Youth XI
F.A. Youth Cup, 1st Round, single-sheet issue.

101

1968-69

FOOTBALL LEAGUE—DIVISION ONE

TOTTENHAM HOTSPUR

v.

QUEEN'S PARK RANGERS

Official Programme

Price SIXPENCE

SEASON 1968-69
Vol. 61   No. 30

Saturday, 30th November, 1968
KICK-OFF 3 p.m.

Spurs v Queen's Park Rangers,
The cover of the programme for the postponed match in November.
Copies of this programme are now very hard to find, however, copies of the
postponed **Ipswich Town** and **Southampton** League matches are not all that rare.

102

1968-69

Inter-City Schools Challenge Match   8th April, 1969   Kick-off 7.30 p.m.

LONDON BOYS
White Shirts, Blue Shorts

LEFT WING

RIGHT WING

G. LONG
(Croydon)

T. SAMPSON
(Blackheath)

M. DAVIES (South London)   A. MARCHANT (Capt.) (Barking)   S. PHILLIPS (Haringey)

J. COKER (West London)   J. FLAHERTY (South London)   T. SPINNER (Aldershot)   R. FULTON (Barnet)

A. TAYLOR (Barking)   P. GREGORY (Havering)

Referee: Mr. J. TRIPPICK (Waltham Cross)

Linesmen: Mr. H. ROWBOTTOM, Haringey (Red Flag)   Mr. A. PEARCE, Edmonton (Orange Flag)

D. HEALEY (St. Clare's)   P. SMITH (Preston Brook High)   H. STRINGER (Harpurhey High)   P. FLETCHER (Whalley Range)   E. O'KEEFE (St. Clare's)

M. BUCKLEY (Capt.) (Brockway High)   R. MANCINI (St. Clare's)   K. JORDAN (St. Peter's Grammar)

M. LESTER (St. Gregory's Tech.)   P. ROBERTS (Charlton High)

M. FINN
(St. Gregory's Tech.)

MANCHESTER BOYS
Red Shirts, Red Shorts

LEFT WING

RIGHT WING

---

this season. Here are biographies of the players of both teams:

MANCHESTER

MICHAEL FINN (St. Gregory's Technical). Goalkeeper. A member of the Manchester team that shared the English Schools Trophy with Waltham Forest last season. A County player.

PHILLIP ROBERTS (Chorlton High School). A full-back who has speed and plenty of ability in making constructive use of his clearances.

MICHAEL LESTER (St. Gregory's Technical). A defender who can look back on a highly satisfactory season. Has a good positional sense.

KEVIN JORDAN (St. Peter's Grammar School). A wing-half who covers a lot of ground, and is noted for his industry. Lightens the work of the players around him.

RUDY MANCINI (St. Clare's Secondary School). A strong centre-half who can spread confidence among the rest of the defence. Good with his head.

MICHAEL BUCKLEY (Brockway High School). Captain of the team, and also a County player. Is best described as a link-man, and is a member of the England Boys squad.

EAMONN O'KEEFE (St. Clare's Secondary School). The smallest player in the Manchester team for years. Compensates for his small stature with good ball control and 'reads' the game well.

PETER FLETCHER (Whalley Range). Another member of the team who is also a County player, appeared in a number of matches for Manchester last season.

HENRY STRINGER (Harpurhey High School). Also a County player. Enjoys a big reputation as a marksman.

PAUL SMITH (Moston Brook High School). A full Schools international, who is also a County player. Shines as a schemer.

DANNY HEALEY (St. Clare's Secondary School). A speedy winger who can use both feet equally well.

Reserves

STEPHEN BARRATT (St. George's), goalkeeper; DAVID CHARLTON (St. John's), full-back; EAMONN KAVANAGH (St. Bede's), utility player;

LONDON

MICHAEL KILBRIDE (Wilbraham High), wing-half.

GRAHAM LONG (Norbury Manor School). Goalkeeper. Has won County representative honours. An agile 'keeper, whose handling of the ball is sound.

THOMAS SAMPSON (Catford Comprehensive). Has played in defence for Blackheath since he was 12. Will not be 15 until August. Captain of Kent County Boys.

JOHN FLAHERTY (Beaufoy Secondary, South London). Left-back or left-half who has won County honours. An international trialist.

MALCOLM DAVIES (Stockwell Manor). Wing-half or inside-forward who plays for South London and has gained County honours.

ANTHONY MARCHANT (Park Modern School, Barking). Captains London from the half-back line. A current England Schools international.

RAYMOND FULTON (Goldbeaters School, Edgware). A strong defender who has played for Barnet Boys for four years. A Middlesex County player and international trialist.

JAMES ADE COKER (Henry Compton School, Fulham). A striker who has played for West London since 1966. Has also played for Middlesex.

STEPHEN PHILLIPS (Somerset School, Tottenham). Plays as a link-man for Haringey Boys, and is an international trialist. Attends the school that produced Jimmy Pearce of Spurs.

TERENCE SPINNER (Cove County School, Farnborough). Centre-forward for Aldershot Boys, and another current international. Scored over 100 goals in each of the past two seasons.

ALAN TAYLOR (Erkenwald School, Dagenham). An inside-forward with an effective shot. Has played for England Boys and also Essex County. A member of Barking Boys team.

PAUL GREGORY (Bush Elms School, Hornchurch). A fast winger who plays for Havering Boys and Essex.

Reserves

IAN SACHS (Grey Court School, Richmond), goalkeeper; JOHN DELVE (Feltham School-Hounslow Boys); ANTHONY WAREING (Salesian College-South London Boys), striker.

London Schools F.A. extend a cordial welcome this evening to Councillor and Mrs. H. J. Worms, the Mayor and Mayoress of Haringey.

The London Schools F.A. expresses its appreciation to the Directors of the Tottenham Hotspur Football Club for their generosity in providing their ground and facilities for tonight's match. The interest taken by the Club in Schoolboy Football has always been greatly appreciated.

The London Schools F.A. offer their thanks to the Haringey Schools F.A. for their valuable help in the organisation of tonight's match, and all spectators for their support. Schools' football depends on public support at these matches for funds with which to carry on the work.

London Boys v Manchester Boys,
The centre spread of the four-page "Reserve team" style programme issued for this Inter-City Schools Challenge Match.

1969-70

Volume 62

1	9th August	Fulham Reserves	Football Combination
2	**13th August**	**Burnley**	**League**
3	**16th August**	**Liverpool**	**League**
4	23rd August	Bristol City Reserves	Football Combination
5	**27th August**	**Chelsea**	**League**
6	**30th August**	**Ipswich Town**	**League**
7	6th September	Leicester City Reserves	Football Combination
8	**13th September**	**Manchester City**	**League**
9	17th September	Aldershot Youth	Southern Junior Floodlight Cup Preliminary Round
10	20th September	West Ham United Reserves	Football Combination
11	**27th September**	**Sunderland**	**League**
12	1st October	Brentford	London Challenge Cup 1st Round
13	4th October	Southampton Reserves	Football Combination
14	**11th October**	**Wolverhampton Wanderers**	**League**
15	**18th October**	**Newcastle United**	**League**
16	25th October	Luton Town Reserves	Football Combination Cup Group
17	29th October	West Ham United Youth	F.A Youth Cup 1st Round
18	**1st November**	**Sheffield Wednesday**	**League**
19	8th November	Norwich City Reserves	Football Combination
20	**15th November**	**West Bromwich Albion**	**League**
21	22nd November	Crystal Palace Reserves	Football Combination
22	26th November	Walsall Reserves	Football Combination Cup Group
23	**29th November**	**Everton (postponed)**	**League**
23	3rd December	Orient Youth	F.A Youth Cup 2nd Round
24	13th December	Ipswich Town Reserves	Football Combination
25	**17th December**	**Everton (abandoned)**	**League**
26	**20th December**	**West Ham United**	**League**
27	**26th December**	**Crystal Palace**	**League**
28	31st December	Arsenal Youth (postponed)	F.A Youth Cup 3rd Round
28	5th January	Arsenal Youth	F.A Youth Cup 3rd Round
29	7th January	Bradford City	F.A Cup 3rd Round Replay
30	**10th January**	**Derby County**	**League**
31	14th January	Northampton Town Reserves	Football Combination Cup Group
32	17th January	Queens Park Rangers Reserves	Football Combination
33	**24th January**	**Crystal Palace**	**F.A Cup 4th Round**
34	28th January	Orient Youth	Southern Junior Floodlit Cup 2nd Round
35	**31st January**	**Southampton**	**League**
36	7th February	Walsall Reserves	Football Combination
37	**14th February**	**Leeds United**	**League**
38	18th February	Stoke City Youth	F.A Youth Cup 5th Round
39	**21st February**	**Stoke City**	**League**
40	25th February	Leicester City Reserves	Football Combination Cup Group
41	28th February	Birmingham City Reserves	Football Combination Cup Group
42	**6th March**	**Manchester United (postponed)**	**League**
42	**11th March**	**Everton**	**League**
43	14th March	Watford v Chelsea	F.A Cup Semi-Final
44	**21st March**	**Coventry City**	**League**
45	24th March	Bristol City Youth	F.A Youth Cup Semi-Final 1st Leg
46	**27th March**	**Nottingham Forest**	**League**
47	1st April	Birmingham City Reserves	Football Combination
48	4th April	Chelsea Reserves	Football Combination
49	**13th April**	**Manchester United**	**League**
50	18th April	Coventry City Youth	F.A Youth Cup Final 1st Leg
51	23rd April	Arsenal Reserves	Football Combination Cup Semi-Final 2nd Leg
52	25th April	Millwall Youth	Southern Junior Floodlit Cup Final 2nd Leg
53	1st May	Coventry City Youth	F.A Youth Cup Final 2nd Replay
54	**2nd May**	**Arsenal**	**League**

1969-70

FOOTBALL LEAGUE—DIVISION ONE

TOTTENHAM HOTSPUR

v.

MANCHESTER UNITED

Official Programme

Price SIXPENCE

SEASON 1969–70
Vol. 62   No. 42

Friday, 6th March, 1970
KICK-OFF 7.30 p.m.

Tottenham Hotspur v Manchester United,
The cover of the programme for the postponed League match.

1969-70

Aerial view of Spurs Ground

THE FOOTBALL ASSOCIATION
CHALLENGE CUP

SEMI-FINAL TIE

WATFORD
v.
CHELSEA

Saturday, 14th March 1970
Kick-off 2.45 p.m.

TOTTENHAM HOTSPUR GROUND

PRICE ONE SHILLING

OFFICIAL
PROGRAMME

Watford v Chelsea,
F.A. Cup Semi-Final.

1969-70

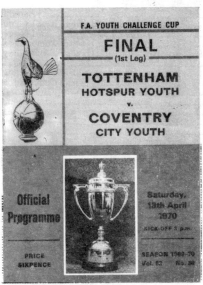

OFFICIAL PROGRAMME
Vol. 62   FRIDAY, 1st MAY, 1970   No. 53

OUR VISITORS TONIGHT
COVENTRY CITY YOUTH

OUR F.A. YOUTH CUP final tie with Coventry City has developed into a marathon, and this evening we meet in a second replay in an attempt to decide the destination of the trophy.

As the Final was played in two legs, this is the fourth meeting between the teams, and if the scores are again level at the end of 90 minutes this evening, 30 minutes' extra time will again be played.

This is proving one of the most remarkable Finals in the history of the competition, and the matches already played between Spurs and Coventry have produced a high standard of football, and a full quota of thrills.

The first leg of the Final, last Saturday week, drew a crowd of 10,700 to this ground, and the second leg, at Coventry, was watched by 9,568 spectators.

For the replay at Coventry on Tuesday evening, the crowd figure was 14,926. Although tonight's second replay had to be hastily arranged, we hope for another good attendance tonight to provide a suitable setting for the efforts of these outstanding and evenly-matched teams.

EARLY GOALS
In the match at Coventry on Tuesday two early goals were scored, and both were spectacular efforts. First Steve Perryman cracked a flashing 25-yard drive off the bar into Coventry's net in the ninth minute, and within a minute Alan Green had headed a brilliant equaliser.

Midway through the second half Johnny Stevenson put Coventry ahead with a right-footed shot following the regrettable incident that led to the sending-off of Graeme Souness, but Spurs struck back in great style for John Oliver to score through a ruck of players.

In the last minute of normal time Spurs had two great chances to score, but Coventry's goal managed to survive. In the second period of extra time, Mike Flanagan was replaced by Ron Gibson.

COVENTRY: Icke; Crossley, Holmes; Mortimer, Dugdale, Parker; Cartwright, Green, Randell, McGuire and Stevenson.

SPURS: Daines; St. Almond, E. Jones; Dillon, M., W. Edwards; Souness; J. Oliver, Turner, Clarke, Perryman and M. Flanagan (sub. R. Gibson).

Tottenham Youth v Coventry City Youth,
F.A. Youth Cup Final, a 16-page issue.

Tottenham Youth v Coventry City Youth,
F.A. Youth Cup Final 2nd Replay,
a 4-page issue.

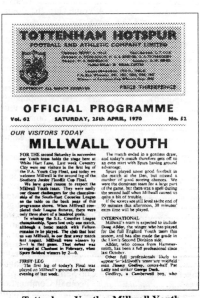

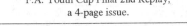

OFFICIAL PROGRAMME
Vol. 62   SATURDAY, 25th APRIL, 1970   No. 52

OUR VISITORS TODAY
MILLWALL YOUTH

FOR THE second Saturday in succession our Youth team holds the stage here at White Hart Lane. Last week Coventry City were our visitors in the first leg of the F.A. Youth Cup Final, and today we welcome Millwall in the second leg of the Southern Junior Floodlit Cup Final.

We have good reason to respect the Millwall Youth team. They were easily our closest challengers for the championship of the South-East Counties League so the table on the back page of this programme shows. When Millwall completed their League fixtures, there were only three short of a hundred goals.

In winning the S.E. Counties League championship, Spurs lost only one match, although a bonus match with Fulham remains to be played. The club that beat us was Millwall, in our first away match last August. Millwall were winners by 3—1 in that game. That defeat was avenged at Chelsea in February, when Spurs finished winners by 2—0.

FIRST LEG
The first leg of today's Final was played on Millwall's ground on Monday evening of last week.

The match ended in a goalless draw, and today's match therefore gets off to an even start with Spurs having ground advantage.

Spurs played some good football in the match at the Den, but missed a number of good scoring chances. We were the dominant team for a large part of the game, but there was a spell during the second half when Millwall caused us quite a bit of trouble.

If the scores are still level at the end of 90 minutes at the end 30 minutes' extra time will be played.

INTERNATIONAL
Millwall's team is expected to include Doug Allder, the winger who has played for the full England Youth team this season, and has also made the grade in the Lion's Second Division side.

Allder, who comes from Hammersmith, has been a full professional since last October.

Other full professionals likely to appear in Millwall's team are midfield man Jimmy Godfrey, centre-half Pat Laity and striker George Duck.

Godfrey, a Camberwell boy, who

Tottenham Youth v Millwall Youth,
Southern Junior Floodlit Cup Final 2nd Leg.

OFFICIAL PROGRAMME
Vol. 62   THURSDAY, 23rd APRIL, 1970   No. 51

OUR VISITORS TONIGHT
ARSENAL RESERVES

THIS EVENING we stage the second leg of the Football Combination Cup Semi-final, and in meeting our near neighbours, Arsenal, we could not wish for more attractive opposition.

The first leg of this Semi-final tie was played at Highbury last Friday evening, and resulted in a 4—2 win for Arsenal. We therefore start two goals behind, and our players are well aware of the task confronting them.

If at the end of 90 minutes' play tonight, Spurs hold a lead of two goals, and the aggregate score is therefore level, an additional extra time will be played.

West Ham United have already qualified for the Final. They beat Ipswich Town, their Semi-final opponents, by an aggregate score of 4—2. Ipswich won their home match 2—1, but West Ham were winners by 3—0 at Upton Park last week.

The double-leg Final of this competition will now be held over until next season.

FIRST LEG
The result of the first leg at Highbury last Friday was a big disappointment to

us. Neil Johnson crashed in an early goal to give Spurs the lead, and although Joe Kinnear cleared off the goal-line on one occasion, we had most of the play and the best of the goalscoring chances in the first half-hour.

Arsenal rallied before half-time, however, and Bobby Gould cracked in a spectacular equaliser.

In rain-soaked conditions Arsenal put on the pressure in the second half, and David Court gave them the lead eight minutes after the restart. Further goals to Arsenal by John Woodward and Paul Davies, Kennedy, Gould and De Garis.

Spurs left us well in arrears, but with only five minutes left to play, Johnson steered the ball into the far corner of the net to improve our chances of making up the leeway in the second leg this evening.

The gate figure at Highbury was 2,241.

The teams were:
ARSENAL: Barnett; Rice, Woodward; Carmichael, Roberts, Court; Marinello, Davies, Kennedy, Gould and De Garis.
SPURS: Daines; Kinnear, Want; Naylor, Collins, P., Pratt; Pearce, Bunkell, Jenkins, Bond and Johnson.

Tottenham Reserves v Arsenal Reserves,
Combination Cup Semi-Final, 2nd Leg

1970-71

Volume 63

1	3rd August	Glasgow Rangers	Friendly
2	15th August	West Ham United	League
3	19th August	Leeds United	League
4	22nd August	Oxford United Reserves	Football Combination
5	26th August	Bournemouth & B.Athletic Reserves	Football Combination
6	29th August	Coventry City	League
7	2nd September	Plymouth Argyle Reserves	Football Combination
8	5th September	Arsenal Reserves	Football Combination
9	9th September	Swansea City	Football League Cup 2nd Round
10	12th September	Blackpool	League
11	16th September	Dunfermline Athletic	Texaco Cup1st Round 1st Leg
12	19th September	Ipswich Town Reserves	Football Combination
13	26th September	Manchester City	League
14	30th September	Dagenham	London Challenge Cup 1st Round Replay
15	3rd October	Bristol Rovers Reserves	Football Combination
16	7th October	Sheffield United	Football League Cup 3rd Round
17	10th October	Liverpool	League
18	17th October	Fulham Reserves	Football Combination
19	21st October	Motherwell	Texaco Cup 2nd Round 1st Leg
20	24th October	Stoke City	League
21	28th October	West Bromwich Albion	Football League Cup 4th Round
22	31st October	Bristol City Reserves	Football Combination
23	2nd November	Millwall Youth	Southern Junior Floodlight Cup 1st Round
24	4th November	West Ham United	London Challenge Cup Semi-Final
25	7th November	Burnley	League
26	14th November	Chelsea Reserves	Football Combination
27	18th November	Coventry City	Football League Cup 5th Round
28	21st November	Newcastle United	League
29	28th November	Swindon Town Reserves	Football Combination
30	30th November	Wimbledon	London Challenge Cup Final
31	2nd December	Charlton Athletic Youth (postponed)	F.A Youth Cup 2nd Round
31	5th December	Manchester United	League
32	8th December	Charlton Athletic Youth	F.A Youth Cup 2nd Round
	(match played 12th December at Cheshunt)		
33	12th December	Cardiff City Reserves	Football Combination
34	19th December	Wolverhampton Wanderers	League
35	23rd December	Bristol City	Football League Cup Semi-Final 2nd Leg
36	26th December	West Ham United Reserves (postponed)	Football Combination
36	2nd January	Sheffield Wednesday	F.A Cup 3rd Round
37	9th January	Southampton Reserves	Football Combination
38	16th January	Southampton	League
39	23rd January	Birmingham City Reserves (postponed)	Football Combination
39	30th January	Everton	League
40	6th February	Swansea City Reserves	Football Combination
41	13th February	Nottingham Forest	F.A Cup 5th Round
42	17th February	West Bromwich Albion	League
43	20th February	Gillingham Reserves	Football Combination
44	22nd February	West Ham United Reserves	Football Combination
	(incorrectly dated, 1970)		
45	3rd March	London Boys v Glasgow Boys	Inter-City Schools Challenge
46	6th March	Leicester City Reserves	Football Combination
47	10th March	Nottingham Forest	League
48	13th March	Chelsea	League
49	16th March	Liverpool	F.A Cup 6th Round Replay
50	20th March	Norwich City Reserves	Football Combination
51	24th March	Birmingham City Reserves	Football Combination
52	3rd April	Crystal Palace Reserves	Football Combination
53	7th April	Derby County	League
54	10th April	Ipswich Town	League
55	15th April	Coventry City Youth	Southern Junior Floodlight Cup Semi-Final Replay
56	17th April	Queens Park Rangers Reserves	Football Combination
57	24th April	Crystal Palace	League
58	28th April	Huddersfield Town	League
59	1st May	Reading Reserves	Football Combination
60	3rd May	Arsenal	League

1970-71

TOTTENHAM HOTSPUR
FOOTBALL AND ATHLETIC COMPANY LIMITED

Chairman: SIDNEY A. WALE   Vice-Chairman: C. F. COX
Directors: A. RICHARDSON, H. G. L. GROVES, G. A. RICHARDSON
Manager: W. E. NICHOLSON   Secretary: G. W. JONES
Medical Officer: Dr. BRIAN CURTIN

League Champions 1950-51, 1960-61
F.A. Cup Winners 1901, 1921, 1961, 1962, 1967
Winners of European Cup Winners Cup 1963

COPYRIGHT ALL RIGHTS RESERVED   **PRICE THREEPENCE**

OFFICIAL PROGRAMME

Vol. 63   TUESDAY, 8th DECEMBER, 1970   No. 32

F.A. Youth Cup, 2nd Round   Kick-off 7.30 p.m.

TOTTENHAM HOTSPUR YOUTH
White Shirts, Blue Shorts

RIGHT WING   LEFT WING

WARD
1

M. JACKSON   JONES
2   3

DILLON   PECK   SOUNESS
4   5   6

BOUGHEY   J. LEWIS
8   10

MABEE   CLARKE   M. FLANAGAN
7   9   11

Referee: **Mr. K. W. RIDDEN**, Essex
Linesmen: **Mr. E. F. MERCHANT**, Essex (Red Flag)
Mr. D. V. REEVES, Middx. (Yellow Flag)

---

11   9   7
BOWMAN   ARNOLD   A. BROWN
        10   8
    I. McGONAGLE   K. BROWN
    6   5   4
O'KANE (Capt.)   WOOD   HOWELL
    3   2
    CORBETT   R. RIBRON

1
CLARKE
LEFT WING   RIGHT WING

CHARLTON ATHLETIC YOUTH
Red Shirts, White Shorts

Substitutes: (Home Club)........................ (Visiting Club)........................

Tottenham Youth v Charlton Athletic Youth
F.A. Youth Cup, 2nd Round
This match was eventually played at Cheshunt with this programme issued.

1970-71

OFFICIAL PROGRAMME

Vol. 63   WEDNESDAY, 3rd MARCH, 1971   **No. 45**

Inter-City Schools Challenge Match   Kick-off 7.30 p.m.

LONDON BOYS
White Shirts, Black Shorts

RIGHT WING   LEFT WING

1
GRAHAM VAN HAMME
(Enfield)

2   **3**
CHRISTOPHER JONES   **GERALD WEALE**
(Haringey)   (Richmond)

4   **5**   **6**
LAWRENCE ELLIS   **CHRIS. STOCKMAN**   **ROBERT PITTAWAY**
(Barking)   (Haringey)   (South London)

         8   **10**
     GARY ALLEN   **STEPHEN BARRETT**
     (Islington)   (Barking)

7   **9**   **11**
DAVID LUCAS   **KEITH OSGOOD**   **DAVID HAYES**
(South London)   (Hounslow)   (Barking)

Referee: Mr. D. W. WARBY, Pinner
Linesmen: Mr. D. LINGE, Wood Green (Red Flag)
Mr. F. R. DEACON, Lewisham (Yellow Flag)

---

11   **9**   **7**
IAN HAIR   **ROSS MACFARLANE**   **FRED WRIGHT**
(Duncanrigg Sec.)   (Hermitage Sec.)   (Govan Sec.)

     10   **8**
WILLIAM MILLER   **PAUL FEENAN**
(John St. Sec.)   (Bellarmine H.S.)

6   **5**   **4**
JIM SCOTLAND   **NEIL CHUDLEIGH**   **JIM CALDERWOOD**
(Carnhill Sec.)   (Clydebank)   (Grange Sec.)

3   **2**
BRIAN FITZPATRICK   **ALAN McCULLOUGH**
(St. Pius Sec.)   (Holyrood Sec.)

1
IAN BROWN
(Carnhill G.S.)

LEFT WING   RIGHT WING

GLASGOW BOYS
Black and White Hoops, White Shorts

Substitutes:

London: **Glasgow:**
Edward Dale,   Barry Cook,   Andreas Constantinou.   Jim Muldoon
(Barnet)   (Croydon)   (Islington)   (Partick H.S.)

London Boys v Manchester Boys
Inter-City Schools Challenge Match.

110

1970-71

Tottenham v Wimbledon
London Challenge Cup Final.
Wimbledon were then a Southern
League club.

Tottenham v Arsenal
League.
Arsenal win to take the Championship.

Tottenham v Wimbledon
London Challenge Cup Final.
The centre-page spread of the four-page programme.
Note the man in the no.6 shirt for the Dons!!

1971-72

Volume 64

1	14th August	Fulham Reserves	Football Combination
2	18th August	**Newcastle United**	**League**
3	21st August	**Huddersfield Town**	**League**
4	25th August	Reading Reserves	Football Combination
5	28th August	Bournemouth Reserves	Football Combination
6	4th September	**Liverpool**	**League**
7	16th September	Crystal Palace Reserves	London Challenge Cup 1st Round
8	18th September	**Crystal Palace**	**League**
9	22nd September	**A.C.Torino**	**Anglo-Italian League Cup Winners Cup 2nd Leg**
10	25th September	Oxford United Reserves	Football Combination
11	28th September	**Keflavik F.C.**	**U.E.F.A Cup 1st Round 2nd Leg**
12	2nd October	**Ipswich Town**	**League**
13	9th October	Cardiff City Reserves	Football Combination
14	16th October	**Wolverhampton Wanderers**	**League**
15	23rd October	**Nottingham Forest**	**League**
16	27th October	**Preston North End**	**Football League Cup 4th Round**
17	30th October	Bristol Rovers Reserves	Football Combination
18	2nd November	**F.C.Nantes**	**U.E.F.A Cup 2nd Round 2nd Leg**
19	6th November	**Everton**	**League**
20	10th November	Bristol City Reserves	Football Combination
21	13th November	Swindon Town Reserves	Football Combination
22	17th November	**Blackpool**	**Football League Cup 5th Round**
23	20th November	**West Bromwich Albion**	**League**
24	24th November	**Arsenal**	**League**
25	27th November	Chelsea Reserves	Football Combination
26	29th November	Gillingham Youth	F.A Youth Cup 2nd Round
	(match played on 1st December, same programme issued)		
27	4th December	**Southampton**	**League**
28	8th December	**Rapid Bucharest**	**U.E.F.A Cup 3rd Round 1st Leg**
29	11th December	Leicester City Reserves	Football Combination
30	18th December	West Ham United Reserves	Football Combination
31	27th December	**West Ham United**	**League**
32	1st January	Arsenal Reserves	Football Combination
33	5th January	**Chelsea**	**Football League Cup Semi-Final 2nd Leg**
34	8th January	**Manchester City**	**League**
35	15th January	**Carlisle United**	**F.A Cup 3rd Round**
36	22nd January	Plymouth Argyle Reserves	Football Combination
37	29th January	**Leeds United**	**League**
38	5th February	**Rotherham United**	**F.A Cup 4th Round**
39	12th February	Norwich City Reserves	Football Combination
40	19th February	**Stoke City**	**League**
41	26th February	Swansea City Reserves	Football Combination
42	4th March	**Manchester United**	**League**
43	11th March	**Derby County**	**League**
44	18th March	Ipswich Town Reserves	Football Combination
45	21st March	**Unizale Textile Arad**	**U.E.F.A Cup 4th Round 2nd Leg**
46	25th March	**Sheffield United**	**League**
47	31st March	**Coventry City**	**League**
48	1st April	Queens Park Rangers Reserves	Football Combination
49	5th April	**A.C.Milan**	**U.E.F.A Cup Semi-Final 1st Leg**
50	8th April	Birmingham City Reserves	Football Combination
51	15th April	**Chelsea**	**League**
52	22nd April	Southampton Reserves	Football Combination
53	26th April	Crystal Palace Reserves	Football Combination
54	29th April	**Leicester City**	**League**
55	17th May	**Wolverhampton Wanderers**	**U.E.F.A Cup Final 2nd Leg**

1971-72

Tottenham v Chelsea
Football League Cup Semi-Final
2nd Leg

**Tottenham v Wolverhampton
Wanderers**
U.E.F.A. Cup Final, 2nd Leg

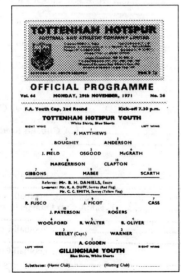

**Tottenham Youth v
Gillingham Youth**
F.A. Youth Cup 2nd Round

**Tottenham Reserves v
Norwich City Reserves**
Football Combination

113

1972-73

Volume 65

1972-73

Tottenham v Feyenoord
Goodbye Greaves Match

Tottenham v Wolverhampton Wanderers
Football League

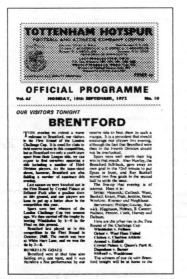

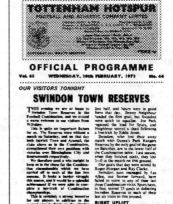

Tottenham v Brentford
London Challenge Cup, 1st Round

Tottenham Reserves v Swindon Town Reserves
Football Combination

1973-74

Volume 66

1	25th August	West Ham United Reserves	Football Combination
2	29th August	Birmingham City Reserves	Football Combination
3	**1st September**	**Leeds United**	**League**
4	**5th September**	**Burnley**	**League**
5	8th September	Ipswich Town Reserves	Football Combination
6	12th September	Luton Town Reserves	Football Combination
7	**15th September**	**Sheffield United**	**League**
8	22nd September	Swansea City Reserves	Football Combination
9	24th September	Wealdstone	London Challenge Cup 1st Round
10	**29th September**	**Derby County**	**League**
11	**3rd October**	**Grasshopper-Club, Zurich**	**U.E.F.A Cup 1st Round 2nd Leg**
12	6th October	Plymouth Argyle Reserves	Football Combination
13	**13th October**	**Arsenal**	**League**
14	20th October	Norwich City Reserves	Football Combination
15	**27th October**	**Newcastle United**	**League**
16	29th October	Orient	London Challenge Cup 2nd Round Replay
17	3rd November	Cardiff City Reserves	Football Combination
18	**7th November**	**Aberdeen**	**U.E.F.A Cup 2nd Round 2nd Leg**
19	**10th November**	**Manchester United**	**League**
20	12th November	Arsenal	London Challenge Cup Semi-Final
21	17th November	Arsenal Reserves	Football Combination
22	21st November	West Ham United Youth	F.A Youth Cup 2nd Round
23	**24th November**	**Wolverhampton Wanderers**	**League**
24	1st December	Leicester City Reserves (postponed)	Football Combination
*	**3rd December**	**Bayern Munich**	**Philip Beal Testimonial**
25	**8th December**	**Stoke City**	League
26	**12th December**	**Dinamo Tbilisi**	**U.E.F.A Cup 3rd Round 2nd Leg**
27	**15th December**	**Manchester City**	League
28	22nd December	Fulham Reserves	Football Combination
29	**26th December**	**Queens Park Rangers**	**League**
30	**29th December**	**West Ham United**	**League**
31	1st January	Queens Park Rangers Reserves	Football Combination
32	5th January	Chelsea Reserves	Football Combination
33	12th January	Bristol City Reserves	Football Combination
34	16th January	Orient Youth	F.A Youth Cup 3rd Round Replay
35	**19th January**	**Coventry City**	**League**
36	2nd February	AFC Bournemouth Reserves	Football Combination
37	**6th February**	**Birmingham City**	**League**
38	**9th February**	**Liverpool (postponed)**	**League**
39	16th February	Swindon Town Reserves	Football Combination
40	**23rd February**	**Ipswich Town**	**League**
41	27th February	Leicester City Reserves	Football Combination
42	2nd March	Crystal Palace Reserves	Football Combination
43	9th March	Reading Reserves	Football Combination
44	**16th March**	**Norwich City**	**League**
45	**20th March**	**1.F.C Cologne**	**U.E.F.A Cup Quarter-Final 2nd Leg**
46	23rd March	Bristol Rovers Reserves	Football Combination
47	**30th March**	**Everton**	**League**
48	**3rd April**	**Chelsea**	**League**
49	6th April	Southampton Reserves	Football Combination
50	9th April	Arsenal Youth	F.A Youth Cup Semi-Final 1st Leg
51	**13th April**	**Southampton**	**League**
52	20th April	Oxford United Reserves	Football Combination
53	**24th April**	**1.F.C Lokomotive Leipzig**	**U.E.F.A Cup Semi-Final 2nd Leg**
54	**27th April**	**Leicester City**	**League**
55	**8th May**	**Liverpool**	**League**
56	11th May	Huddersfield Town Youth	F.A Youth Cup Final 1st Leg
57	**21st May**	**Sportclub Feyenoord**	**U.E.F.A Cup Final 1st Leg**

1973-74

F.A. YOUTH CHALLENGE CUP
FINAL (1st Leg)

TOTTENHAM HOTSPUR

Official Programme

Price Five Pence

HUDDERSFIELD TOWN

Saturday, 11th May, 1974

Kick-off 3 p.m.

SEASON 1973-74   Vol. 66 No. 56

Tottenham Hotspur Youth v Huddersfield Town Youth
F.A. Youth Cup Final, 1st Leg

1973-74

TOTTENHAM HOTSPUR
FOOTBALL AND ATHLETIC COMPANY LIMITED

Chairman: SIDNEY A. WALE   Vice-Chairman: C. F. COX
Directors: A. RICHARDSON, H. G. S. GROVES, G. A. RICHARDSON
Manager: W. E. NICHOLSON   Secretary: G. W. JONES
Medical Officer: Dr. BRIAN CURTIN
League Champions: 1950-51, 1960-61
F.A. Cup Winners: 1901, 1921, 1961, 1962, 1967
Winners of European Cup Winners Cup: 1963
Winners of Football League Cup: 1971, 1973
Winners of U.E.F.A. Cup: 1972

COPYRIGHT ALL RIGHTS RESERVED   PRICE 1p

OFFICIAL PROGRAMME

Vol. 66   **SATURDAY, 1st DECEMBER, 1973**   **No. 24**

OUR VISITORS TODAY

LEICESTER CITY RESERVES

THIS AFTERNOON we welcome Leicester City Reserves in the Football Combination, and will have to improve on our last home display, against Arsenal Reserves, if we are to beat our visitors from the midlands.

Leicester, who defeated Luton Town 3—0 in a home Combination fixture last Saturday, occupy a higher position in the table than ourselves. Last season Leicester finished in fourteenth position, and their record to date this season therefore shows considerable improvement.

Last season Leicester held us to a 1—1 draw here in the Combination. It was a scrappy game and we hope the standard of play reaches a higher level today.

Jimmy Neighbour gave Spurs an early lead following a free-kick by Phil Holder, but Leicester were quick to equalise from the penalty spot. The away Combination match with Leicester was in April, when the only goal, scored by John Margerrison, gave Spurs both points.

GOOD WIN

The Reserves pulled off a good 2—0 away win over Southampton last Saturday. It was as good a display as the Reserves have given away from home, and we would not have been flattered by a bigger margin of victory.

Spurs were well on top from the start and both Mike Dillon and Neighbour failed with scoring chances during the early play. Late in the first half Holder gave us the lead with a magnificent shot from about 25 yards on the half volley.

It followed a move on the right and a cross by Terry Naylor. Coming shortly before half-time, this goal came at the right time, and Spurs continued in confident mood in the second half.

Barry Daines made a couple of good saves, but Spurs were still in command. Our second goal, late in the game, was headed home from about 10 yards' range by Joe Peck. Again it was a move down the right wing, and again Naylor crossed the ball.

Team: Daines; Osgood, Anderson, Dillon, Collins, Naylor, Neighbour, Clapton, Peck, Holder and Jones.

Next Wednesday the Reserves are away to Oxford United in the Combination.

ANOTHER REVERSE

After suffering another reverse on our ground in losing 3—1 to Wolverhampton Wanderers last Saturday,

Tottenham Reserves v Leicester City Reserves,
The postponed Football Combination match.

1973-74

Tottenham v Liverpool,
the postponed League match.

Tottenham v Sportclub Feyenoord
U.E.F.A. Cup Final, 1st Leg.

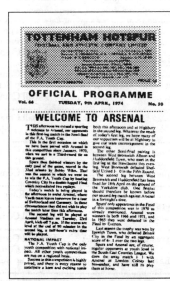

Tottenham Youth v Arsenal Youth
F.A. Youth Cup, Semi-Final 1st Leg.

Tottenham v Bayern Munich,
Philip Beal Testimonial.

1974-75

Volume 67

1	**17th August**	**Ipswich Town**	**League**
2	21st August	Norwich City Reserves	Football Combination
3	24th August	Swansea City Reserves	Football Combination
4	**28th August**	**Manchester City**	**League**
5	**31st August**	**Derby County**	**League**
6	4th September	AFC Bournemouth Reserves	Football Combination
7	7th September	Bristol City Reserves	Football Combination
8	**11th September**	**Middlesbrough**	**Football League Cup 2nd Round**
9	**14th September**	**West Ham United**	**League**
10	21st September	Ipswich Town Reserves	Football Combination
11	**28th September**	**Middlesbrough**	**League**
12	**5th October**	**Burnley**	**League**
13	8th October	Millwall Youth	Southern Junior Floodlit Cup 1st Round
14	12th October	Chelsea Reserves	Football Combination
15	**16th October**	**Carlisle United**	**League**
16	**19th October**	**Arsenal**	**League**
17	26th October	Luton Town Reserves	Football Combination
18	2nd November	Leicester City Reserves	Football Combination
19	**9th November**	**Everton**	**League**
20	16th November	Birmingham City Reserves (postponed)	Football Combination
20	**23rd November**	**Birmingham City**	**League**
*	**27th November**	**Red Star Belgrade**	**Alan Gilzean Testimonial**
21	30th November	Viking Sports	F.A Youth Cup 2nd Round
	(match played at Cheshunt)		
22	30th November	Cardiff City Reserves	Football Combination
23	4th December	England Youth XI	Friendly
24	**7th December**	**Newcastle United**	**League**
25	14th December	Fulham Reserves	Football Combination
26	18th December	Wolverhampton Wanderers Youth	F.A Youth Cup 3rd Round
27	**21st December**	**Queens Park Rangers**	**League**
28	**28th December**	**Coventry City**	**League**
29	4th January	Plymouth Argyle Reserves	Football Combination
30	**8th January**	**Nottingham Forest**	**F.A Cup 3rd Round Replay**
31	11th January	Reading Reserves	Football Combination
32	**18th January**	**Sheffield United**	**League**
33	25th January	Crystal Palace Reserves (postponed)	Football Combination
33	29th January	Chelsea Youth	South East Counties League Division One Cup Semi-Final
34	1st February	Swindon Town Reserves	Football Combination
35	**8th February**	**Stoke City**	**League**
36	15th February	Bristol Rovers Reserves	Football Combination
37	18th February	Burnley Youth	F.A Youth Cup 4th Round
38	**22nd February**	**Leicester City**	**League**
39	26th February	Birmingham City Reserves	Football Combination
40	1st March	Southend United Youth	South East Counties League Division One
41	15th March	Oxford United Reserves	Football Combination
42	**22nd March**	**Liverpool**	**League**
43	25th March	Middlesbrough Youth	F.A Youth Cup 5th Round Replay
44	**28th March**	**Wolverhampton Wanderers**	**League**
45	29th March	Crystal Palace Reserves	Football Combination
46	**5th April**	**Luton Town**	**League**
47	9th April	Queens Park Rangers Reserves	Football Combination
48	12th April	Southampton Reserves	Football Combination
*	14th April	Chelsea Juniors	South East Counties League Division 2 Cup Semi-Final
49	**19th April**	**Chelsea**	**League**
50	23rd April	West Ham United Reserves	Football Combination
51	26th April	Arsenal Reserves	Football Combination
52	**28th April**	**Leeds United**	**League**
*	29th April	West Ham Utd. Juniors	South East Counties Lge Div.2 Cup Final 1st Leg

120

1974-75

OFFICIAL PROGRAMME

Vol. 67   SATURDAY, 30th NOVEMBER, 1974   No. 21

F.A. Youth Cup, 2nd Round   **Kick-off 1.30 p.m.**

TOTTENHAM HOTSPUR YOUTH
White Shirts, White Shorts

RIGHT WING   LEFT WING

1
CRANSTONE

2   3
WADE   STEAD

4   5   6
KEELEY   WALFORD   SMITH

8   10
HODDLE   BACON

7   9   11
BROTHERSTON   ROBINSON   HYAMS

Referee: **Mr. B. M. L. JAMES**, Surrey
Linesmen: **Mr. P. G. OGGELSBY**, Herts (Red Flag)
Mr. E. J. HASKELL, Herts (Yellow Flag)

---

11   9   7
I. COVENTRY   R. BUTLER   D. HILL

10   8
J. ASHE   G. CHURCHOUSE

6   5   4
M. BULLOCK   S. MITROVIC   I. PAYNE

3   2
P. HUMBLE   N. LAWRENCE

1
B. SURMAN

LEFT WING   RIGHT WING

VIKING SPORTS
Amber Shirts, Blue Shorts

Substitutes: (Home Club).................................   (Visiting Club).......................

Tottenham Youth v Viking Sports,
F.A. Youth Cup, 2nd Round, one of many single-sheets issued during the season,
but this match was played at Cheshunt, not at White Hart Lane.

121

1974-75

TOTTENHAM HOTSPUR FOOTBALL & ATHLETIC CO. LTD.

Price 2p.

SOUTH EAST COUNTIES LEAGUE DIVISION II CUP, SEMI-FINAL

Monday, 14th April, 1975. K.O. 3.00 p.m.

	TOTTENHAM HOTSPUR			CHELSEA	
	(White shirts, blue shorts)			(Blue shirts, blue shorts)	
1	Nick	MARKWICK	1	Ken	DODDS
2	Paul	VAN GELDER	2	Mike	PINCHIN
3	Mike	CLEAVER	3	John	WEBBERLEY
4	Fred	BARWICK	4	John	BUMSTEAD
5	Terry	BOYLE	5	Paul	HAMMOND
6	Steve	CAVANAGH	6	Danny	GODWIN
7	Andy	BRADBURY	7	Lee	FROST
8	Gary	LUCAS	8	Ian	SOUNESS
9	Kevin	STEAD	9	Nigel	ROGGOFF
10	Barry	PACE	10	David	STRIDE
11	Gary	HYAMS	11	Ken	GILBERT
12			12		
14			13		

REFEREE: Mr. G. KUBERSKI, London

Linesmen: Mr. F.G.T. MACDONALD, London   Mr. D.J.PALMER, Chigwell
(Red Flag)   (Yellow Flag)

The rules of the competition allow TWO substitute players for each team.
This competition is organised on a League basis, the first four teams in the
final table then compete in the Semi-Finals. All players in this competition
must be under the age of 17 years on 1st August in the current season.

DIVISION TWO CUP, FINAL TABLE

	P	W	D	L	F	A	Ps.
TOTTENHAM HOTSPUR	10	6	3	1	18	10	15
SOUTHEND UNITED	10	5	3	2	24	13	13
CHELSEA	10	5	1	4	23	22	11
WEST HAM UNITED	10	4	2	4	14	17	10
ORIENT	10	4	0	6	17	18	8
WATFORD	10	1	1	8	19	35	3

NEXT MATCHES HERE -

Saturday, 19th April

C H E L S E A, Football League, KO 3 pm.

Wednesday, 23rd April

W E S T H A M U N I T E D,
Football Combination, KO 7.30 pm.

Tottenham Juniors v Chelsea Juniors,
South East Counties League Division II Cup, Semi-Final,
a single duplicated sheet issue.

1974-75

Tottenham v Red Star Belgrade,
Alan Gilzean Testimonial Match.

Tottenham v Carlisle United,
Football League.

Tottenham Reserves v
Birmingham City Reserves,
the postponed Football
Combination match.

Tottenham Reserves v
Birmingham City Reserves,
the reverse side of the single-sheet issue
for the re-arranged Football Combination
match in February 1975.

1975-76

1975-76

T O T T E N H A M   H O T S P U R

FOOTBALL AND ATHLETIC COMPANY LIMITED

PRICE 1p.

MATCH PROGRAMME

WEDNESDAY, 10th SEPTEMBER 1975

LONDON YOUTH F.A. CHALLENGE CUP, FINAL

for SEASON 1974/75

TOTTENHAM HOTSPUR		v.	CRYSTAL PALACE	
White shirts	Ian CRANSTONE	1	Peter CASWELL	Blue & Red
Blue shorts	Ian SMITH	2	Phil McQUEEN	Striped shirts
	Mike STEAD	3	Kevin DARE	Blue shorts
	Terry BOYLE	4	Neil SMILLIE	
	Steve WALFORD	5	Bill GILBERT	
	Garry BACON	6	Peter COKER	
	Noel BROTHERSTON	7	Steve BRENNAN	
	Fred BARWICK	8	Vince HILLAIRE	
	Martin ROBINSON	9	Gerry MURPHY	
	Glenn HODDLE	10	Ian WELSH	
	Gary HYAMS	11	Steven LEAHY	
		12		

Referee: MR. W. G. BRADFORD, Sydenham

Linesmen: MR. R.E.PARKER,Forest Hill   MR. F.A.BUTTIGIEG,Herne Hill
(Red Flag)   (Orange Flag)

Crystal Palace, to whom we extend a warm welcome, reached this
evening's Final by defeating West Ham United in the Semi-Final by
3 - 1 last week. This match was held over from last season owing
to a combination of bad weather causing postponements, and a run
of cup successes by West Ham, creating a very crowded fixture list.
Spurs own path to the final was by wins over Millwall and Charlton.

Because this final is for the 1974/75 season, players tonight are
those who were eligible at Youth level last season, i.e. aged under
18 on 31.8.74.   If the scores are level at 90 minutes, then extra
time will be played.

F O R T H C O M I N G   M A T C H E S

Saturday, 13th September 1975, Football League, v. DERBY COUNTY. KO 3 p.m.

Saturday, 20th September 1975, Football Combination v. PLYMOUTH ARGYLE
KO 3 pm.

Please note that our FOOTBALL LEAGUE match v. EVERTON on Wednesday,
24th September 1975 HAS BEEN POSTPONED.

Tottenham Youth v Crystal Palace Youth,
London Youth F.A. Challenge Cup Final, 1974-75,
a single duplicated sheet issue for this match held over until the new season.

1975-76

L O N D O N   S C H O O L S   F . A .

PROGRAMME
PRICE 2p.

LONDON   v.   BRISTOL

at TOTTENHAM HOTSPUR F.C. GROUND
MONDAY, 27th OCTOBER 1975. K.O. 7.15. p.m.

LONDON (White shirts)		BRISTOL (Yellow shirts)
MASON, Nicholas(West London)	1	FEARNLEY, Kevin(Hengrove)
DICKSON, Andrew(Enfield)	2	COOK, Martin(Merrywood)
HILL, Mark (Hounslow)	3	FRANCIS, Lennox (Monks Park)
BRIGNULL, Philip(Newham)	4	STONE, Robert(Speedwell)
ASHER, Gary(Haringey)	5	CLARKE, Tony(Bedminster Down)
VINCENT, Tim(Ealing)	6	MABBUTT, Gary(Cotham)
ALLEN, Clive(Havering)	7	CLARKE, Craig(Hengrove)
MULLINGS, Winston(Waltham F.)	8	JAMESON, Clive(Lockleaze)
LOVELL, Mark(West London)	9	GREGSON, Stephen(Brislington)
DURRANT, Kevin(Newham)	10	JASPER, Stephen(Hartcliffe)
PHILLIPS, Nicholas(Newham)	11	SHORTMAN, Bradley(Speedwell)
	Subs.	
	12	
	13	

Referee: Mr. P. NEWSOME(Thornton Heath)
Linesmen: Mr. D. JACOBS(Islington)   Mr. J.MURRAY(Forest Gate)
           (Red flag)   (Orange flag)

Two substitutes are allowed during the match, which is of two periods of 40 minutes duration each.

This is the first Inter-City match to be played between London and Bristol, and we have much pleasure in welcoming our visitors from the West Country this evening.

The London team was chosen following trials held at the end of September. The London Schools Football Association are indebted to Tottenham Hotspur F.C. for the use of their training ground at Cheshunt for our trials, and also wish to thank the Directors of Tottenham Hotspur for allowing tonight's match to be played at White Hart Lane, together with all the attendant facilities. Our thanks also to the Club staff for their help on this and many other occasions.

Further London Schools matches are planned for this season, the next fixture being against Liverpool Schools at the Liverpool F.C. ground on Friday, the 28th November. K.O. 7.30 p.m.

****

London v Bristol,
Inter-City Schools Challenge Match,
but did it mark the first appearances on the White Hart Lane of Clive Allen and Gary Mabbutt?

1975-76

Tottenham v Newcastle United,
Football League Cup Semi-Final,
1st Leg.

Tottenham v Manchester City,
Football League.
A special edition to commemorate
Pat Jennings' record appearance for
the club.

Tottenham v Arsenal,
Cyril Knowles Testimonial Match.

**Tottenham Reserves v
West Ham United Reserves,**
Football Combination.

1976-77

Volume 69

1	16th August	Royal Antwerp F.C.	**Friendly**
2	21st August	Swindon Town Reserves	Football Combination
3	25th August	Newcastle United	**League**
4	28th August	Middlesbrough	**League**
5	4th September	Orient Reserves	Football Combination
6	11th September	Leeds United	**League**
7	18th September	Norwich City Reserves	Football Combination
8	22nd September	Wrexham	**Football League Cup 3rd Round**
9	25th September	Norwich City	**League**
10	2nd October	Chelsea Reserves	Football Combination
11	16th October	Plymouth Argyle Reserves	Football Combination
12	20th October	Birmingham City	**League**
13	23rd October	Coventry City	**League**
14	30th October	Everton	**League**
15	6th November	Southampton Reserves	Football Combination
16	13th November	Bristol City	**League**
17	20th November	Crystal Palace Reserves	Football Combination
*	23rd November	Arsenal	**Pat Jennings Testimonial**
18	27th November	Stoke City	**League**
19	4th December	Queens Park Rangers Reserves	Football Combination
*	7th December	London Schools v Liverpool Schools (postponed)	Inter-City Schools Challenge
20	11th December	Manchester City	**League**
*	13th December	Norwich City Youth	F.A Youth Cup 2nd Round
21	18th December	Luton Town Reserves	Football Combination
22	27th December	Arsenal	**League**
23	1st January	West Ham United	**League**
*	12th January	Orient Youth	F.A Youth Cup 3rd Round
	(away match, played at Tottenham)		
24	15th January	Arsenal Reserves (postponed)	Football Combination
24	17th January	Orient v Darlington	F.A Cup 3rd Round 2nd Replay
25	22nd January	Ipswich Town	**League**
*	24th January	Gillingham Youth	S.E Counties League Div. One Cup Semi-Final
26	2nd February	Oxford United Reserves	Football Combination
27	5th February	Bristol Rovers Reserves	Football Combination
	(played at Cheshunt)		
28	12th February	Manchester United	**League**
*	15th February	Portsmouth Youth	F.A Youth Cup 4th Round
29	1st March	Hereford United Reserves	Football Combination
30	5th March	Reading Reserves	Football Combination
*	9th March	West Ham United Reserves	Football Combination
	(match played at Cheshunt)		
31	9th March	Liverpool	**League**
32	12th March	West Bromwich Albion	**League**
33	16th March	Ipswich Town Reserves	Football Combination
34	19th March	Birmingham City Reserves	Football Combination
*	22nd March	Arsenal Reserves	Football Combination
	(played at Cheshunt)		
35	23rd March	Derby County	**League**
*	28th March	Liverpool Youth	F.A Youth Cup 5th Round
36	2nd April	Cardiff City Reserves	Football Combination
37	9th April	Queens Park Rangers	**League**
38	13th April	Crystal Palace Youth	F.A Youth Cup Semi-Final 2nd Leg
39	16th April	Sunderland	**League**
*	18th April	London Schools v Liverpool Schools	Inter-City Schools
40	23rd April	Bristol City Reserves	Football Combination
*	27th April	Fulham Reserves	Football Combination
	(match played at Cheshunt)		
*	27th April	Queens Park Rangers Youth	S.E Counties Lge Div.1 Cup Final 1st Leg
41	30th April	Aston Villa	**League**
*	2nd May	Queens Park Rangers Youth	S.E Counties Lge Div.1 Cup Final 2nd Leg
	(away match played at Tottenham, QPR issue dated 30th April)		
42	7th May	Leicester City Reserves	Football Combination
*	10th May	Queens Park Rangers Reserves	Football Combination
	(away match played at Tottenham)		
43	14th May	Leicester City	**League**
*	16th May	West London Schools v South London Schools	Bill Nicholson Trophy

1976-77

TOTTENHAM HOTSPUR FOOTBALL & ATHLETIC CO. LTD.

MATCH PROGRAMME   PRICE 2p.

SOUTH EAST COUNTIES LEAGUE DIVISION 1 CUP FINAL
1st leg

Wednesday, 27th April 1977 - K.O. 7.30 p.m.

TOTTENHAM HOTSPUR   v.   QUEENS PARK RANGERS

White shirts	Paul	BATCHELOR	1	Peter HUCKER		Shirts
	Martin	PERRY	2	Gary MANEY		Red and
Navy shorts	Chris	HUGHTON	3	Barry WALLIS		white
	Phil	HOLYOAK	4	Micky IRONTON		halves
White socks	Nicholas	LAWS	5	Paul GODDARD		Black
	Mike	HAZARD	6	Paul HAVERSON		shorts
	Gary	BROOKES	7	Craig RICHARDS		
	Stuart	BEAVON	8	Bobby HALE		Black
	Kevin	STEAD	9	Clive ALLEN		socks
	Mark	FALCO	10	Terry DIBBLE		
	Imre	VARADI	11	John DOCKER		
	Toyan	OKITIKPI	12	Mark HILL		
	Richard	COOK	14	Keith WEAVER		

REFEREE: Mr. A. GIRDLESTONE(Herts)
LINESMEN: Mr. B. SMITH (Kent)   Mr. P. PULHAM(Essex)
(Red flag)   (Yellow flag)

This evening we extend a warm welcome to the officials, players and supporters of Queens Park Rangers Football Club for the first leg of our South East Counties League Division 1 Cup Final.

Spurs played in the Final of this competition last year, losing to Ipswich Town on aggregate by 5 goals to one.

PATH TO SEMI-FINAL

SPURS				Q.P.R.	
1st round	Crystal Palce(H)	1-0	1st round	Norwich(H)	6-1
2nd round	Arsenal(H)	5-0	2nd round	Ipswich Town(A)	4-2
Semi-Final	Gillingham(H)	1-0	Semi-Final	Portsmouth(A)	1-1
				Replay (H)	4-2

The second leg of this Final will be played at Loftus Road next Saturday, the 30th April 1977, kick-off 3.00 p.m.

Tottenham Youth v Queen's Park Rangers Youth,
South East Counties League Division 1 Cup Final 1st Leg.

129

1976-77

LONDON SCHOOLS' FOOTBALL ASSOCIATION.

BILL NICHOLSON TROPHY

SOUTH v WEST.

Tottenham Hotspur F.C. Ground, White Hart Lane, N.17.

Monday, 16th May, 1977.

6.30.p.m.

The Bill Nicholson Trophy competition is a London Schools' F.A. Inter-Divisional tourney for boys at the Under 14 age level. The finalists this evening meet for the second year in succession.

The South team is drawn from an area south of the Thames extending west to Aldershot; the West team covers the area of Middlesex. All the boys playing this evening have gained County Under 14 honours during the year.

The London Schools' F.A. wishes to thank Tottenham Hotspur F.C. for so kindly presenting the Bill Nicholson Trophy to the Association. To the Directors of Tottenham Hotspur F.C. sincere appreciation for granting us permission to use the ground and other facilities for the match. Our grateful thanks to the Club staff for all the help given to the L.S.F.A. in the staging of this match.

SOUTH.		SKY BLUE.	WEST.		TANGERINE.
1.	M.London	....Wandsworth	1.	M.Turner	....Hillingdon
2.	T.Shea	....South London	2.	M.McLaren	....Hillingdon
3.	I.Bowes	....Croydon	3.	T.Hurrell	....Hillingdon
4.	M.O'Connor	....Aldershot	4.	T.Neill	....Ealing
5.	J.Smith	....Blackheath	5.	G.Tyler	....Brent
6.	T.Elmes	....Croydon	6.	A.Roe	....Hillingdon
7.	J.Hodge	....Merton	7.	G.West	....Ealing
8.	J.Bolton	....Merton	8.	T.Moore	....Ealing
9.	K.Davidson	....South London	9.	C.Thorne	....Hounslow
10.	J.Finnegan	....Wandsworth	10.	M.Neary	....Ealing
11.	P.Lazarus	....Blackheath	11.	D.Imson	....Harrow

Substitutes:			Substitutes:		
P.Saith	....South London		D.Taylor	....Brent	
S.Carolan	....Blackheath		B.Wilde	....Harrow	
S.Hodge	....Aldershot		R.Martin	....Harrow	
C.Gentle	....Blackheath		M.Marshall	....Hillingdon	

Referee: G.Day   Linesmen H.Chadwick   T.A.C.Lomas

Duration of play - 35 minutes each way; extra time of 10 minutes each way if necessary.

Two substitutes allowed at any time during the match.

South v West,
London Schools' F.A.
Bill Nicholson Trophy

OFFICIAL PROGRAMME

VOL. 69   MONDAY, 17th JANUARY, 1977   NO. 24

ORIENT v DARLINGTON

F.A. CUP, THIRD ROUND—2nd REPLAY.   Kick-off 7.30 p.m.

THIS evening we stage the second replay of the Third Round F.A. Cup-tie between Orient and Darlington, and we extend a warm welcome to the officials, players and supporters of both clubs.

We also hope many Spurs supporters are here this evening to watch what promises to be a tense and hard-fought cup-tie. Our own aspirations in the competition were brought to an early end at Cardiff last Saturday week, but we wish the winners of tonight's match further success on the road to Wembley. The winners will be away to Blackburn Rovers in the fourth round.

The first match of the tie, played at Darlington, ended with a score-line of 2–2. The first goal was scored by DEREK POSSEE in the 6th minute, and Orient led by this goal up to half-time.

Darlington equalised two minutes into the second half, JIMMY SEAL scoring from close range. Midway through the second half, Orient again took the lead with a header by PHIL HOADLEY.

As the minutes ticked away, Orient looked set for victory, but close on time Darlington earned themselves a replay when Seal netted his second goal with a low cross shot.

The replay at Leyton last Tuesday evening ended in a goalless draw after extra time, and tonight's third attempt to reach a conclusive result has therefore become necessary. IF THE SCORES ARE STILL LEVEL AFTER 90 MINUTES' PLAY TONIGHT, A FURTHER PERIOD OF 30 MINUTES' EXTRA TIME WILL AGAIN BE PLAYED.

After last week's replay had ended in another draw, the clubs tossed for choice of venue, Orient won and therefore gained the advantage of playing the third match in the south.

THE MANAGERS

GEORGE PETCHEY (ORIENT)

An East Londoner, who started his football career as a half-back with West Ham United. He then had an eight-year spell with Queen's Park Rangers before moving to Crystal Palace later to become first-team coach. He has been Orient's manager since 1971.

PETER MADDEN (DARLINGTON)

A Yorkshireman from Bradford, who made his name with Rotherham United. A centre-half, he played late for Bradford Park Avenue (then in the League), Aldershot and Scunthorpe. He was in the Rotherham team beaten in the 1961 League Cup final.

Orient v Darlington,
F.A. Cup 3rd Round, 2nd Replay.
A four-page edition.

TOTTENHAM HOTSPUR

FOOTBALL AND ATHLETIC COMPANY LIMITED

Chairman: SIDNEY A. WALE   Vice-Chairman: F. J. COX
Directors: A. RICHARDSON, H. G. S. GROVES, G. A. RICHARDSON
Manager: K. H. BURKINSHAW   Secretary: G. W. JONES

COPYRIGHT ALL RIGHTS RESERVED   Price 2p

OFFICIAL PROGRAMME

Vol. 69   SATURDAY, 16th JANUARY, 1977   No. 24

Football Combination   Kick-off 3 p.m.

Tottenham Hotspur Res. v Arsenal Res.

White Shirts Blue Shorts				Red Shirts White Shorts
DAINES	1		PARKER	
WADE	2		TYLER	
STEAD, M.	3		MATTHEWS	
KEELEY	4		ARMSTRONG, P.	
WALFORD	5		DEVINE	
BARWICK	6		CANT	
BROTHERSTON	7		HOWARD	
BEAVON	8		TOWNSEND	
ARMSTRONG	9		RIX	
MOORES	10		PRICE	
ROBINSON	11		ROSTRON	
	12			

Referee: Mr. P. G. DALY, Glasgow

Linesmen: Mr. R. G. GARDNER, Surrey (Red Flag)   Mr. J. N. SCOTT, Hampshire (Yellow Flag)

FOOTBALL COMBINATION	HALF TIME SCORES

NEXT MATCHES HERE—

Monday, 17th January, 1977   F.A. Cup 3rd Rd., 2nd Replay, 7.30 p.m.

ORIENT v DARLINGTON

Saturday, 22nd January, 1977   Football League, Division 1, 3 p.m.

IPSWICH TOWN

Printed by Knight & Co. Ltd., Tiny Clock House Press, Hoddesdon, Herts

Tottenham Reserves v Arsenal Reserves,
Football Combination,
the postponed match.

130

1976-77

Tottenham v Arsenal,
Pat Jennings Testimonial Match

Tottenham v Royal Antwerp F.C.,
Friendly Match

QPR's Don Givens strikes a shot past Arsenal's Pat Rice.
(Photo: Monte Fresco)

**Tottenham Youth v
Crystal Palace Youth,**
F.A. Youth Cup Semi-Final, 2nd Leg.

Q.P.R. v Tottenham,
S.E.C.L Div.1 Cup Final, 2nd Leg,
match played at White Hart Lane on
Monday, May 2nd 1977.

1977-78

Volume 70

1	**20th August**	**Sheffield United**	**League**
2	**27th August**	**Notts County**	**League**
3	**31st August**	**Wimbledon**	**Football League Cup 2nd Round**
4	3rd September	Fulham Reserves	Football Combination
5	**10th September**	**Fulham**	**League**
6	14th September	Oxford United Reserves	Football Combination
7	17th September	Reading Reserves	Football Combination
8	21st September	Plymouth Argyle Reserves	Football Combination
9	**24th September**	**Luton Town**	**League**
10	28th September	Hereford United Reserves	Football Combination
11	1st October	Luton Town Reserves	Football Combination
12	**8th October**	**Oldham Athletic**	**League**
13	15th October	Swindon Town Reserves	Football Combination
14	**22nd October**	**Bristol Rovers**	**League**
15	**26th October**	**Coventry City**	**Football League Cup 3rd Round**
16	31st October	Bristol Rovers Reserves	Football Combination
17	**5th November**	**Burnley**	**League**
18	9th November	Norwich City Reserves	Football Combination
19	12th November	Southampton Reserves	Football Combination
20	**19th November**	**Brighton & Hove Albion**	**League**
21	23rd November	Arsenal Reserves	Football Combination
22	**3rd December**	**Southampton**	**League**
*	7th December	Norwich City Youth	F.A Youth Cup 2nd Round
23	**17th December**	**Crystal Palace**	**League**
24	**27th December**	**Mansfield Town**	**League**
25	**31st December**	**Blackburn Rovers**	**League**
26	**7th January**	**Bolton Wanderers**	**F.A Cup 3rd Round**
27	14th January	Cardiff City Reserves	Football Combination
*	16th January	Aston Villa Youth	F.A Youth Cup 3rd Round
28	**21st January**	**Cardiff City**	**League**
29	4th February	Birmingham City Reserves (postponed)	Football Combination
29	**11th February**	**Blackpool**	**League**
30	18th February	Ipswich Town Reserves	Football Combination
31	**25th February**	**Orient**	**League**
32	4th March	Orient Reserves	Football Combination
33	**11th March**	**Charlton Athletic**	**League**
34	18th March	Chelsea Reserves	Football Combination
35	**22nd March**	**Stoke City**	**League**
36	**27th March**	**Millwall**	**League**
37	29th March	Leicester City Reserves	Football Combination
38	1st April	West Ham United Reserves	Football Combination
39	**8th April**	**Bolton Wanderers**	**League**
*	10th April (match played at Cheshunt)	Queens Park Rangers Reserves	Football Combination
*	12th April (match played at Cheshunt)	Birmingham City Reserves	Football Combination
40	15th April	Bristol City Reserves	Football Combination
41	**22nd April**	**Sunderland**	**League**
42	**26th April**	**Hull City**	**League**
*	27th April	East Division v South Division	Bill Nicholson Trophy
43	29th April	Crystal Palace Reserves	Football Combination
*	2nd May	Oxford United Youth (postponed)	S.E.Counties Lge Div.2 Cup Final 1st Leg
*	3rd May	Metropolitan Police v West Midlands Police	Police Athletic Assoc. Cup Final
*	**12th May**	**Arsenal**	**John Pratt Testimonial**
*	13th May	Oxford United Youth	S.E Counties Lge Div.2 Cup Final 2nd Leg

1977-78

TOTTENHAM HOTSPUR
FOOTBALL AND ATHLETIC COMPANY LIMITED

Chairman: SIDNEY A. WALE   Vice-Chairman: C. F. COX
Directors: A. RICHARDSON, H. G. S. GROVES, G. A. RICHARDSON
Manager: K. H. BURKINSHAW   Secretary: G. W. JONES

COPYRIGHT ALL RIGHTS RESERVED

Price 2p

OFFICIAL PROGRAMME

Vol. 70   **SATURDAY, 4th FEBRUARY, 1978**   **No. 29**

Football Combination   Kick-off 3.00 p.m.

Tottenham Hotspur Res. v Birmingham City Res.

White Shirts
Blue Shorts

Royal Blue with
White Stripe
Blue Shorts

KENDALL	1	LATCHFORD
HOLYOAK	2	RATHBONE
HUGHTON	3	STYLES
HEFFERNAN	4	BROADHURST
BOWGETT	5	SBRAGIA
COATES	6	WRIGHT
MOORES	7	FOX
HAZARD	8	HODGSON
JONES, C.	9	McDONOUGH
ROBINSON	10	DAVIES
GALVIN	11	VAN DEN HAUWE
	12	

Referee: **Mr. A. G. HALES**, Norfolk

Linesmen: **Mr. D. J. CLARK**, London (Red Flag)   **Mr. J. GILMARTIN**, Essex (Yellow Flag)

FOOTBALL COMBINATION

Up to and incl 2nd February

	P.	W.	D.	L.	F.	A.	Ps.
Southampton	24	16	2	6	51	22	34
West Ham United	24	13	5	6	44	22	31
Chelsea	27	12	7	8	46	24	31
Tottenham Hotspur	25	10	11	4	44	28	31
Norwich City	26	11	9	6	33	29	31
Ipswich Town	23	13	4	6	42	21	30
Crystal Palace	25	11	7	7	38	27	29
Leicester City	27	12	5	10	38	34	29
Queen's Park Rangers	23	11	6	6	38	20	28
Hereford United	24	12	4	8	41	34	28
Arsenal	25	9	8	8	32	25	26
Plymouth Argyle	23	11	4	8	32	26	26
Fulham	24	7	8	9	28	32	22
Bristol Rovers	22	8	6	8	28	35	22
Bristol City	22	6	9	7	33	35	21
Birmingham City	25	6	11	9	22	27	21
Luton Town	26	7	5	14	38	54	19
Oxford United	27	6	6	15	26	45	18
Orient	23	4	7	12	16	36	15
Cardiff City	25	4	7	14	24	50	15
Swindon Town	20	5	4	11	20	48	14
Reading	22	4	3	15	18	53	11

SCOREBOARD

A   Fulham v. Tottenham Hotspur
B   Blackpool v. Blackburn Rovers
C   Burnley v. Southampton
D   Hull City v. Brighton & Hove Albion
E   Luton Town v. Bristol Rovers
F   Millwall v. Mansfield Town
G   Oldham Athletic v. Bolton Wand.
H   Orient v. Charlton Athletic
J   Sheffield United v. Stoke City
K   Sunderland v. Crystal Palace
L   Arsenal v. Aston Villa
M   Derby County v. Chelsea
N   Manchester United v. Manchester City
O   Nottingham Forest v. Wolverhampton
P   Queen's Park R. v. West Ham United

NEXT MATCHES HERE

Saturday, 11th February, 1978

BLACKPOOL

Football League, Division II   Kick-off 3 p.m.

Saturday, 18th February, 1978

IPSWICH TOWN RESERVES

Football Combination   Kick-off 3 p.m.

Thomas Knight & Co. Ltd., The Clock House Press, Hoddesdon, Herts

Tottenham Reserves v Birmingham City Reserves,
the programme for the postponed Football Combination match.

133

1977-78

TOTTENHAM HOTSPUR FOOTBALL & ATHLETIC CO. LTD.

MATCH PROGRAMME   PRICE 2p.

FOOTBALL ASSOCIATION YOUTH CHALLENGE CUP, 2nd Round

Wednesday, 7th December 1977   K.O. 7.30 p.m.

	TOTTENHAM HOTSPUR		v.	NORWICH CITY		
White	Paul BATCHELOR	1		Bill	BENNETT	Yellow
shirts	Simon MABEY	2		Stephen	PERLMAN	shirts
Navy blue	Mark WYATT	3		David	POWNALL	Green
shorts	Gerry REARDON	4		Peter	MENDHAM	shorts
White	Gary O'REILLY	5		Richard	SYMONDS	Yellow
socks	Joe SIMMONDS	6		Mark	HALSEY	socks
	Garry BROOKE	7		Philip	LYTHGOE	
	Paul MILLER	8		Peter	MOUNTFORD	
	Mark FALCO	9		David	LITTLECHILD	
	Peter SOUTHEY	10		David	MORTON	
	Mike HAZARD	11		Steven	GOBLES	
	Owsun ABEBRESE	12		Kevin	BIRD	

REFEREE: Mr. M. DIMBLEBEE - Herts F.A.
LINESMEN: Mr. D.B. SHAW - Middx. F.A.   Mr. D.L. CUTLER - Middx. F.A.
(Red flag)   (Yellow flag)

This evening it is our pleasure to welcome again to White Hart Lane the Youth Team and officials of Norwich City F.C.

We have played Norwich City in this competition in the last two seasons, winning on both occasions, after replays. Of tonight's teams only Paul Miller and Mike Hazard played in the Competition for us last season, whilst Norwich City include Peter Mendham, Mark Halsey, Philip Lythgoe, Richard Symonds and Steven Gobles, who all have similar experience.

Norwich City played Cambridge United in the First Round of this Competition this season, winning by six goals to one in the Replay at Carrow Road, after drawing 2-2 at Cambridge.

Having been exempt until the Second Round, it is our first match in the competition this season.

FORTHCOMING MATCHES AT WHITE HART LANE

Sat., 10th December v. Q.P.R. (Football Combination)   K.O. 3 p.m.
Sat., 17th December v. Crystal Palace (Football League, Div.2) K.O. 3 p.m.

FORTHCOMING MATCHES AT CHESHUNT

Sat., 17th December v. Norwich City (S.E.C.L. Div.1)   K.O. 11 a.m.
              v. West Ham Utd. (S.E.C.L. Div.2)   K.O. 11 a.m.

Tottenham Youth v Norwich City Youth,
F.A. Youth Cup, 2nd Round.

134

1977-78

(right):
Tottenham v Bristol Rovers,
Football League, the match won 9-0 to create a
"Match of the Day" record.

(below):
Metropolitan Police
v
West Midlands Police,
Police Athletic Association Cup Final.

(right):
Tottenham v Arsenal,
John Pratt Testimonial Match.

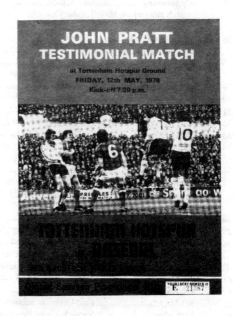

1978-79

Volume 71

1	19th August	Queens Park Rangers Reserves	Football Combination
2	**23rd August**	**Aston Villa**	**League**
3	**26th August**	**Chelsea**	**League**
4	2nd September	Chelsea Reserves	Football Combination
5	**6th September**	**Swansea City**	**Football League Cup 2nd Round Replay**
6	**9th September**	**Bristol City**	**League**
7	16th September	Arsenal Reserves	Football Combination
8	20th September	Fulham Reserves	Football Combination
9	23rd September	Plymouth Argyle Reserves	Football Combination
10	**30th September**	**Coventry City**	**League**
11	7th October	Birmingham City Reserves	Football Combination
12	**14th October**	**Birmingham City**	**League**
13	**28th October**	**Bolton Wanderers**	**League**
14	1st November	Luton Town Reserves	Football Combination
15	4th November	Norwich City Reserves	Football Combination
16	**11th November**	**Nottingham Forest**	**League**
17	18th November	Swindon Town Reserves	Football Combination
18	**22nd November**	**Liverpool**	**League**
19	**25th November**	**Wolverhampton Wanderers**	**League**
20	2nd December	West Ham United Reserves	Football Combination
21	**9th December**	**Ipswich Town**	**League**
22	16th December	Crystal Palace Reserves	Football Combination
23	**23rd December**	**Arsenal**	**League**
24	**1st January**	**Southampton (postponed)**	**League**
24	**6th January**	**Altrincham**	**F.A Cup 3rd Round**
	(match played on 10th January)		
25	13th January	Orient Reserves	Football Combination
26	**20th January**	**Leeds United**	**League**
*	22nd January	Crystal Palace Youth	F.A Youth Cup 3rd Round
27	**3rd February**	**Manchester City**	**League**
28	10th February	Leicester City Reserves	Football Combination
29	**12th February**	**Wrexham**	**F.A Cup 4th Round**
30	24th February	Bristol Rovers Reserves	Football Combination
31	**3rd March**	**Derby County**	**League**
32	**10th March**	**Manchester United**	**F.A Cup 6th Round**
33	**17th March**	**Norwich City**	**League**
34	20th March	Hereford United Reserves	Football Combination
35	24th March	Bristol City Reserves	Football Combination
36	**28th March**	**Southampton**	**League**
37	31st March	Cardiff City Reserves	Football Combination
*	2nd April	Reading Reserves	Football Combination
	(match played at Cheshunt)		
38	**7th April**	**Middlesbrough**	**League**
39	**14th April**	**Queens Park Rangers**	**League**
40	**21st April**	**Manchester United**	**League**
41	25th April	Southampton Reserves	Football Combination
42	28th April	Oxford United Reserves	Football Combination
*	**30th April**	**West Ham United**	**Steve Perryman Testimonial**
43	**5th May**	**Everton**	**League**
*	8th May	East Division Schools v West Division Schools	Bill Nicholson Trophy
44	11th May	Ipswich Town Reserves	Football Combination
45	**14th May**	**West Bromwich Albion**	**League**

1978-79

Tottenham v West Ham United,
Steve Perryman Testimonial Match.

Tottenham v Southampton,
the postponed League match.

London Schools' Football Association.
Bill Nicholson Trophy Final.
Tottenham Hotspur F.C. Ground, White Hart Lane, N.17.
Tuesday, 8th May, 1979. 5.30.p.m.

The Bill Nicholson Trophy is for competition among the divisional representative teams of London Schools' F.A. at the Under 14 age level. In the final this evening the East Division, covering much of Essex, meets the West Division, covering Middlesex. All of the boys playing have gained representative honours for their counties as Under 14 this season.

The London Schools' F.A. expresses grateful thanks to the Directors of Tottenham Hotspur F.C. for once again allowing us the use of the ground at White Hart Lane for this final; it is sincerely appreciated. Our thanks also to the many members of the Club for making all the arrangements for the staging of the match.

To the match officials this evening, thank you gentlemen for your services on this and so many other occasions during the season.

EAST.	WHITE.	WEST.	BLUE.
1.	G.COLLINS (Walthamstow Forest)	1.	R.HANNEN (Harrow)
2.	D.JACKSON (Walthamstow Forest)	2.	G.AMPOFO (Brent)
3.	J.CONNELLY (Barking)	3.	S.MILLER (Hounslow)
4.	J.BOLLE (Redbridge)	4.	R.D.DUFFIELD (Ealing)
5.	J.PHILIP (Basildon)	5.	J.COXES (Harrow)
6.	G.FRANKIS (Redbridge)	6.	B.ROSS (West London) capt.
7.	G.GRANGER (Newham)	7.	A.WADDOCK (Hillingdon)
8.	A.DICKENS (Newham)	8.	I.CREEDY (Staines)
9.	J.MARKELOW (Walthamstow Forest)	9.	S.JONES (West London)
10.	B.TODD (Waltham Forest)	10.	P.NICHOLAS (Harrow)
11.	D.HIGGINS (Barking)	11.	S.GODNIAC (Ealing)

Substitutes:		Substitutes:	
P.COLLINS (Thurrock)		P.TARA (Hounslow)	
S.WILLIAMS (Barking)		S.WATKINS (Ealing)	
D.COOPER (Barking)		S.BLOXFIELD (Hounslow)	
M.BYRNE (Barking)		H.FRANCIS (Staines)	
		J.EVERSFIELD (Harrow)	

REFEREE: M.MOFFATT. LINESMEN: M.FLAHERTY, D.JACOBS.

Duration of play: 35 minutes each way. Extra time of ten minutes each way if necessary.

If the result is a draw after extra time the trophy will be shared.

Two substitutes plus goalkeeper substitute allowed to each team at any time during the match.

East v West,
Bill Nicholson Trophy Final

TOTTENHAM HOTSPUR
FOOTBALL AND ATHLETIC COMPANY LIMITED

Chairman: SIDNEY A. WALE Vice-Chairman: C. F. COX
Directors: A. RICHARDSON, G. A. RICHARDSON, D. W. KENNARD
Manager: L. M. BURKINSHAW Secretary: D. W. JONES

COPYRIGHT ALL RIGHTS RESERVED   Price 2p

OFFICIAL PROGRAMME

Vol. 71   SATURDAY, 10th FEBRUARY, 1979   **No. 28**

Football Combination   Kick-off 3 p.m.

Tottenham Hotspur Reserves v Leicester City Reserves

White Shirts, Blue Shorts   Blue Shirts, White Shorts

1	DAINES		RAFTER	1
2	HUGHTON		WELSH	2
3	SMITH		SMITH	3
4	MILLER		KELLY	4
5	BOWGETT		FARMER	5
6	BEAVON		LINEKER	6
7	GALVIN		WHITE	7
8	HEFFERNAN		R. ATKINS	8
9	JONES, C.		DAVIS	9
10	P. STONE		HUGHES	10
11	FALCO		LEE	11
12				12

Referee: Mr. P. W. HEARNEY, Norfolk

Linesmen: Mr. M. POTTER, Mid-Essex (Red Flag)   Mr. J. M. TYFACETT, Norfolk (Yellow Flag)

NEXT MATCHES HERE

Monday, 12th February, 1979

WREXHAM

F.A. Cup, 4th Round   Kick-off 7.30 p.m.

**Tottenham Reserves v
Leicester City Reserves,**
Football Combination match, with Gary
Lineker at No.6 for the opposition.

137

1979-80

Volume 72
From this season onwards Reserve programmes were printed by the club, and numbered in their own sequence

1		**18th August**	**Middlesbrough**	**League**
	1	22nd August	Reading Reserves	Football Combination
	3	25th August	Hereford United Reserves	Football Combination
		(incorrectly numbered)		
2		**29th August**	**Manchester United**	**Football League Cup 2nd Round 1st Leg**
3		**1st September**	**Manchester City**	**League**
4		**8th September**	**Brighton & Hove Albion**	**League**
	3	15th September	Southampton Reserves	Football Combination
	4	19th September	Queens Park Rangers Reserves	Football Combination
5		**22nd September**	**West Bromwich Albion**	**League**
	4	29th September	Plymouth Argyle Reserves	Football Combination
		(incorrectly numbered, sequence not rectified until No.8 was omitted)		
	5	6th October	Crystal Palace Reserves	Football Combination
6		**10th October**	**Norwich City**	**League**
7		**13th October**	**Derby County**	**League**
	6	20th October	Swindon Town Reserves	Football Combination
8		**27th October**	**Nottingham Forest**	**League**
	7	3rd November	West Ham United Reserves	Football Combination
9		**10th November**	**Bolton Wanderers**	**League**
	9	17th November	Cardiff City Reserves	Football Combination
	10	24th November	Ipswich Town Reserves	Football Combination
10		**1st December**	**Manchester United**	**League**
	11	8th December	Fulham Reserves	Football Combination
11		**15th December**	**Aston Villa**	**League**
	12	19th December	Luton Town Reserves	Football Combination
12		**29th December**	**Stoke City**	**League**
13		**1st January**	**Wolverhampton Wanderers (postponed)**	**League**
13		**5th January**	**Manchester United**	**F.A Cup 3rd Round**
	13	12th January	Arsenal Reserves	Football Combination
	14	19th January	Orient Reserves	Football Combination
	15	23rd January	Oxford United Reserves	Football Combination
14		**30th January**	**Swindon Town**	**F.A Cup 4th Round Replay**
15		**2nd February**	**Southampton**	**League**
	*	7th February	Watford Youth	F.A Youth Cup 4th Round
		(incorrectly dated 7th January, and opponents named Watford Town)		
16		**16th February**	**Birmingham City**	**F.A Cup 5th Round**
17		**27th February**	**Coventry City**	**League**
18		**1st March**	**Leeds United**	**League**
19		**8th March**	**Liverpool**	**F.A Cup 6th Round**
20		**15th March**	**Crystal Palace**	**League**
	16	22nd March	Chelsea Reserves	Football Combination
21		**29th March**	**Liverpool**	**League**
22		**2nd April**	**Ipswich Town**	**League**
23		**7th April**	**Arsenal**	**League**
	17	12th April	Bristol City Reserves	Football Combination
	18	14th April	Norwich City Reserves	Football Combination
24		**19th April**	**Everton**	**League**
25		**23rd April**	**Wolverhampton Wanderers**	**League**
	19	24th April	Charlton Athletic Youth	S.E Counties Lge Div.2 Cup Semi-Final
	20	26th April	Leicester City Reserves	Football Combination
*		**29th April**	**Crystal Palace**	**Terry Naylor Testimonial**
	22	30th April	Birmingham City Reserves	Football Combination
		(incorrectly numbered)		
26		**3rd May**	**Bristol City**	**League**
	22	6th May	Bristol Rovers Reserves	Football Combination
*		8th May	North Division Schools v West Division Schools	Bill Nicholson Trophy
*		9th May	Wimbledon Youth	S.E Counties Lge Div.2 Cup Final 2nd Leg

1979-80

TOTTENHAM HOTSPUR FOOTBALL AND ATHLETIC COMPANY LTD
Registered Offices: 748 High Road, Tottenham, London N17 0AP

Board of Directors
A. Richardson *(Chairman)*
C.F. Cox *(Vice Chairman)*
S.A. Wale
G.A. Richardson
D.W. Kennard

Administration
Manager: K.H. Burkinshaw
Secretary: G.W. Jones
Commercial Manager: M.J. Lewis
Medical Officer: Dr. Brian Curtin

Honours League Champions: 1950-51, 1960-61. F.A. Cup Winners: 1901, 1921, 1961, 1962, 1967.
European Cup Winners Cup: 1963. Football League Cup: 1971, 1973. U.E.F.A. Cup: 1972.

Designed and Printed by Maybank Press Ltd., Hainault, Essex.   Copyright   All rights reserved

OFFICIAL PROGRAMME FRIDAY, 9th MAY 1980

TOTTENHAM HOTSPUR
v WIMBLEDON

SOUTH EAST COUNTIES LEAGUE DIVISION 2 CUP
FINAL — 2ND LEG   KICK-OFF 7 p.m.

We extend a sporting welcome this evening to WIMBLEDON for the second leg of the South East Counties League Division 2 Cup final, a competition often described as the Junior League Cup, and also thank every spectator here tonight for his and her support.

The importance of the South East Counties League lies in its function as a competition for the development of young players to Football League status, and for this reason alone, matches of this description are worthy and needful of public support.

The first leg was played at Wimbledon last Friday evening, and resulted in a 4-2 win for the home team. We could not complain at the result. Wimbledon were well organised and defended well. Moreover, they took their scoring chances, whereas our finishing was less accurate. On two occasions we struck the woodwork.

After Wimbledon had taken an early lead, PAT CORBETT equalised for Spurs with a 30-yard drive. The Dons regained the lead from a penalty kick, and scored a third goal early in the second half.

PAUL WILKINS then netted for Spurs from close in, but Wimbledon were again on the mark with a late fourth goal.

Our team at Plough Lane was P. Burke; M. Entwistle, P. Baxter, S. Webster, Corbett, Harvey, Emms, S. Cox (sub. P. Wilkins), M. Jones, Bolton and A. Rollock. Wilkins replaced Steve Cox in the 65th minute.

If Spurs wipe out Wimbledon's two-goal lead this evening, and the scores are still level after 90 minutes, a further 30 minutes' extra time will be played.

This competition takes the form of four separate league sections, the respective winners qualifying for the semi-finals. Thus, the twelve clubs were split into four sections of three each. Our group was completed by Cambridge United and Peterborough United, Spurs winning the section by picking up seven of the eight points.

Wimbledon were grouped with Oxford United and Chelsea, and won all their four matches. In the semi-finals we defeated Charlton Athletic 4-1 on this ground and Wimbledon won 2-1 away to Bristol Rovers.

THE CUP WILL BE PRESENTED TO THE WINNERS, AND MOMENTOES TO INDIVIDUAL PLAYERS, BY MR. RICHARD BAILEY, SECRETARY OF THE SOUTH EAST COUNTIES LEAGUE.

PRICE 2p

Tottenham v Wimbledon,
South East Counties League Division 2 Cup Final, 2nd Leg.

1979-80

TOTTENHAM HOTSPUR
FOOTBALL AND ATHLETIC COMPANY LIMITED

Chairman SIDNEY A WALE   Vice Chairman C F. COX
Directors: A. RICHARDSON, G A. RICHARDSON, D. W. KENNARD
Manager K. H. BURKINSHAW   Secretary G. W. JONES

COPYRIGHT ALL RIGHTS RESERVED

Price 2p

OFFICIAL PROGRAMME

Vol. 72   Wednesday, 22nd August 1979   **No.** 1

Football Combination   Kick-off 7.30 p.m.

Tottenham Hotspur Reserves v READING Reserves

White Shirts, Blue Shorts		Blue & White shirts, white shorts	
1	M. Kendall	1	A. Beales
2	P. Southey	2	J. Cullen
3	C. Hughton	3	T. Evans
4	G. Mazzon	4	N. Webb
5	P. Miller	5	D. Bailey
6	M. Hazzard	6	P. Alexander
7	T. Galvin	7	E. Jack
8	S. Beavon	8	M. Mathews
9	G. Armstrong	9	A. Hay
10	P. Grayling	10	K. Bright
11	T. Gibson	11	S. Pentland
12	G. Brooke	12	S. Head

Referee: Mr. H. Taylor (Leics)

Linesmen Mr. M. Potter (Middx) and Mr. J.R. Dickenson (Herts)
(Red flag)   (Yellow flag)

NEXT MATCHES HERE

Football Combination	Football League Cup 2nd Round (1st Leg)
SPURS v HEREFORD UTD. Reserves Reserves	SPURS v MANCHESTER UTD.
Saturday, 25th August k.o. 3p.m.	Wednesday, 29th August k.o. 7.30pm

Tottenham Reserves v Reading Reserves,
Football Combination.

140

1979-80

Tottenham v Wolverhampton,
the postponed League match.

Tottenham v Bristol City,
Football League.

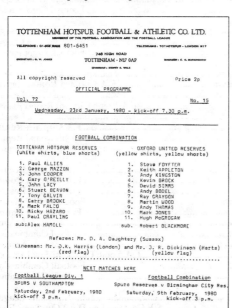

Tottenham Reserves v Oxford Utd. Reserves,
the revised Combination programme style.

Tottenham v Crystal Palace,
Terry Naylor Testimonial Match.

1980-81

Volume 73
From this volume the title "Reserves" was dropped from Reserve programmes.

1		16th August .... Nottingham Forest .... League
	1	20th August .... Swindon Town .... Football Combination
2		23rd August .... Brighton & Hove Albion .... League
	2	30th August .... West Ham United .... Football Combination
3		3rd September .... Orient .... Football League Cup 2nd Round 2nd Leg
4		6th September .... Manchester United .... League
	3	13th September .... Oxford United .... Football Combination
5		20th September .... Sunderland .... League
6		24th September .... Crystal Palace .... Football League Cup 3rd Round
	4	27th September .... Bristol City .... Football Combination
		(incorrectly dated, 13th September)
	5	4th October .... Crystal Palace .... Football Combination
7		11th October .... Middlesbrough .... League
	6	18th October .... Ipswich Town .... Football Combination
	7	22nd October .... Cardiff City .... Football Combination
8		25th October .... Coventry City .... League
9		27th October .... Arsenal .... Football League Cup 4th Round
		(match played 4th November)
	8	1st November .... Orient .... Football Combination
10		8th November .... Wolverhampton Wanderers .... League
11		12th November .... Crystal Palace .... League
	9	15th November .... Bristol Rovers .... Football Combination
		(incorrectly dated, 22nd November, match played at Cheshunt)
	10	22nd November .... Norwich City .... Football Combination
		(match played at Cheshunt)
12		29th November .... West Bromwich Albion .... League
	11	6th December .... Plymouth Argyle .... Football Combination
		(match played at Cheshunt)
13		13th December .... Manchester City .... League
14		17th December .... Ipswich Town .... League
	12	20th December .... Reading .... Football Combination
		(match played at Cheshunt)
15		26th December .... Southampton .... League
16		7th January .... Queens Park Rangers .... F.A Cup 3rd Round Replay
17		10th January .... Birmingham City .... League
	*	12th January .... Chelsea .... F.A Youth Cup 3rd Round Replay
18		17th January .... Arsenal .... League
19		24th January .... Hull City .... F.A Cup 4th Round
*		28th January .... Enfield v Barnsley .... F.A Cup 4th Round Replay
	13	31st January .... Arsenal .... Football Combination
		(match played at Cheshunt)
20		7th February .... Leeds United .... League
21		14th February .... Coventry City .... F.A Cup 5th Round
22		21st February .... Leicester City .... League
	15	25th February .... Queens Park Rangers .... Football Combination
23		7th March .... Exeter City .... F.A Cup 6th Round
24		11th March .... Stoke City .... League
	16	16th March .... Birmingham City .... Football Combination
25		21st March .... Aston Villa .... League
*		23rd March .... Manchester United .... F.A Youth Cup Semi-Final 1st Leg
	17	28th March .... Luton Town .... Football Combination
	18	1st April .... Hereford United .... Football Combination
		(match played at Cheshunt)
26		4th April .... Everton .... League
	*	6th April .... Swindon Town .... S.E Counties Lge Div.2 Cup Semi-Final
	19	8th April .... Southampton .... Football Combination
	20	13th April .... Fulham .... Football Combination
27		18th April .... Norwich City .... League

142

1980-81

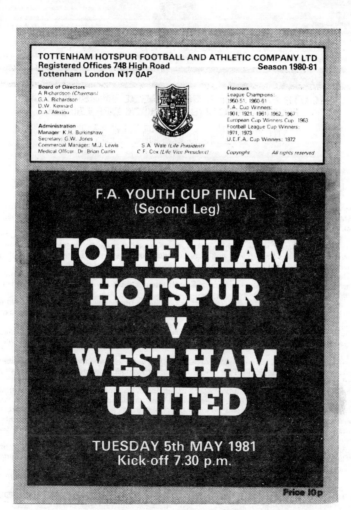

Tottenham v West Ham United,
F.A. Youth Cup Final, 2nd Leg,
an 8-page edition.

143

1980-81

SOUTH EAST COUNTIES LEAGUE, DIVISION 2 CUP FINAL — SECOND LEG. KICK-OFF 7.30 pm.

TOTTENHAM HOTSPUR
v
CAMBRIDGE UNITED

This evening we extend a cordial welcome to the officials, players and supporters of CAMBRIDGE UNITED, our visitors for the second leg of the South East Counties Division 2 Cup, and we also thank every spectator here tonight for his and her support.

The players in tonight's teams spend most of the season playing their matches on minor grounds, and a match on the main ground is always a special occasion for them. The bigger the crowd, the better the atmosphere, and an appreciative audience can do a lot in urging the players to raise their game.

The South East Counties League is a vitally important competition, providing a platform from which young players can develop to professional status, and for this reason alone is deserving of public support.

The first leg of tonight's final was played at Cambridge on the evening of Saturday, 2nd May and Spurs finished winners by 4-2. We therefore hold a two-goal advantage at the start of tonight's second leg.

The opening play at Cambridge was even and well-contested, but after STEVE COX had scored following an upfield kick, we struck a spell in which we were well on top, and held a 3-0 lead at half-time.

Our second goal was scored by ALLAN COCKRAM, who beat a number of opponents before lobbing the ball over the goal-keeper's head from a narrow angle. Towards half-time Cox netted a third goal for Spurs from close in.

Early in the second half PAUL WILKINS scored Spurs' fourth goal following a good through pass by Cockram, but to their credit, Cambridge refused to be daunted by the score against them.

They rallied well and put us under a lot of pressure in a spell that yielded them two goals, and gives them a better chance tonight than looked likely earlier in the game at the Abbey Stadium.

In the last 15 minutes Spurs came back into the game, but the Cambridge defence prevented us from adding to our score.

Our team at Cambridge was Hughes; Dixon (sub. P. Shirt), Baxter, I. Culverhouse, Webster, Cockram, Bowen, Rollock, Cox, Wilkins and Brace. Kenny Dixon sustained a leg injury and was replaced by Paul Shirt at half-time.

If the scores are level after ninety minutes' play this evening, a further thirty minutes' extra time will be played.

THE CUP WILL BE PRESENTED TO THE WINNERS, AND MEMENTOES TO INDIVIDUAL PLAYERS, BY MR. RICHARD BAILEY, SECRETARY OF THE SOUTH EAST COUNTIES LEAGUE.

Price 10p

Tottenham v Cambridge United,
South East Counties League, Division 2 Cup Final, 2nd Leg.

144

1980-81

Tottenham v West Ham United,
Barry Daines Testimonial Match

Tottenham v West Bromwich Albion,
Football League, the first match without
the old West Stand in use.

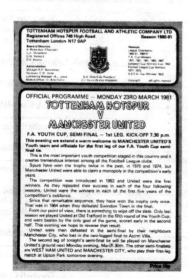

Tottenham v Manchester United,
F.A. Youth Cup Semi-Final, 1st Leg.

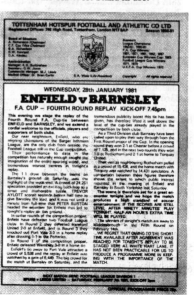

Enfield v Barnsley,
F.A. Cup 4th Round Replay.

145

1981-82

	1	29th August	Bristol Rovers	Football Combination
1		**2nd September**	**West Ham United**	**League**
2		**5th September**	**Aston Villa**	**League**
	3	12th September	Swindon Town	Football Combination
		(incorrectly numbered)		
	*	14th September	Coventry City	Southern Junior Floodlight Cup Prel.Round
3		**19th September**	**Everton**	**League**
	3	26th September	Chelsea	Football Combination
4		**29th September**	**Ajax**	**European Cup Winners Cup 1st Round 2nd Leg**
5		**3rd October**	**Nottingham Forest**	**League**
6		**7th October**	**Manchester United**	**Football League Cup 2nd Round 1st Leg**
7		**10th October**	**Stoke City**	**League**
	*	15th October	Charlton Athletic	Southern Junior Floodlight Cup 1st Round
	4	17th October	Leicester City	Football Combination
8		**24th October**	**Brighton & Hove Albion**	**League**
	6	31st October	Norwich City	Football Combination
		(incorrectly numbered)		
9		**4th November**	**Dundalk**	**European Cup Winners Cup 2nd Round 2nd Leg**
10		**7th November**	**West Bromwich Albion**	**League**
11		**11th November**	**Wrexham**	**Football League Cup 3rd Round**
	*	14th November	Gillingham	S.E Counties League Div.One
	6	16th November	Hereford United	Football Combination
12		**21st November**	**Manchester United**	**League**
	7	25th November	Luton Town	Football Combination
	8	28th November	Oxford United	Football Combination
13		**2nd December**	**Fulham**	**Football League Cup 4th Round**
14		**5th December**	**Coventry City**	**League**
15		**28th December**	**Arsenal (postponed)**	**League**
15		**2nd January**	**Arsenal**	**F.A Cup 3rd Round**
	*	4th January	Fulham	F.A Youth Cup 4th Round
	9	6th January	Ipswich Town	Football Combination
		(match played at Cheshunt)		
17		**18th January**	**Nottingham Forest**	**Football League Cup 5th Round**
		(programme incorrectly numbered)		
	10	23rd January	Crystal Palace	Football Combination
		(match played at Cheshunt)		
17		**23rd January**	**Leeds United**	**F.A Cup 4th Round**
18		**27th January**	**Middlesbrough**	**League**
	11	28th January	Fulham	Football Combination
		(match played at Cheshunt)		
	12	30th January	Plymouth Argyle	Football Combination
19		**6th February**	**Wolverhampton Wanderers**	**League**
	13	8th February	Reading	Football Combination
		(match played at Cheshunt)		
20		**10th February**	**West Bromwich Albion**	**Football League Cup Semi-Final 2nd Leg**
	*	11th February	Sunderland	F.A Youth Cup 4th Round
	14	13th February	West Ham United	Football Combination
		(match played at Cheshunt)		
21		**13th February**	**Aston Villa**	**F.A Cup 5th Round**
22		**20th February**	**Manchester City**	**League**
	15	25th February	Orient	Football Combination
		(match played at Cheshunt)		
	16	27th February	Birmingham City	Football Combination
		(match played at Cheshunt)		
23		**3rd March**	**Eintracht Frankfurt**	**European Cup Winners Cup 3rd Round 1st Leg**
	17	11th March	Southampton	Football Combination
24		**20th March**	**Southampton**	**League**
	18	27th March	Watford	Football Combination
25		**29th March**	**Arsenal**	**League**
26		**7th April**	**F.C Barcelona**	**European Cup Winners Cup Semi-Final 1st Leg**

1981-82

(above left):
Tottenham v F.C. Barcelona,
European Cup Winners Cup
Semi-Final 1st Leg.

(above right):
Tottenham v Arsenal,
the postponed League match,
the same cover picture was then used
for the F.A. Cup 3rd Round tie
between the two clubs.

(right):
Tottenham v Wolverhampton Wanderers,
a special edition to mark the
opening of the New West Stand.

1982-83

148

1982-83

(left):
Tottenham v Bayern Munich,
European Cup Winners Cup
2nd Round, 1st Leg.

(right):
Tottenham v Liverpool,
Football League.

1982-83

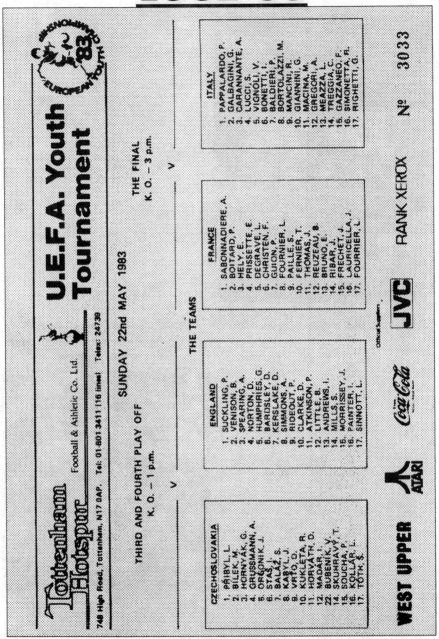

U.E.F.A. Youth Tournament,
The single-sheet issue for the matches played at White Hart Lane, however, only the Final
was played there with the 3rd place play-off game being moved to Watford.

1982-83

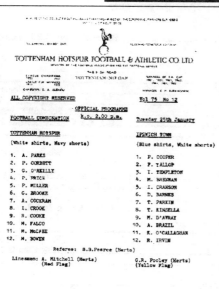

TOTTENHAM HOTSPUR FOOTBALL & ATHLETIC CO LTD

TOTTENHAM · N17 0AP

Vol 75 No 12

OFFICIAL PROGRAMME

FOOTBALL COMBINATION   K.O. 2.00 p.m.   Tuesday 25th January

TOTTENHAM HOTSPUR   IPSWICH TOWN

(White shirts, Navy shorts)   (Blue shirts, White shorts)

1.	A. PARKS		1.	P. COOPER
2.	P. CORBETT		2.	F. TALLON
3.	G. O'REILLY		3.	I. TEMPLETON
4.	P. PRICE		4.	M. BRENNAN
5.	P. MILLER		5.	I. CRANSON
6.	G. BROOKE		6.	D. BARNES
7.	A. COCKRAM		7.	T. PARKIN
8.	I. CROOK		8.	T. KINSELLA
9.	R. COOKE		9.	M. D'AVRAY
10.	M. FALCO		10.	A. BRAZIL
11.	M. McCABE		11.	K. O'CALLAGHAN
12.	M. BOWEN		12.	R. IRVIN

Referee: B.S.Pearce (Herts)

Linesmen: A. Mitchell (Herts)   G.R. Pooley (Herts)
              (Red Flag)   (Yellow Flag)

(left):
Tottenham v Ipswich Town,
Football Combination,
the style used for the
first part of the season.

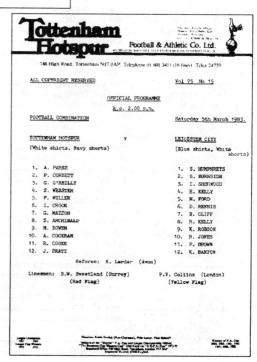

Tottenham Hotspur Football & Athletic Co. Ltd.

748 High Road, Tottenham N17 0AP. Telephone 01 801 3411 (16 lines) Telex 24739

Vol 75 No 15

OFFICIAL PROGRAMME
K.O. 2.00 p.m.

FOOTBALL COMBINATION   Saturday 5th March 1983.

TOTTENHAM HOTSPUR   v   LEICESTER CITY

(White shirts, Navy shorts)   (Blue shirts, White shorts)

1.	A. PARKS		1.	S. HUMPHREYS
2.	P. CORBETT		2.	S. BURNSIDE
3.	G. O'REILLY		3.	I. SHERWOOD
4.	S. WEBSTER		4.	E. KELLY
5.	P. MILLER		5.	M. FORD
6.	I. CROOK		6.	D. RENNIE
7.	G. MAZZON		7.	B. CLIFF
8.	S. ARCHIBALD		8.	R. KELLY
9.	M. BOWEN		9.	K. ROBSON
10.	A. COCKRAM		10.	R. JONES
11.	R. COOKE		11.	P. BROWN
12.	J. PRATT		12.	K. BAXTON

Referee: K. Larder (Avon)

Linesmen: B.W. Sweetland (Surrey)   P.V. Collins (London)
                  (Red Flag)   (Yellow Flag)

(right):
Tottenham v Leicester City,
Football Combination,
the style used during the
latter stages of the season.

1983-84

Volume 76

*		21st August .... West Ham United .... Bill Nicholson O.B.E Testimonial		

21st August .... West Ham United .... Bill Nicholson O.B.E Testimonial
(team sheet also issued)
    1 27th August .... Watford .... Football Combination
1 29th August .... Coventry City .... League
2 3rd September .... West Ham United .... League
    2 10th September .... Reading .... Football Combination
3 17th September .... Everton .... League
    3 24th September .... Leicester City .... Football Combination
4 28th September .... Drogheda .... U.E.F.A Cup 1st Round 2nd Leg
5 2nd October .... Nottingham Forest .... League
(team sheet also issued)
    4 5th October .... Swansea City .... Football Combination
(match played at Cheshunt)
6 5th October .... Lincoln City .... Milk Cup 2nd Round 1st Leg
    * 10th October .... Gillingham .... Southern Junior Floodlit Cup 1st Round Replay
    5 15th October .... Millwall .... Football Combination
7 19th October .... Feyenoord .... U.E.F.A Cup 2nd Round 1st Leg
    6 22nd October .... Swindon Town .... Football Combination
8 29th October .... Notts County .... League
    7 5th November .... Norwich City .... Football Combination
9 9th November .... Arsenal .... Milk Cup 3rd Round
10 12th November .... Liverpool .... League
    8 19th November .... Bristol Rovers .... Football Combination
11 26th November .... Queens Park Rangers .... League
    * 30th November .... Millwall .... F.A Youth Cup 2nd Round
    8 3rd December .... Luton Town .... Football Combination
(incorrectly numbered, sequence not rectified all season)
12 7th December .... Bayern Munich .... U.E.F.A Cup 3rd Round 2nd Leg
13 10th December .... Southampton .... League
    9 17th December .... Chelsea .... Football Combination
14 26th December .... Arsenal .... League
15 2nd January .... Watford .... League
    10 3rd January .... Crystal Palace .... Football Combination
16 11th January .... Fulham .... F.A Cup 3rd Round Replay
17 14th January .... Ipswich Town .... League
    11 18th January .... Southampton ....:........... Football Combination
(match played at Cheshunt)
    12 21st January .... West Ham United .... Football Combiantion
(match played at Cheshunt)
18 28th January .... Norwich City .... F.A Cup 4th Round
    13 4th February .... Ipswich Town (postponed) .... Football Combination
19 8th February .... Sunderland .... League
20 11th February .... Leicester City .... League
    14 15th February .... Queens Park Rangers .... Football Combination
21 25th February .... Birmingham City .... League
    15 28th February .... Birmingham City .... Football Combination
22 3rd March .... Stoke City .... League
23 7th March .... F.K. Austria Memphis .... U.E.F.A Cup 4th Round 1st Leg
    16 13th March .... Arsenal .... Football Combination
24 17th March .... West Bromwich Albion .... League
    17 24th March .... Oxford United (postponed) .... Football Combination
25 31st March .... Wolverhampton Wanderers .... League
    17 7th April .... Charlton Athletic .... Football Combination
    18 9th April .... Brighton & Hove Albion .... Football Combination
26 14th April .... Luton Town .... League
    19 16th April .... Oxford United .... Football Combination
(match played at Cheshunt)
27 18th April .... Aston Villa .... League
28 25th April .... Hajduk Split .... U.E.F.A Cup Semi-Final 2nd Leg

1983-84

<table>
<tr><td>29</td><td></td><td>5th May</td><td>Norwich City</td><td>League</td></tr>
<tr><td>30</td><td></td><td>12th May</td><td>Manchester United</td><td>League</td></tr>
<tr><td></td><td>20</td><td>15th May</td><td>Ipswich Town</td><td>Football Combination</td></tr>
<tr><td></td><td>21</td><td>21st May</td><td>Fulham</td><td>Football Combination</td></tr>
<tr><td></td><td></td><td colspan="4">(match played at Cheshunt)</td></tr>
<tr><td>31</td><td></td><td>23rd May</td><td>R.S.C. Anderlecht</td><td>U.E.F.A Cup Final 2nd Leg</td></tr>
<tr><td>*</td><td></td><td>29th May</td><td>England XI</td><td>Keith Burkinshaw Testimonial</td></tr>
</table>

Abridged Particulars

Application has been made to the Council of The Stock Exchange for the ordinary shares of Tottenham Hotspur plc issued, to be issued and now being issued, to be admitted to the Official List. These abridged particulars do not constitute an offer for any of the ordinary shares.

Tottenham Hotspur plc

(Incorporated in England under the Companies Acts 1948 to 1981 – No 1706358)

Offer for Sale
by
Sheppards and Chase
of
3,800,000 new ordinary shares of 25p each at 100p per share payable in full on application

Authorised	Share Capital	Issued, to be issued and now being issued fully paid
£3,000,000	in ordinary shares of 25p each	£2,295,300

The Application List for the ordinary shares now being offered for sale will open at 10.00 a.m. on Thursday, 6th October, 1983 and may be closed at any time thereafter.

Copies of the Offer for Sale on the terms of which alone applications will be considered, with a Form of Application, are available from:

Barclays Bank PLC
Tottenham Hotspur plc, — New Issues Department, — Sheppards and Chase,
748 High Road, — P.O. Box 123, — Clements House,
Tottenham, — Floriston House, — Gresham Street,
London N17 0AP — 26 Farringdon Street, — London EC2V 7AU
London EC4A 4HD

and the principal branches of Barclays Bank PLC in Tottenham and the surrounding boroughs.

The Offer for Sale is being advertised in full, with an application form, in the Financial Times and Daily Telegraph on Monday, 3rd October, 1983.

Live TV Sunday Football comes to Tottenham.

Tottenham v Nottingham Forest,
(right):
The rather strange cover of the programme for this League match, the first to be shown live on ITV. It was a four page wrapper enclosing the normal programme, advertising the forthcoming share issue.

(below):
The single-sheet teamsheet that was distributed through the turnstiles upon admission to the ground.

153

1983-84

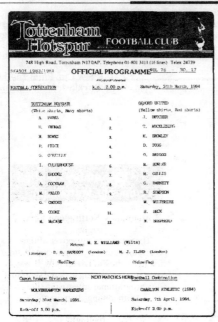

(left):
Tottenham v Oxford United,
the postponed Football Combination
match, the style adopted during
the season, and was still being used
at the end of the 1991-92 season.

(right):
Tottenham v Milwall,
Football Combination,
the style used during the
early stages of the season.

1983-84

Tottenham v Aston Villa,
Football League.

Tottenham v R.S.C. Anderlecht,
U.E.F.A. Cup Final, 2nd Leg.

Tottenham v West Ham United,
Bill Nicholson O.B.E. Testimonial Match.

Tottenham v England XI,
Keith Burkinshaw Testimonial Match.

1984-85

Volume 77

*		20th August	Fulham	Peter Southey Memorial Match
1		27th August	Leicester City	League
2		1st September	Norwich City	League
	1	8th September	Crystal Palace	Football Combination
3		15th September	Queens Park Rangers	League
	2	22nd September	Reading	Football Combination
4		29th September	Luton Town	League
	3	1st October	Swindon Town	Football Combination
		(match played at Cheshunt)		
5		3rd October	Sporting Clube De Braga	U.E.F.A Cup 1st Round 2nd Leg
	4	6th October	Swansea City	Football Combination
6		9th October	Halifax Town	Milk Cup 2nd Round 2nd Leg
7		12th October	Liverpool	League
	5	16th October	Norwich City	Football Combination
	6	20th October	Bristol Rovers	Football Combination
8		27th October	Stoke City	League
9		31st October	Liverpool	Milk Cup 3rd Round
	7	2nd November	Charlton Athletic	Football Combination
		(match played at Cheshunt)		
10		3rd November	West Bromwich Albion	League
11		7th November	Club Brugge K.V.	U.E.F.A Cup 2nd Round 2nd Leg
	*	10th November	Millwall	Friendly
	*	17th November	Wokingham Town	Friendly
	8	19th November	Millwall	Football Combination
12		24th November	Chelsea	League
	9	26th November	Chelsea	Football Combination
		(match played at Cheshunt)		
13		28th November	Bohemians Prague	U.E.F.A Cup 3rd Round 1st Leg
	10	1st December	Watford	Football Combination
14		5th December	Sunderland	Milk Cup 4th Round Replay
15		8th December	Newcastle United	League
	11	18th December	Portsmouth	Football Combination
16		26th December	West Ham United	League
17		29th December	Sunderland	League
18		5th January	Charlton Athletic	F.A Cup 3rd Round
	*	22nd January	Queens Park Rangers	Football Combination
		(match played at Q.P.R)		
	12	25th January	Ipswich Town	Football Combination
		(match played at Cheshunt)		
	13	29th January	Luton Town	Football Combination
19		9th February	Sheffield Wednesday (postponed)	League
	14	2nd March	Oxford United	Football Combination
		(match played at Cheshunt)		
	15	4th March	Brighton & Hove Albion	Football Combination
		(match played at Cheshunt)		
19		6th March	Real Madrid	U.E.F.A Cup 4th Round 1st Leg
*		9th March	Birmingham City	F.A Youth Cup 5th Round
20		12th March	Manchester United	League
	16	16th March	Southampton	Football Combination
	17	18th March	West Ham United	Football Combination
21		23rd March	Southampton	League
	17	26th March	Portsmouth	South East Counties League Cup Semi-Final
		(incorrectly numbered, sequence not rectified)		
22		30th March	Aston Villa	League
23		3rd April	Everton	League
	18	13th April	Arsenal	Football Combination
24		17th April	Arsenal	League
25		20th April	Ipswich Town	League

1984-85

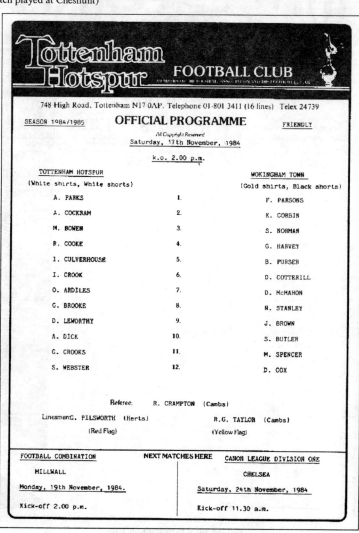

Tottenham v Wokingham Town,
Reserve Friendly.

157

1984-85

Tottenham v Birmingham City,
F.A. Youth Cup 5th Round,
a four-page issue.

1984-85

Tottenham v Sporting Clube De Braga,
U.E.F.A. Cup 1st Round, 2nd Leg.

Tottenham v Sheffield Wednesday,
the postponed League match.

Tottenham v Arsenal,
South East Counties League Cup Final
2nd Leg, a four page issue.

Tottenham Hotspur v Fulham

Tottenham v Fulham,
Peter Southey Memorial Match,
a 12-page editiion.

1985-86

Volume 78

*		4th August	Arsenal	Glenn Hoddle Testimonial
		(team sheet also issued)		
1		17th August	Watford	League
	1	20th August	Reading	Football Combination
1		26th August	Everton	League
		(incorrectly numbered)		
	2	31st August	Watford	Football Combination
3		4th September	Chelsea	League
4		7th September	Newcastle United	League
	3	14th September	Chelsea	Football Combination
5		21st September	Sheffield Wednesday	League
	4	25th September	Bristol Rovers	Southern Junior Floodlit Cup 1st Round
	5	28th September	Swansea City	Football Combination
6		2nd October	Southampton	Screen Sport Super Cup
	6	5th October	Birmingham City	Football Combination
	*	15th October	Essex v Greater Manchester	Schools F.A Under-16 Final
	7	19th October	Norwich City	Football Combination
7		26th October	Leicester City	League
8		30th October	Orient	Milk Cup 2nd Round 2nd Leg
	8	2nd November	West Ham United	Football Combination
9		6th November	Wimbledon	Milk Cup 3rd Round
10		9th November	Luton Town	League
11		20th November	Portsmouth	Milk Cup 4th Round
12		23rd November	Queens Park Rangers	League
	9	26th November	Queens Park Rangers	Southern Junior Floodlit Cup 2nd Round
	10	30th November	Luton Town	Football Combination
	11	3rd December	Gillingham	F.A Youth Cup 2nd Round
13		7th December	Oxford United	League
	12	14th December	Portsmouth	Football Combination
14		21st December	Ipswich Town	League
15		26th December	West Ham United	League
	13	4th January	Oxford United	Football Combination
16		8th January	Oxford United	F.A Cup 3rd Round Replay
	14	9th January	West Ham United	F.A Youth Cup 3rd Round
17		11th January	Nottingham Forest	League
18		14th January	Liverpool	Screen Sport Super Cup
19		18th January	Manchester City	League
	15	25th January	Ipswich Town	Football Combination
20		29th January	Notts County	F.A Cup 4th Round Replay
21		5th February	Everton	Screen Sport Super Cup Semi-Final 1st Leg
22		8th February	Coventry City	League
23		16th February	Everton (postponed)	F.A Cup 5th Round
	16	25th February	Charlton Athletic	Football Combination
23		2nd March	Liverpool	League
		(team sheet also issued)		
24		4th March	Everton	F.A Cup 5th Round
25		8th March	West Bromwich Albion	League
	17	11th March	Swindon Town	Football Combination
	18	18th March	Crystal Palace	Football Combination
	19	20th March	Coventry City	F.A Youth Cup 5th Round Replay
	20	22nd March	Arsenal	Football Combination
*		23rd March	Tottenham Hotspur Staff XI v Parliamentary XI	Charity Match
26		29th March	Arsenal	League
*		5th April	Southampton v Liverpool	F.A Cup Semi-Final
	21	12th April	Queens Park Rangers	Football Combination
27		16th April	Birmingham City	League
28		19th April	Manchester United	League
	22	22nd April	Arsenal	Southern Junior Floodlit Cup Semi-Final
	23	26th April	Brighton & Hove Albion	Football Combinatio

160

1985-86

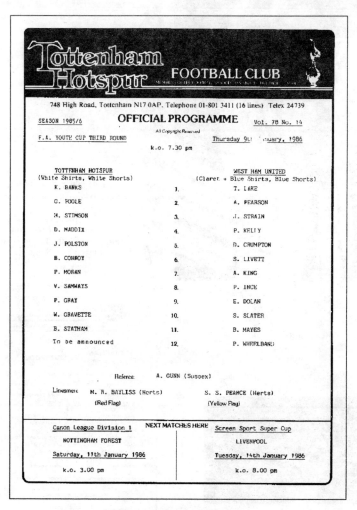

Tottenham v West Ham United,
F.A. Youth Cup 3rd Round.

1985-86

Official souvenir programme Price £1

Tottenham v Inter Milan,
Ossie Ardiles Benefit Match.

(below left):
Tottenham v Arsenal
Glenn Hoddle Testimonial Match.

(below):
Tottenham v Liverpool
Team-sheet for the League match
played on a Sunday.

· GLENN HODDLE ·
· TESTIMONIAL MATCH ·

Tottenham Hotspur FC
Vs
Arsenal FC

Sunday 4th August 1985 - K.O. 3.00p.m.

Price
£1

Sponsored by BLUE ARROW PLC

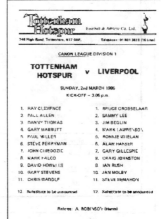

Tottenham Hotspur Football & Athletic Co. Ltd.

748 High Road, Tottenham, N17 0AP.   Telephone: 01 801 3811 (16 lines)

CANON LEAGUE DIVISION 1

TOTTENHAM HOTSPUR v **LIVERPOOL**

SUNDAY, 2nd MARCH 1986
KICK-OFF - 3.06 p.m.

1. RAY CLEMENCE	1. BRUCE GROBBELAAR
2. PAUL ALLEN	2. SAMMY LEE
3. DANNY THOMAS	3. JIM BEGLIN
4. GARY MABBUTT	4. MARK LAWRENSON
5. PAUL MILLER	6. RONNIE WHELAN
6. STEVE PERRYMAN	6. ALAN HANSEN
7. JOHN CHIEDOZIE	7. GARY GILLESPIE
8. MARK FALCO	8. CRAIG JOHNSTON
9. DAVID HOWELLS	9. IAN RUSH
10. GARY STEVENS	10. JAN MOLBY
11. CHRIS WADDLE	11. STEVE McMAHON
12. Substitute to be announced	12. Substitute to be announced

Referee: A. ROBINSON (Herts)

Linesmen: A.J. BURCE (Oxon) A.P. MURPHY (Herts)

162

1985-86

Tottenham v Arsenal,
South East Counties League Cup
Final. 1st Leg.

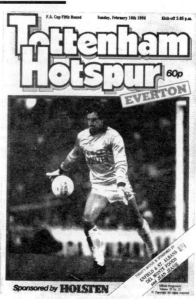

Tottenham v Everton,
the postponed F.A. Cup 5th Round issue.

Tottenham Staff XI v Parliamentary XI,
Charity Match.

Southampton v Liverpool,
F.A. Cup Semi-Final.

1986-87

*		**2nd August**	**Glasgow Rangers**	**Paul Miller Testimonial**
1		23rd August	Charlton Athletic	Football Combination
1		**25th August**	**Newcastle United**	**League**
2		**30th August**	**Manchester City**	**League**
	2	6th September	Watford	Football Combination
3		**13th September**	**Chelsea**	**League**
	3	20th September	Reading	Football Combination
4		**27th September**	**Everton**	**League**
	4	2nd October	Swindon Town	Football Combination
5		**4th October**	**Luton Town**	**League**
6		**8th October**	**Barnsley**	**Littlewoods Challenge Cup 2nd Round 2nd Leg**
	5	11th October	Bristol Rovers	Football Combination
7		**18th October**	**Sheffield Wednesday**	**League**
	6	25th October	Luton Town	Football Combination
8		**29th October**	**Birmingham City**	**Littlewoods Challenge Cup 3rd Round**
9		**1st November**	**Wimbledon**	**League**
10		**4th November**	**Hamburg**	**Friendly**
	7	8th November	Norwich City	Football Combination
11		**15th November**	**Coventry City**	**League**
	8	22nd November	Ipswich Town	Football Combination
	9	25th November	Swindon Town	Southern Junior Floodlit Cup 2nd Round Replay
12		**29th November**	**Nottingham Forest**	**League**
	10	2nd December	Epsom & Ewell	F.A Youth Cup 2nd Round
	11	6th December	Arsenal	Football Combination
	12	10th December	Queens Park Rangers	Southern Junior Floodlit Cup 3rd Round
13		**13th December**	**Watford**	**League**
	13	20th December	Millwall	Football Combination
14		**26th December**	**West Ham United**	**League**
15		**4th January**	**Arsenal**	**League**
		(contains reprint of the first Woolwich Arsenal v Spurs programme)		
		(team sheet also issued)		
16		**10th January**	**Scunthorpe United**	**F.A Cup 3rd Round**
	14	13th January	Oxford United	F.A Youth Cup 3rd Round
	15	17th January	Chelsea	Football Combination
17		**24th January**	**Aston Villa**	**League**
18		**31st January**	**Crystal Palace**	**F.A Cup 4th Round**
19		**2nd February**	**West Ham United**	**Littlewoods Challenge Cup 5th Round Replay**
	16	7th February	Brighton & Hove Albion	Football Combination
	17	10th February	Nottingham Forest	F.A Youth Cup 4th Round
20		**14th February**	**Southampton**	**League**
21		**21st February**	**Newcastle United**	**F.A Cup 5th Round**
22		**25th Febraury**	**Leicester City**	**League**
23		**1st March**	**Arsenal**	**Littlewoods Challenge Cup Semi-Final 2nd Leg**
		(team sheet also issued)		
24		**4th March**	**Arsenal**	**Littlewoods Challenge Cup Semi-Final Replay**
25		**7th March**	**Queens Park Rangers**	**League**
	18	14th March	Queens Park Rangers	Football Combination
26		**22nd March**	**Liverpool**	**League**
		(team sheet also issued)		
	19	28th March	Fulham	Football Combination
27		**4th April**	**Norwich City**	**League**
	20	9th April	Southampton	Football Combination
28		**18th April**	**Charlton Athletic**	**League**
	21	23rd April	West Ham United	Football Combination
29		**25th April**	**Oxford United**	**League**
	22	2nd May	Portsmouth	Football Combination
30		**4th May**	**Manchester United**	**League**
	23	5th May	Crystal Palace	Football Combination
	24	9th May	Oxford United	Football Combination
	*	10th May	Ridgeway Rovers v Forest United	U-12 Sunday Youth Cup Final

1986-87

THE TODAY LEAGUE
DIVISION ONE

Sunday, January 4th 1987
Kick-off 3.05 p.m.

Tottenham Hotspur 80p

Sponsored by **HOLSTEN**

ARSENAL

Bumper souvenir programme

Inside — your own re-print of the programme for the first-ever meeting between the two clubs.

Spurs v Arsenal
— the 100th League meeting

support spurs – buy Holsten

Friendly foes!

Today's match is sponsored by
ENFIELD & ST. ALBANS CO-OP
BIRDS EYE WALLS   CASHMAN ERECTORS

Official Programme
Volume 79 No. 15
© Copyright All Rights Reserved

Tottenham v Arsenal,
the 100th League match special issue.

1986-87

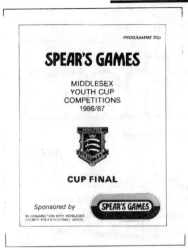

PROGRAMME 50p

SPEAR'S GAMES

MIDDLESEX
YOUTH CUP
COMPETITIONS
1986/87

CUP FINAL

Sponsored by   SPEAR'S GAMES

IN CONJUNCTION WITH MIDDLESEX
COUNTY YOUTH FOOTBALL ASSOC.

MIDDLESEX COUNTY YOUTH

FOOTBALL ASSOCIATION

UNDER 12

COUNTY CUP

FINAL

RIDGEWAY ROVERS

v

FOREST UNITED

SUNDAY 10th MAY 1987
TOTTENHAM HOTSPUR F.C.
Kick Off 11 am.

Ridgeway Rovers v Forest United,
Middlesex County Youth F.A. Under-12 County Cup Final,
(left): the programme cover, (right): page 3.

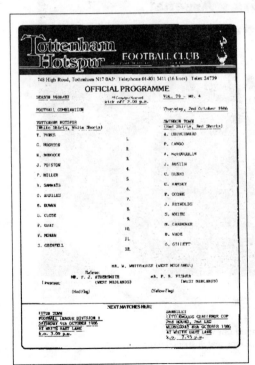

Tottenham v Swindon Town,
Football Combination.

166

1986-87

Tottenham v Hamburg,
Friendly.

Tottenham v Birmingham City,
Littlewoods Challenge Cup 3rd Round.

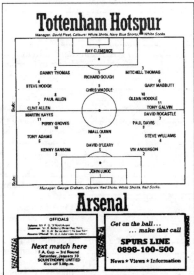

Tottenham v Arsenal,
the team-sheet issued for the 100th League
match, on this team-sheet the teams differed
from those printed in the programme.

Tottenham v Glasgow Rangers,
Paul Miller Testimonial Match.

1987-88

*		10th August .... Arsenal .... Chris Hughton Testimonial
	*	15th August .... Watford .... Friendly
1		19th August .... Newcastle United .... League
2		22nd August .... Chelsea .... League
	1	29th August .... Brighton & Hove Albion .... Football Combination
3		1st September .... Oxford United .... League
	2	5th September .... Reading .... Football Combination
4		12th September .... Southampton .... League
	3	19th September .... Chelsea .... Football Combination
	4	26th September .... West Ham United .... Football Combination
5		3rd October .... Sheffield Wednesday .... League
6		7th October .... Torquay United .... Littlewoods Challenge Cup 2nd Round 2nd Leg
7		18th October .... Arsenal .... League
		(team sheet also issued)
*		20th October .... West Ham United .... Tony Galvin Testimonial
*		24th October .... Frank Bruno v Joe Bugner .... Boxing
8		31st October .... Wimbledon .... League
	5	7th November .... Bristol Rovers .... Football Combination
	6	10th November .... Leyton Orient .... Southern Junior Floodlit Cup 2nd Round
9		14th November .... Queens Park Rangers .... League
	7	21st November .... Fulham .... Football Combination
10		28th November .... Liverpool .... League
	8	5th December .... Arsenal .... Football Combination
	9	8th December .... Bristol Rovers .... F.A Youth Cup 2nd Round
11		13th December .... Charlton Athletic .... League
		(team sheet also issued)
	10	19th December .... Ipswich Town .... Football Combination
	11	22nd December .... Crystal Palace .... Football Combination
12		28th December .... West Ham United .... League
13		1st January .... Watford .... League
	12	9th January .... Oxford United .... Football Combination
14		16th January .... Coventry City .... League
	13	21st January .... Charlton Athletic .... F.A Youth Cup 3rd Round Replay
	14	23rd January .... Southampton .... Football Combination
	15	13th February .... Watford .... Football Combination
15		15th February .... A.S Monaco .... Friendly
	16	20th February .... Luton Town .... Football Combination
16		23rd February .... Manchester United .... League
17		1st March .... Derby County .... League
	17	3rd March .... Chelsea .... F.A Youth Cup 4th Round
18		9th March .... Everton .... League
19		12th March .... Norwich City .... League
	18	22nd March .... Reading .... F.A Youth Cup 5th Round Replay
20		26th March .... Nottingham Forest .... League
*		28th March .... Manchester United .... Danny Thomas Benefit Match
21		2nd April .... Portsmouth .... League
*		9th April .... Wimbledon v Luton Town .... F.A Cup Semi-Final
	*	12th April .... Norwich City .... Football Combination
		(programme undated)
*		14th April .... Doncaster Rovers .... F.A Youth Cup Semi-Final 2nd Leg
	*	16th April .... Portsmouth .... Football Combination
		(programme undated)
	21	21st April .... Swindon Town .... Football Combination
	22	23rd April .... Charlton Athletic .... Football Combination
*		27th April .... Southampton .... South East Counties League Cup Final 1st Leg
	23	28th April .... Queens Park Rangers .... Football Combination
22		4th May .... Luton Town .... League
	24	5th May .... Millwall .... Football Combination

1987-88

Tottenham v Southampton,
Football Combination.

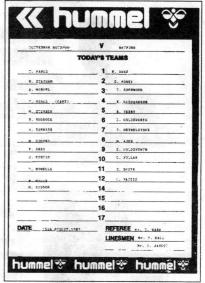

Tottenham v Watford,
Reserve Team Friendly.

Tottenham v Doncaster Rovers,
F.A. Youth Cup Semi-Final, 2nd Leg.

Tottenham v Southampton,
South East Counties League
Cup Final, 1st Leg.

1987-88

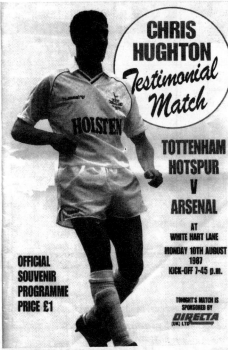

(left):
Tottenham v Arsenal,
Chris Hughton Testimonial Match.

(below left):
Wimbledon v Luton Town,
F.A. Cup Semi-Final.

(below):
Frank Bruno v Joe Bugner,
Boxing.

1987-88

Tottenham v A.S. Monaco,
Friendly.

Tottenham v Newcastle United,
League.

Tottenham v Manchester United,
Danny Thomas Benefit Match.

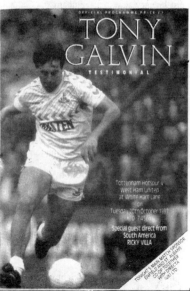

Tottenham v West Ham United,
Tony Galvin Testimonial Match.

1988-89

1988-89

SEASON 1988/89

OFFICIAL PROGRAMME

VOL.81 - 20
KICK-OFF 7PM

All Copyright Reserved

F A YOUTH CUP 5TH ROUND
WEDNESDAY 15TH MARCH 1989

Tottenham Hotspur Football Club

TOTTENHAM HOTSPUR WHITE/BLUE/WHITE		MANCHESTER CITY MAROON&WHITE/MAROON/MAROON
IAN WALKER	1.	MARTIN MARGETSON
DAVID MCDONALD	2.	NEIL LENNON
STEPHEN SMART	3.	JOHN WILLS
IAN HENDON	4.	MARK PETERS
ANDY THEODOSIOU	5.	GERALD TAGGART
STEPHEN CARNEY	6.	COLIN SMALL
SCOTT HOUGHTON	7.	MICHAEL HUGHES
PETER GARLAND	8.	ASHLEY WARD
NEIL SMITH	9.	JASON HASFORD
SHAUN MURRAY	10.	MICHAEL QUIGLEY
MATTHEW EDWARDS	11.	MICHAEL WALLACE
DAVID TUTTLE	12.	IAN THOMPSTONE
KEVIN SMITH	14.	MICHAEL SHERON

Referee: G R POOLEY (HERTFORDSHIRE)

Linesmen: N J LUDLOW (BERKSHIRE)   D J DOUGLAS (MIDDLESEX)

(Red Trim)   (Yellow Trim)

NEXT MATCHES HERE

SATURDAY 18TH MARCH 1989
TOTTENHAM HOTSPUR v. WATFORD
OVENDEN PAPERS FOOTBALL COMBINATION
KICK-OFF 2PM

SUNDAY 26TH MARCH 1989
TOTTENHAM HOTSPUR v LIVERPOOL
BARCLAYS LEAGUE DIVISION 1
KICK-OFF 3.05PM

Tottenham v Manchester City,
F.A. Youth Cup 5th Round.

1988-89

Tottenham v Coventry City,
the postponed League match.

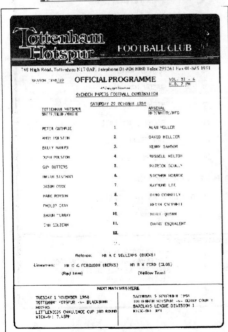

Tottenham v Arsenal,
Football Combination.

Tottenham v Nottingham Forest,
team-sheet for the Sunday match.

1988-89

Tottenham v Derby County,
League.

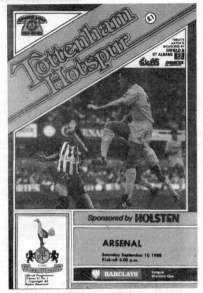

Tottenham v Arsenal.
League.

Tottenham v A.S. Monaco,
Friendly.

Tottenham v Bordeaux,
Friendly.

1989-90

Volume 82

1		**19th August** .... **Luton Town** .... **League**
	1	26th August .... Arsenal .... Football Combination
	2	2nd September .... Charlton Athletic .... Football Combination
	3	9th September .... Luton Town .... Football Combination
2		**16th September** .... **Chelsea** .... **League**
3		**20th September** .... **Southend United** .... **Littlewoods Challenge Cup 2nd Round 1st Leg**
	4	23rd September .... Queens Park Rangers .... Football Combination
4		**30th September** .... **Queens Park Rangers** .... **League**
	5	7th October .... West Ham United .... Football Combination
	6	14th October .... Reading .... Football Combination
5		**18th October** .... **Arsenal** .... **League**
6		**21st October** .... **Sheffield Wednesday** .... **League**
	*	26th October .... Wimbledon .... Southern Junior Floodlit Cup 2nd Round
	7	28th October .... Brighton & Hove Albion .... Football Combination
	8	4th November .... Southampton .... Football Combination
7		**11th November** .... **Wimbledon** .... **League**
	9	18th November .... Crystal Palace .... Football Combination
8		**25th November** .... **Derby County** .... **League**
9		**29th November** .... **Tranmere Rovers** .... **Littlewoods Challenge Cup 4th Round Replay**
	10	2nd December .... Fulham .... Football Combination
10		**9th December** .... **Everton** .... **League**
	11	16th December .... Watford (postponed) .... Football Combination
11		**26th December** .... **Millwall** .... **League**
12		**30th December** .... **Nottingham Forest** .... **League**
13		**6th January** .... **Southampton** .... **F.A Cup 3rd Round**
14		**13th January** .... **Manchester City** .... **League**
	12	20th January .... Millwall .... Football Combination
15		**24th January** .... **Nottingham Forest** .... **Littlewoods Challenge Cup 5th Round Replay**
	13	27th January .... Ipswich Town .... Football Combination
	*	30th January .... Wolverhampton Wanderers (postponed) .... F.A Youth Cup 4th Round
16		**4th February** .... **Norwich City** .... **League**
	*	8th February .... Leyton Orient .... Southern Junior Floodlit Cup 3rd Round
	14	10th February .... Chelsea .... Football Combination
		(from this match onwards all Reserve programme were incorrectly printed as Volume 88)
	*	13th February .... Wolverhampton Wanderers .... F.A Youth Cup 4th Round
	15	17th February .... Watford .... Football Combination
17		**21st February** .... **Aston Villa** .... **League**
	16	24th February .... Portsmouth .... Football Combination
18		**3rd March** .... **Crystal Palace** .... **League**
	*	5th March .... Charlton Athletic .... John Ullman Cup 3rd Round
19		**10th March** .... **Charlton Athletic** .... **League**
	*	13th March .... Watford .... Southern Junior Floodlit Cup Semi-Final Replay
	17	17th March .... Wimbledon .... Football Combination
20		**21st March** .... **Liverpool** .... **League**
	18	31st March .... Norwich City .... Football Combination
*		4th April .... Manchester United .... F.A Youth Cup Semi-Final 1st Leg
	19	7th April .... Oxford United .... Football Combination
21		**14th April** .... **Coventry City** .... **League**
*		19th April .... Arsenal .... Southern Junior Floodlit Cup Final 1st Leg
22		**21st April** .... **Manchester United** .... **League**
	20	24th April .... Swindon Town .... Football Combination
*		**1st May** .... **Northern Ireland XI** .... **Danny Blanchflower Benefit Match**
23		**5th May** .... **Southampton** .... **League**
*		13th May .... Middlesbrough .... F.A Youth Cup Final 2nd Leg
	21	14th May .... Fisher Athletic .... John Ullman Cup Final

1989-90

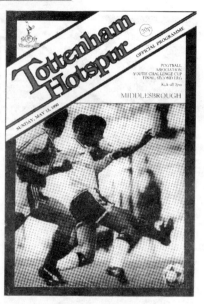

Tottenham v Manchester United,
F.A. Youth Cup Semi-Final, 1st Leg
a 4-page edition.

Tottenham v Middlesbrough,
F.A. Youth Cup Final, 2nd Leg,
a 8-page edition.

Tottenham v Wolverhampton Wanderers,
F.A. Youth Cup 4th Round,
the programme for the postponed match.

1989-90

Tottenham v Arsenal,
Southern Junior Floodlit Cup Final,
1st Leg, a 4-page edition.

Tottenham v Fisher Athletic,
John Ullman Cup Final.

1989-90

Tottenham v Charlton Athletic,
League.

Tottenham v Northern Ireland XI,
Danny Blanchflower Benefit Match.

1990-91

Volume 83

*		17th August .... West Ham United	**Ray Clemence Benefit Match**
1		25th August .... Manchester City	**League**
	1	28th August .... Oxford United	Football Combination
	2	1st September .... Chelsea	Football Combination
2		8th September .... Derby County	**League**
	3	15th September .... Fulham	Football Combination
	*	19th September .... Northampton Town	Southern Junior Floodlit Cup 1st Round
3		22nd September .... Crystal Palace	**League**
4		26th September .... Hartlepool United	**Rumbelows League Cup 2nd Round 1st Leg**
5		29th September .... Aston Villa	**League**
	*	2nd October .... Birmingham City	Southern Junior Floodlit Cup 2nd Round
	4	6th October .... Queens Park Rangers	Football Combination
	5	13th October .... Crystal Palace	Football Combination
*		16th October .... England v Poland	U.E.F.A Under-21 International
6		20th October .... Sheffield United	**League**
	6	26th October .... Swindon Town	Football Combination
		(incorrectly dated, should be 27th October)	
7		30th October .... Bradford City	**Rumbelows League Cup 3rd Round**
8		4th November .... Liverpool	**League**
		(also issued with "The Match" wrapper	
9		10th November .... Wimbledon	**League**
	7	17th November .... Millwall	Football Combination
10		24th November .... Norwich City	**League**
	8	1st December .... Portsmouth	Football Combination
11		8th December .... Sunderland	**League**
	9	15th December .... Southampton	Football Combination
*		18th December .... England XI v Italia 90 XI	Peter Shilton International Farewell
12		22nd December .... Luton Town	**League**
	10	29th December .... Arsenal	Football Combination
13		1st January .... Manchester United	**League**
14		12th January .... Arsenal	**League**
	11	19th January .... Watford	Football Combination
15		23rd January .... Chelsea	**Rumbelows League Cup 5th Round Replay**
16		26th January .... Oxford United	**F.A Cup 4th Round**
	12	29th January .... Charlton Athletic	Football Combination
17		2nd February .... Leeds United	**League**
	13	23rd February .... Luton Town	Football Combination
18		2nd March .... Chelsea	**League**
19		10th March .... Notts County	**F.A Cup 6th Round**
	14	16th March .... Brighton & Hove Albion	Football Combination
	15	19th March .... Norwich City	Football Combination
20		23rd March .... Queens Park Rangers	**League**
21		30th March .... Coventry City	**League**
22		6th April .... Southampton	**League**
	16	16th April .... West Ham United	Football Combination
	17	18th April .... V.C.D Athletic	John Ullman Cup 2nd Round
	18	20th April .... Reading	Football Combination
23		24th April .... Everton	**League**
	19	27th April .... Ipswich Town	Football Combination
24		4th May .... Nottingham Forest	**League**
*		7th May .... Arsenal	South East Counties League Div.1
	20	8th May .... Wimbledon	Football Combination

1990-91

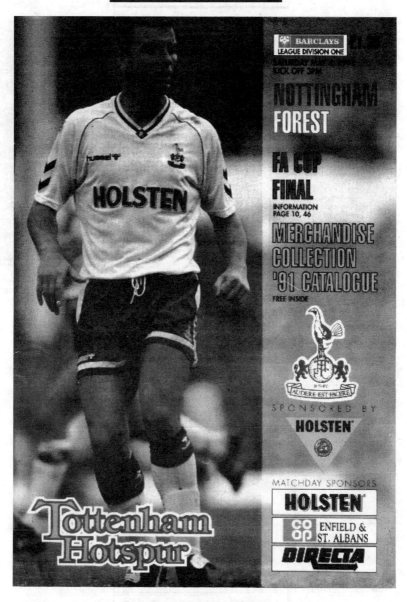

Tottenham v Nottingham Forest,
League.

1990-91

England v Poland,
U.E.F.A. Under-21 International.

England XI v Italia '90 XI,
Peter Shilton International Farewell.

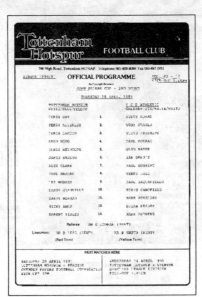

Tottenham v V.C.D. Athletic,
John Ullman Cup, 2nd Round.

1990-91

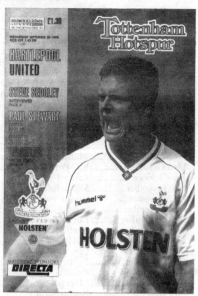

Tottenham v Liverpool,
"The Match" 8-page wrapper around
the usual League edition.

Tottenham v Hartlepool United,
Rumbelows Cup 2nd Round, 1st Leg.

Tottenham v West Ham United,
Ray Clemence Benefit Match.

1991-92

	1	17th August	Brighton & Hove Albion	Football Combination
		(programme undated)		
1		**24th August**	**Chelsea**	**League**
	2	31st August	Charlton Athletic	Football Combination
2		**4th September**	**Sparkasse Stockerau European Cup Winners Cup Prel.Round 2nd Leg**	
	3	7th September	Chelsea	Football Combination
3		**14th September**	**Queens Park Rangers**	**League**
*		21st September	Chris Eubank v Michael Watson	Boxing
4		**28th September**	**Manchester United**	**League**
5		**2nd October**	**Hajduk Split**	**European Cup Winners Cup 1st Round 2nd Leg**
	4	5th October	Ipswich Town	Football Combination
6		**9th October**	**Swansea City**	**Rumbelows League Cup 2nd Round 2nd Leg**
	5	12th October	Luton Town	Football Combination
7		**19th October**	**Manchester City**	**League**
8		**23rd October**	**F.C Porto**	**European Cup Winners Cup 2nd Round 1st Leg**
	6	26th October	Arsenal	Football Combination
	7	2nd November	Millwall	Football Combination
	8	9th November	Crystal Palace	Football Combination
*		10th November	Spurs 81-82 v Spurs 90-91 etc	Cyril Knowles Memorial Match
9		**16th November**	**Luton Town**	**League**
10		**23rd November**	**Sheffield United**	**League**
	9	30th November	Portsmouth	Football Combination
*		3rd December	Coventry City	F.A Youth Cup 2nd Round
11		**7th December**	**Notts County**	**League**
	10	14th December	Reading (abandoned)	Football Combination
12		**18th December**	**Liverpool**	**League**
13		**26th December**	**Nottingham Forest**	**League**
14		**28th December**	**Norwich City**	**League**
	11	4th January	Queens Park Rangers	Football Combination
15		**8th January**	**Norwich City**	**Rumbelows League Cup 5th Round**
	12	11th January	Southampton	Football Combination
16		**14th January**	**Aston Villa**	**F.A Cup 3rd Round Replay**
17		**18th January**	**Southampton**	**League**
*		20th January	A.F.C. Bournemouth	F.A Youth Cup 3rd Round
18		**25th January**	**Oldham Athletic**	**League**
	13	1st February	Swindon Town	Football Combination
	14	3rd February	Reading	Football Combination
	15	14th February	West Ham United	Football Combination
		(match played at Leyton Orient FC)		
19		**16th February**	**Crystal Palace**	**League**
*		18th February	Birmingham City	Southern Junior Floodlit Cup Semi-Final
20		**22nd February**	**Arsenal**	**League**
*		26th February	Everton	F.A Youth Cup 5th Round
21		**1st March**	**Nottingham Forest**	**Rumbelows League Cup Semi-Final 2nd Leg**
	16	4th March	Oxford United	Football Combination
		(match played at Hendon FC)		
22		**7th March**	**Leeds United**	**League**
23		**14th March**	**Sheffield Wednesday**	**League**
24		**18th March**	**Feyenoord**	**European Cup Winners Cup 3rd Round 2nd Leg**
	17	21st March	Norwich City	Football Combination
*		25th March	Manchester United	F.A Youth Cup Semi-Final 2nd Leg
25		**28th March**	**Coventry City**	**League**
26		**1st April**	**West Ham United**	**League**
27		**4th April**	**Aston Villa**	**League**
*		8th April	Arsenal	Southern Junior Floodlit Cup Final 1st Leg
	18	11th April	Watford	Football Combination
	19	15th April	Wimbledon	Football Combination
28		**18th April**	**Wimbledon**	**League**
29		**25th April**	**Everton**	**League**
	20	2nd May	Fulham	Football Combination
*		5th May	Chelsea	South East Counties League Cup Final 2nd Leg

1991-92

Tottenham v Feyenoord,
European Cup Winners Cup.
3rd Round, 2nd Leg.

Tottenham v Chelsea,
League.

Tottenham v Everton,
League.

1991-92

Tottenham v Arsenal,
Southern Junior Floodlit Cup,
Final, 1st Leg.

Tottenham v Manchester United,
F.A. Youth Cup, Semi-Final,
2nd Leg.

Tottenham v Chelsea,
South East Counties League Cup,
Final, 2nd Leg.

Tottenham v Everton,
F.A. Youth Cup, 5th Round.

1991-92

Cyril Knowles Memorial Match.

Chris Eubank v Michael Watson,
Boxing.

Spurs at Hoddesdon & Cheshunt

For the first couple of full seasons after the end of the War, Tottenham Hotspur fielded only two sides in competitive football, the First team and the Reserves, with occasional appearances being made by the "A" team in friendly games. All that changed at the start of the 1948-49 season when the "A" team entered the Eastern Counties League. However, the lack of a second ground meant that most matches had to be played away from home, with just a few being fitted into the schedule at White Hart Lane. This situation existed for two seasons, but from the start of the 1950-51, Spurs, having entered the London Professional Midweek League as well, were able to use the home ground of Hoddesdon Town Football Club for these matches. First at Lowfield in Brocket Road, before moving to the Hoddesdon Sports Arena in Essex Road. Many younger collectors may not be aware but programmes for these matches were printed. Like the normal Spurs home programme, they were printed by Thomas Knight & Co. Ltd., but they were in fact Hoddesdon Town programmes. Spurs played at Hoddesdon for two seasons before acquiring the Brookfield Lane ground at Cheshunt, and an example for each season has been reproduced on the following pages. The first example, opposite, is numbered in sequence, but the sequence is for Hoddesdon Town programmes. The following season, 1951-52, Eastern Counties League home matches reverted to a few at White Hart Lane with the remainder played away. Instead the club entered their "B" team in the Metropolitan League, and these matches as well as the Midweek League games were played there. The programme, whilst retaining Hoddesdon's advertisements, as you will see, made no mention of that club at all, using a Tottenham Hotspur heading in place of the Hoddesdon Town heading. A small editorial section appeared on the second page, with the team line-ups on the third. The two League tables appeared on the back cover.

Then from the 1952-53 season the ground at Cheshunt came into operation, and the club produced its own duplicated single-sheet programmes for matches played there. At first they were un-numbered but a numbering system began with Volume 1 from the start of the 1956-57 season.

At the end of the 1968-69 season the "A" team was finally disbanded and only South East Counties League matches were played at Cheshunt regularly, and as far as know no further programmes were produced for matches at that ground, unless they were for Football Combination matches or other matches switched from White Hart Lane, and these are listed within the individual seasons earlier in the book.

Unfortunately we do not possess a complete record of every programme issued for these matches at Hoddesdon or Cheshunt, but if there is anyone we can help us with us our enquiries as they possess information or programmes, we would be only to pleased to hear from them. Please send information to the publishing company, whose address appears on page two of this volume.

Tottenham Hotspur v Charlton Athletic
London Professional Midweek League
The team line-ups

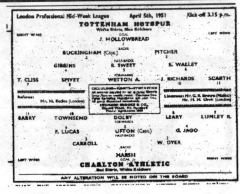

Spurs at Hoddesdon & Cheshunt

Tottenham Hotspur v Charlton Athletic,
London Professional Midweek League,
April 5th, 1951

Spurs at Hoddesdon & Cheshunt

TOTTENHAM HOTSPUR FOOTBALL & ATHLETIC COMPANY LTD

President: The Right Hon. LORD MORRISON, P.C., D.L., J.P.

Official Programme

Secretary: R. S. JARVIS

Team Manager:
ARTHUR S. ROWE

Medical Officer:
Dr. A. E. TUGHAN

Chairman: FRED J. BEARMAN

Directors: F. JOHN BEARMAN, Wm. J. HERYET,
E. DEWHURST HORNSBY, G. WAGSTAFFE SIMMONS, F.J.I.,
HARRY TAYLOR, FREDK. WALE

PRICE
TWOPENCE

HODDESDON SPORTS ARENA :: ESSEX ROAD

TOTTENHAM HOTSPUR v. SKYWAYS

Kick-off 3.15 p.m.

METROPOLITAN LEAGUE   **MONDAY, APRIL 14th, 1952**

Tottenham Hotspur v Skyways,
Metropolitan League,
April 14th, 1952

Spurs at Hoddesdon & Cheshunt

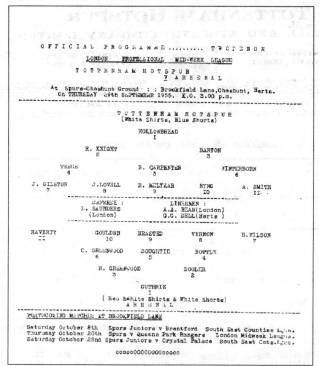

OFFICIAL PROGRAMME .... TWOPENCE

LONDON PROFESSIONAL MID-WEEK LEAGUE

TOTTENHAM HOTSPUR
v ARSENAL

At Spurs-Cheshunt Ground : : Brookfield Lane, Cheshunt, Herts.
On THURSDAY 29th SEPTEMBER 1955. K.O. 3.00 p.m.

TOTTENHAM HOTSPUR
(White Shirts, Blue Shorts)

HOLLOWBREAD
1

R. KNIGHT   BARTON
2   3

TREGE   B. CARPENTER   WINTERBORN
4   5   6

J. GILSTON   J.LOVELL   R. MELYZAR   BYNG   A. SMITH
7   8   9   10   11

REFEREE :   LINESMEN :
L. SAUNDERS   A.A. BEAN (London)
(London)   G.C. DELL (Herts)

HAVERTY   GOULDEN   BRASTED   VERNON   H. WILSON
11   10   9   8   7

C. GREENWOOD   DOUGHTIE   BOTTLE
6   5   4

R. GREENWOOD   DOOLER
3   2

GUTHRIE
1
(Red &White Shirts & White Shorts)
ARSENAL

FORTHCOMING MATCHES AT BROOKFIELD LANE

Saturday October 8th   Spurs Juniors v Brentford   South East Counties Lge.
Thursday October 20th   Spurs v Queens Park Rangers London Midweek League.
Saturday October 22nd   Spurs Juniors v Crystal Palace South East Cnts.Lgue.

oooooOOOOOOoooooo

Tottenham Hotspur "A" v Arsenal, London Professional Midweek League, September 29th, 1955

Tottenham Hotspur v Skyways, Metropolitan League, April 14th, 1952. The team line-ups on page three of the four-page programme.

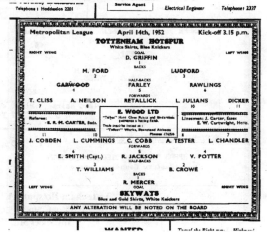

Telephone : Hoddesdon 2201   Service Agent   Electrical Engineer   Telephone: 2337

Metropolitan League   April 14th, 1952   Kick-off 3.15 p.m.

TOTTENHAM HOTSPUR
White Shirts, Blue Knickers

RIGHT WING   LEFT WING
GOAL
D. GRIFFIN
1
BACKS
M. FORD   LUDFORD
2   3
HALF-BACKS
GARWOOD   FARLEY   RAWLINGS
4   5   6
FORWARDS
T. CLISS   A. NEILSON   RETALLICK   L. JULIANS   DICKER
7   8   9   10   11

                    E. WOOD LTD
Referees :   "Talbot" Hire Glass Rubbish and Underfelts   Linesmen: J. Carter, Essex
R. M. CARTER, Beds.   Contractors & Rolling Finish.   E. W. Cartwright, Herts.
                  Their enquiries invited at :
                  "Talbot" Works, Bentstead Abbotts
                         Phone 174/56
11   10   8   7
J. COBDEN   L. CUMMINGS   C. COBB   A. TESTER   L. CHANDLER
FORWARDS
6   5   4
E. SMITH (Capt.)   R. JACKSON   V. POTTER
HALF-BACKS
3   2
T. WILLIAMS   B. CROWE
BACKS
1
R. MERCER
GOAL
SKYWAYS
Blue and Gold Shirts, White Knickers

ANY ALTERATION WILL BE NOTED ON THE BOARD

Spurs at Hoddesdon & Cheshunt

TOTTENHAM HOTSPUR
FOOTBALL AND ATHLETIC COMPANY LIMITED

MEMBERS OF THE FOOTBALL LEAGUE

WINNERS OF THE F.A. CUP 1900-1, 1920-1

Telephone: TOTTENHAM No. 1828

Telegrams: SPURS, LOWER TOTTENHAM

Secretary
R. S. JARVIS.
748 HIGH ROAD
TOTTENHAM, N. 17

BROOKFIELD LANE GROUND, CHESHUNT, HERTS.

Vol. 6. No. 5. PROGRAMME Price — ONE PENNY.

Sat. 3rd November 1962. EASTERN COUNTIES LEAGUE Kick-off 11 a.m.

V . ELY CITY

R. 'SPURS "A" L.
(White shirts, Blue shorts)

BROWN (R)

D. WALKER LYE
2. 3.

REED ELBERY SAINTY
4. 5. 6.

A. TURLEY J. HOLSGROVE BROWN (C) GILLINGWATER AITCHISON
7. 8. 9. 10. 11.

Referee:- Mr. V. Hemmings. Linesmen:- Mr. J. Adams (Essex) — Amber Flag.
(Herts.) Mr. D. Anderson (Beds.) — Red Flag.

11. 10. 9. 8. 7.
GRANGER COTMAN WILLSON PAYNE RACE

6. 5. 4.
GARNETT DOWNES HOPKINSON

3. 2.
YATES WISBEY

HENRY

(Red shirts, Black shorts)
L. ELY CITY R.

NEXT FIXTURE ON THIS GROUND:- SATURDAY 10TH NOVEMBER —

'SPURS "A" v. BIGGLESWADE TOWN — KICK-OFF 2.30 P.M.
(Eastern Counties League)

Tottenham Hotspur "A" v Ely City,
Eastern Counties League,
November 3rd, 1962

192

The Official Handbooks

U nlike many League clubs, Tottenham Hotspur have regularly produced an annual Official Handbook. The first such publication was issued at the start of the 1898-99 season, and apart from war years intervened, it has appeared every season since the last century.

Paper rationing prevented Tottenham from publishing an Official Handbook after World War II until the 1948-49 season, and for many collectors and supporters, acquiring copies is an essential factor in boosting their collection of Tottenham Hotspur artifacts. Pre-war copies now command very high prices indeed.

Over the next few pages we have reproduced all the covers of the Handbooks published since the war, along with any relevant detail, such as the pagenation including the cover, the price, and the dimensions, height by width.

From seasons 1948-49 until 1980-81 inclusive, the Handbooks were printed by Thomas Knight & Co. Ltd. Then from 1981-82 until 1986-87 inclusive, the printing was entrusted to the Maybank Press Ltd. The Valentine Press Ltd. took over for seasons 1987-88 to 1990-91, the 1991-92 edition being printed by M Press (Sales) Ltd. Colour was used for the first time on the cover of the 1978-79 edition, but not internally until the 1981-82 edition.

1948-49
64 pages - price 6d.
148mm x 102mm

1949-50
72 pages - price 6d.
152mm x 102mm

1950-51
88 pages - price 6d.
150mm x 105mm

1951-52
100 pages - price 1s.
154mm x 110mm

1952-53
108 pages - price 1s.
153mm x 105mm

1953-54
88 pages - price 1s.
152mm x 104mm

The Official Handbooks

1954-55
92 pages - price 1s.
157mm x 105mm

1955-56
72 pages - price 1s.
158mm x 108mm

1956-57
60 pages - price 1s.
157mm x 105mm

1957-58
84 pages - price 1s.
156mm x 108mm

1958-59
76 pages - price 1s.
158mm x 108mm

1959-60
76 pages - price 1s.
159mm x 108mm

1960-61
84 pages - price 1s.
158mm x 108mm

1961-62
88 pages - price 1s.
158mm x 108mm

1962-63
88 pages - price 1s.
158mm x 108mm

The Official Handbooks

1963-64
88 pages - price 1s.
158mm x 108mm

1964-65
76 pages - price 1s.
159mm x 108mm

1965-66
88 pages - price 1s.
158mm x 108mm

1966-67
96 pages - price 1/6d.
159mm x 108mm

1967-68
100 pages - price 2s.
158mm x 108mm

1968-69
104 pages - price 2s.
159mm x 108mm

1969-70
108 pages - price 2s.
159mm x 108mm

1970-71
104 pages - price 2s.
158mm x 108mm

1971-72
100 pages - price 12p.
158mm x 108mm

The Official Handbooks

1972-73
100 pages - price 12p.
158mm x 108mm

1973-74
100 pages   price 15p.
158mm x 109mm

1974-75
100 pages - price 15p.
158mm x 107mm

1975-76
92 pages - price 20p.
158mm x 108mm

1976-77
84 pages - price 25p.
160mm x 108mm

1977-78
68 pages - price 30p.
160mm x 108mm

1978-79
84 pages - price 45p.
179mm x 127mm

1979-80
84 pages - price 50p.
179mm x 129mm

1980-81
84 pages - price 60p.
180mm x 127mm

The Official Handbooks

1981-82
84 pages - price 75p.
210mm x 147mm

1982-83
84 pages - price 85p.
209mm x 148mm

1983-84
84 pages - price £1.
206mm x 149mm

1984-85
84 pages - price £1.
209mm x 148mm

1985-86
104 pages - price £1.50p.
210mm x 148mm

1986-87
104 pages - price £2.
209mm x 148mm

1987-88
108 pages - price £2.50p.
242mm x 165mm

1988-89
112 pages - price £2.75p.
240mm x 165mm

1989-90
120 pages - price £3.50p.
239mm x 167mm

197

The Official Handbooks

1990-91
132 pages - price £3.95.
240mm x 165mm

1991-92
80 pages - price £3.50p.
239mm x 165mm

Other collectable publications

As is the case with most major football clubs, just about everything they produce can be construed as collectable, and any item which has anything to do with Tottenham Hotspur is no exception.

A glance through any of the major Programme Dealers' catalogue will reveal a plethora of memorabilia for collectors to purchase. Items vary from match tickets to bubble gum cards, and from brochures to enamel badges and Supporters' club badges. Even today as publications like The Lilywhite and Team, produced by the Spurs Supporters Club, have become sought-after publications, their more recent distant cousins, the fanzines are also now attracting reasonable prices for their early editions.

On the following couple of pages we have reproduced some of the items that are collected and that were produced by the club.

Tottenham Hotspur v Feyenoord,
U.E.F.A. Cup Final (1st Leg),
a 60p Terrace ticket.

Other collectable publications

Spurs 1961
Spurs Players Publication
52 pages - price 2/6d.
204mm x 127mm

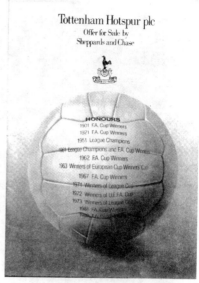

1983 Tottenham Hotspur plc
Share Prospectus
40 pages.
294mm x 210mm

Spurs 1961-62
Autograph Sheet
254mm x 146mm

1982 New West Stand
Season Ticket Prices
213mm x 194mm

Other collectable publications

(above left):
1981 F.A. Cup Final Brochure,
24 pages - price £1.50p,
294mm x 210mm.

(above right):
1991 F.A. Cup Final Brochure,
68 pages - price £5.00,
296mm x 210mm.

(left):
1990-91 Information Booklet,
12 pages,
210mm x 147mm.